SUCCESSFUL CORPORATE AQUISITIONS

A Complete Guide for Acquiring Companies for Growth and Profit

SUCCESSFUL CORPORATE AQUISITIONS

A Complete Guide for Acquiring Companies for Growth and Profit

Jerold Freier

PRENTICE HALL
Englewood Cliffs, New Jersey 07632

Prentice-Hall International (UK) Limited, *London*
Prentice-Hall of Australia Pty. Limited, *Sydney*
Prentice-Hall Canada, Inc., *Toronto*
Prentice-Hall Hispanoamericana, S.A., *Mexico*
Prentice-Hall of India Private Limited, *New Delhi*
Prentice-Hall of Japan, Inc., *Tokyo*
Simon & Schuster Asia Pte. Ltd., *Singapore*
Editora Prentice-Hall do Brasil, Ltda., *Rio de Janeiro*

© 1990 *by*

PRENTICE-HALL, Inc.
Englewood Cliffs, NJ

10 9 8 7 6 5 4 3 2 1

Library of Congress Cataloging-in-Publication Data

Freier, Jerold L.
  Successful corporate acquisitions : a complete guide for acquiring
companies for growth and profit / Jerold Freier.

    p.   cm.
  Includes index.
  ISBN 0-13-860503-3
  1. Consolidatin and merger of corporations.   I. Title.
HD2746.5.F736 1990   90-41679
658.1'6—dc20   CIP

ISBN 0-13-860503-3

PRENTICE HALL
BUSINESS & PROFESSIONAL DIVISION
A division of Simon & Schuster
Englewood Cliffs, New Jersey 07632

PRINTED IN THE UNITED STATES OF AMERICA

HOW THIS BOOK WILL HELP YOUR COMPANY INCREASE ITS SIZE AND PROFITS

Surprisingly few companies use acquisitions to pursue their growth objectives. There are approximately 50,000 companies in the United States which are large enough to make acquisitions valued at $1 million or higher. Over a five-year period, approximately 13,000 such acquisitions will be reported in the national press (e.g., *The Wall Street Journal*). However these 13,000 reported acquisitions will be made by fewer than 1,800 companies. A small group of fewer than 800 of these acquirers will make over 75% of these 13,000 acquisitions.

In discussions with hundreds of company presidents, the author and other merger/acquisition professionals have rarely found a profitable company which was not "in the market to make a good acquisition." Over a five-year period, at least 60% of the larger U.S. companies will have launched what they considered to be acquisition programs. Yet few of these companies have completed any acquisitions. Since there are approximately 13,000 companies sold every five years for prices over $1 million (and perhaps as many as 7,000 other companies which were sold for prices over $1 million but were not reported in the national press), the problem is not a shortage of suitable acquisition candidates. Rather, the problem is that few companies which are not already active acquirers utilize the strategies and techniques which comprise an effective acquisition program.

The strategies and techniques which will enable your company to develop and implement a successful acquisition program are not especially complex, nor do they require special management or technical skills. They are however somewhat different from those which your company uses to manage and operate its ongoing business successfully. Utilizing these acquisition program strategies and techniques will generally require more advance planning and preparation than your executives expected to devote to your company's acquisition program.

The objective of this book is to enable you to develop and implement an acquisition program which will work successfully for your company. Since each company is different, you will obtain the best results with the least effort by selecting the combination of acquisition program strategies and techniques which best fits your own company's unique needs, objectives, and resources. In order to help you make these choices, sections of this book will cover other relevant aspects of corporate growth planning.

CONTENTS

C·H·A·P·T·E·R O·N·E

ACQUISITIONS FOR CORPORATE GROWTH

WHY YOUR COMPANY SHOULD GROW LARGER

There are three principal reasons why your company should grow in size. These are:

1. *Increased earnings.*

   Growth in company size is the principal way in which a company can hope to produce significantly higher profits for its owners.

2. *Management recruitment and retention.*

   Growing companies are more likely to be able to attract and retain talented executives and other key personnel. Corporate growth does this in three ways. They are:

   a. It produces career advancement opportunities for a company's junior and mid-level executives.

   b. It creates opportunities for a company's executives to use more of their creative talents and management skills. This makes their jobs more interesting and fulfilling.

   c. It generally produces higher salary levels for a company's executives and other key employees. Compensation studies indicate that company size is the single most important factor which determines salary levels for executives and staff.

3. *Business survival.*

Over the past 20 years the minimum company size required to compete successfully in most industry segments has been steadily increasing. This change is clearly indicated in company size statistics for various industry segments.

THE RISK OF GROWING LARGER

As your company grows larger, it loses some of the key management and operating characteristics which helped it to survive and compete successfully as a smaller company. Examples of these "smaller company" characteristics include:

1. *Operating flexibility.* This refers to a company's ability to recognize and respond quickly to changes in market conditions.

2. *Financial flexibility.* This refers to a company's ability to quickly adjust its operating expenses in response to changes in its sales volume.

3. *Management efficiency.* This refers to the ability to manage a business using a relatively small number of executives who perform multiple job functions. As companies grow larger and more complex, they require a larger, more specialized management structure.

FACTORS WHICH HELP YOUR COMPANY SURVIVE AND PROSPER AFTER IT BECOMES LARGER

There are four key factors which help larger companies to survive and prosper. These are:

1. *Cost savings.*

Larger companies use their greater purchasing power to obtain lower prices for many of the goods and services which they buy. For example, significant quantity discounts are often available for larger purchases of raw materials, machinery, electric power, office supplies, manufactured components, advertising, and insurance. Larger companies also benefit from their ability to have more functions (e.g., accounting) performed in-house.

2. *Fixed asset productivity.*

Larger companies usually have higher production volumes for each product and service which they produce. This enables them to utilize more efficient specialized equipment and systems.

3. *Diversification.*

Larger companies tend to be more diversified. This reduces their vulnerability to depressed economic conditions in a single-market area or industry segment.

4. *Management depth.*

Larger companies tend to have more management depth. This reduces their vulnerability to the unexpected loss of one or more key employees.

COMPANY-SIZE SAFETY ZONES

An industry segment refers to companies in the same line of business. For industrial companies these are companies in the same industry (e.g., textiles) which perform the same function (e.g., manufacturing). For service businesses these are companies which perform a broad function in a specialized manner. Railroads, trucking companies, and barge lines are examples of industry segments within the transportation industry.

Within an industry segment (e.g., manufacturing generic drugs) there are usually two, three, or four different company size ranges within which most companies are concentrated. At the least of these size ranges the companies have the smaller-company–type competitive characteristics outlined earlier in this chapter. At the highest of these size ranges you find companies which have lost these smaller-company competitive advantages but have realized many of the larger-company–type competitive advantages outlined in the preceding section. When there are concentrations of companies in one or two intermediate size ranges, these companies have gained enough larger-company–type competitive advantages to offset their loss of some of the small-company advantages. These company size ranges in which a company obtains sufficient smaller- and/or larger-company–size benefits to survive and to compete successfully are called company-size safety zones.

When a growing company in a particular industry segment is in between two company safety-zone size levels, it loses some of the characteristics which helped it to survive and compete successfully as a smaller company but does not yet obtain the larger-company competitive benefits characteristic of companies in the next highest company-size safety zone. This "in-between" company-size level is a danger zone for a growing company. Companies in the danger-zone size range have the higher administrative expenses and management difficulties of somewhat larger companies without realizing their competitive advantages (e.g., cost savings). An important potential benefit of making an acquisition is to enable a growing company to junp over these danger zones. For example, assume that the safety zones in a particular industry segment are for companies with annual revenues of $1 million to $3 million, $5 million to $7 million, and over $10 million. The danger zone for a company with annual revenues of $2.5 million is the $3 million to $5 million size range. By acquiring a company in the same industry segment with annual revenues of $3 million, the acquiring company could jump over this danger-zone size level since the combined companies would have annual revenues of $5.5 million.

HOW TO IDENTIFY THE COMPANY-SIZE
SAFETY AND DANGER ZONES

There are two techniques which you can use to find the company-size safety and danger zones in your industry segment or in a different industry segment which you are considering entering. These are:

1. Make a chart which indicates the number of companies in each equal size range. When there are no critical danger zones in an industry segment, the number of companies in each size category will decline at a steady rate as company size increases. The following company-size distribution illustrates this pattern.

ANNUAL REVENUES	NUMBER OF COMPANIES
$1 to $3 million	450
$3 to $5 million	307
$5 to $7 million	149
$7 to $9 million	80
$9 to $11 million	56

When there are danger zones you can spot them because there will be either a greater number, or a similar number, of companies in the next larger size category. The following company-size distribution illustrates this pattern.

ANNUAL REVENUES	NUMBER OF COMPANIES
$1 to $3 million	450
$3 to $5 million	307
$5 to $7 million	55 (danger zone)
$7 to $9 million	80
$9 to $11 million	56

2. Compare the average pretax profit margins (pretax income divided by revenues) for groups of companies in each size range category. Sources where you can find these comparative financial statistics are listed in Chapter 7. Then

make a chart showing the average pretax profit margins for companies in each size range category. The danger-zone company-size levels will show up as company-size ranges which have lower pretax profit margins than both the next higher and the next lower size range categories. The following chart illustrated this concept.

COMPANY SIZE RANGE	AVERAGE PRETAX PROFIT MARGIN
$1 to $3 million	3%
$3 to $5 million	1 1/2% (danger zone)
$5 to $7 million	3%
$7 to $9 million	1 (danger zone)
$9 to $11 million	2%

HOW TO USE THIS INFORMATION TO GUIDE YOUR COMPANY'S GROWTH

1. When your company is approaching a danger-zone size level, consider using an acquisition of another company in your industry segment to leapfrog over this danger zone and reach the next company-size safety zone. In the previous example a company with annual revenues of $6 million should consider acquiring a company in its same industry segment with annual revenues of $3 million rather than gradually increasing its own business and winding up in the $7 to $9 million company-size danger zone.

2. In your own industry segment look for acquisition candidates which have annual revenues in the company-size danger zone, but which when added to your company would put the combined business at a safety-zone size level. Since acquisition candidates which are in the danger-zone size range tend to have low earnings relative to their sales levels and book value, they can often be acquired for an attractive (low) price.

3. Avoid acquiring a company in your industry segment which when added to your company, would create a combined company which would have annual sales in a danger-zone size level.

4. When you are considering acquiring a company which operates in an industry segment different from your present business, check to be sure that this company is not operating at a revenue level which places it in a company-size danger zone for that industry segment.

5. When your company has grown into a danger-zone size level for its industry segment, look for ways either to rapidly accelerate your growth (acquisitions, opening new branches, etc.) or to scale back and become a somewhat smaller company again. As long as your company remains at a danger-zone size level,

it is likely to be especially vulnerable to business downturns which affect your industry segment.

SIX CORPORATE GROWTH STRATEGIES WHICH YOUR COMPANY COULD USE

Corporate growth means increasing the size of your company both in terms of its annual revenues and its annual earnings. There are six basic strategies which your company can use to seek to achieve these dual growth objectives. The first four of these growth strategies are ways in which your company could expand within the industry segment which it now operates in (e.g., book publishing). They are:

1. *Market intensification.*

Increase your market share by selling more of the goods and services which your company now produces to customers in the geographic markets you now serve. Examples of the techniques which your company might use to implement this growth strategy include:

   a. Increased advertising

   b. Employing more sales representatives

   c. Acquiring a competitor

2. *Product line extension.*

Expanding your product line by adding complimentary products or services which can be marketed and distributed by your existing sales organization. Examples of the techniques which your company might use to implement this growth strategy include:

   a. Internal product development

   b. Purchasing the rights to sell products manufactured by another company

   c. Acquiring a company which manufactures products which your company could sell to its present customer base

3. *Market extension.*

Expanding into new geographic markets. Examples of the techniques which your company might use to implement this growth strategy include:

   a. Opening a branch office

   b. Acquiring a business which produces similar products to those which you now produce, but which operates in a different geographic market

4. *Customer extension.*

Selling your company's products or services to new types of customers. For example, a manufacturer of defense communications equipment might be able to sell similar equipment to nondefense customers such as police departments. Two of the techniques which your company might use to implement this growth strategy are:

a. Set up a new marketing organization to market your products to different types of customers.
b. Acquire a company which sells similar products to those which you now produce, but to a different type of customer.

Your company can also grow by expanding into a different segment of your present industry or entering a different industry than the industry which you now operate in. The two growth strategies which correspond to this type of corporate growth are:

5. *Vertical integration.*

Expand into a business which either supplies your company's present business (backward vertical integration) or which purchases the products or services which your company produces (forward vertical integration). The most common type of vertical integration is when a company enters a different segment of the industry in which it now operates. For example, an oil/gas producer enters the oil field services business. Vertical integration could also be implemented by entering a different but related industry. For example, a book publisher enters the book printing industry.

6. *Diversification.*

Expand into a business which is unrelated to your company's present business. For example, a single-family home builder starts or acquires an FM radio station.

Your company may use either acquisitions or internal growth investment (e.g., new product development) to implement each of the six alternative corporate growth strategies.

REASONS FOR USING ACQUISITIONS TO GROW YOUR COMPANY

There are four potential advantages to using acquisitions in preference to internal growth investment to grow your company. One of these, avoiding company-size danger zones was discussed earlier in this chapter. The other potential advantages are:

1. *To save time.*

A company can often use an acquisition to achieve a corporate growth objective (e.g., obtaining a 10% market share in a new geographic market) which could take several years to realize using internal growth investments (e.g., building and staffing a new manufacturing facility).

2. *To obtain capital financing.*

It is generally much easier to obtain long-term financing to acquire an existing profitable business than it is to obtain long-term financing to start similar new ventures.

3. *To reduce short-term losses.*

New corporate ventures (e.g., developing a new product line) generally require a period of months or years to reach the point where they generate sufficient revenues to be profitable. In contrast, you can often acquire a business which will achieve the same objective (e.g., product line extension) but which has already reached a profitable sales level.

REASONS FOR USING INTERNAL INVESTMENT PROJECTS TO GROW YOUR COMPANY

There are two primary reasons for using internal investment projects in preference to making acquisitions to achieve one of your company's growth objectives. These are:

1. *Higher potential return on investment.*

Typical smaller internal investment projects (e.g., developing and introducing additions to your product line) pay for themselves in 2 to 4 years, even though they may produce no earnings for the first 6 to 18 months. Acquiring an already profitable business to achieve a similar objective (e.g., product extension) avoids this period of no earnings. However, it usually takes 5 to 7 years for an acquisition to pay for itself. (An investment "pays for itself" when the investor has recovered its initial investment out of the annual cash flow produced by that investment.) Over the longer term (7 to 10 years), many larger internal investment projects (e.g., a new manufacturing facility) produce an average annual after-tax profit of 25% to 30% per year. In contrast, similar acquisition investments are likely to produce an average annual after-tax profit of 15% to 25% per year over this same period (7 to 10 years).

2. *Lower risk of failure.*

Failure is defined as an investment project which fails to generate satisfactory profits and is therefore liquidated or sold at a loss within 5 years. It is widely recognized that acquisitions have a higher failure rate than internal growth projects which seek to achieve similar growth objectives (e.g., expansion into new market areas). The following chart compares estimated failure rates for different types of acquisitions and internal growth investments. It is based upon the author's experience and that of other corporate development consultants.

	TYPE OF INVESTMENT	
CORPORATE GROWTH STRATEGY	INTERNAL	ACQUISITION
Market intensification	20%	25%
Geographic extension	25%	30%
Product line extension	25%	30%
Customer extension	30%	35%
Vertical integration	35%	50%
Diversification	45%	60%

Failure rates vary widely from industry to industry. However, this general pattern applies to most industries.

WHEN TO SEEK ACQUISITION OPPORTUNITIES

Acquisitions save time, but have a somewhat higher failure rate than do internal growth projects used to implement the same growth strategy. When your company seeks to achieve a business objective which would take more than three years to accomplish using internal growth investment (e.g., new product development), the benefits of using an acquisition will often outweigh this higher risk of failure. However, when internal investment projects would be likely to achieve your objective (e.g., capturing a 5% market share in an adjacent market area), within three years it is usually unnecessary to incur the higher risk of making an acquisition which would achieve the same objective. This guideline for deciding when to seek acquisition opportunities to achieve your company's business objectives is called the "three-year rule." The following examples illustrate this concept:

USE INTERNAL INVESTMENT WHEN YOUR OBJECTIVE IS TO	SEEK ACQUISITION OPPORTUNITIES WHEN YOUR OBJECTIVE IS TO
Increase sales by 10%	Increase sales by 40%
Add two sales representatives	Add a new marketing network
Expand your present product line	Add a new product line
Expand your present manufacturing capacity	Add a new type of manufacturing operation
Capture a 5% market share in a new market area	Obtain a 20% market share in a new market area

There is one other factor which you should consider before choosing to seek acquisition opportunities to accomplish one or more of your company's business objectives. An acquisition program usually requires significantly more management time and effort than does planning and implementing an internal-growth project which seeks to achieve the same type of business objective. When your company's present business is encountering problems which are absorbing a substantial portion of your senior executive's time and energy, you should postpone launching an acquisition program until either their work load has decreased or you are able to free up their time by employing additional junior executives.

VALID BUSINESS GOALS THAT MAY MOTIVATE YOUR COMPANY TO SEEK ACQUISITIONS

The following are examples of good business reasons for seeking to make an acquisition:

1. Improving your company's competitive position in its industry.
2. Reducing your company's reliance on a particular product line, market area, or type of customer.
3. Improving your company's growth prospects.
4. Obtaining economy of scale cost savings in manufacturing, distribution, marketing, or purchasing.

PERSONAL GOALS THAT MAY MOTIVATE YOUR COMPANY TO SEEK ACQUISITIONS

Personal goals of your company's owners and senior executives may motivate your company to seek acquisitions. The following are examples of these "personal" reasons for seeking to make an acquisition:

1. Providing employment opportunities for the owner's children and relatives who wish to join company.

2. Retaining your key executives and employees by creating career advancement opportunities.

3. Developing new management and marketing challenges for your company's senior executives.

4. Creating a business rationale for the company's senior executives to spend time in an area with a pleasant climate (e.g., Florida), or an interesting culture (e.g., Europe).

5. Enhancing your company's reputation and image by becoming involved in exciting projects.

6. Creating an opportunity for your company's executives to use their "deal-making" skills.

7. Reducing the boredom of managing a business that is no longer growing.

BUSINESS AND PERSONAL GOALS ARE BOTH IMPORTANT

A successful acquisition program requires the active involvement and support of your company's senior executives and its owners. This involvement and support are required both before and after your company makes an acquisition. Since these individuals are motivated by a combination of business and personal goals, they are less likely to devote the time and effort necessary to produce a successful acquisition unless it will achieve both types of goals.

The following are examples of acquisitions which will probably fail because they lack this balance between achieving both business and personal goals:

- A company is headquartered in Iowa. Its key executives dislike coming to New York City because of the dirt, noise, and congestion. The company acquires a New York City–based company in its same industry because the purchase price is low.

- A company is headquartered in Boston. Its senior executives frequently vacation in Arizona. The company pays an inflated price to acquire a company located in Arizona.

- A manufacturer of janitor sinks acquires a computer company because its senior executives want to be in a glamour industry.

TWO RISK FACTORS TO CONSIDER WHEN ANALYZING ALTERNATIVE ACQUISITION STRATEGIES

The following two risk factors are the primary reasons why acquisitions have a higher failure rate than internal growth projects which seek to implement the same corporate growth strategy (e.g., market extension).

Postacquisition management problems

Every company is a unique combination of management systems, styles, personalities, strengths, and weaknesses. Combining two companies always produces postacquisition management problems because of these differences. The greater the differences between the businesses of the acquiring company and the acquired company, the more numerous the postacquisition management problems which are likely to occur.

A second factor which produces postacquisition management problems is the loss of management and other key personnel at the acquired company during the 3 months prior to the change in ownership and the 12 months following the acquisition. Even when the acquiring company makes a good faith effort to retain the executives and other key employees at the selling company, a high turnover rate among these personnel can rarely be avoided.

The number of postacquisition management problems tends to be reduced when:

1. Both the acquiring company and the acquired company operate in the same industry segment.
2. Both the acquiring company and the acquired company operate in the same or nearby geographic markets.

These two circumstances (operating in the same industry segment and operating in the same geographic area) also increase the likelihood that the management of the acquiring company will be able to handle the loss of executives and other key personnel at the acquired company.

Near-term depressed market conditions

This refers to the risk that a newly acquired business will become unprofitable due to depressed market conditions in its industry segment or its geographic markets. When depressed market conditions occur during the first 12 months after you purchase a business (the "near term"), this situation could cause your company to lose some or all of its acquisition investment. The reason is that making an acquisition absorbs financial resources which the acquired business and its new owners need to continue operating an unprofitable business until either:

1. Market demand increases.
2. Reduced competition (as other firms withdraw from the market) permits a surviving business to increase its market share and its profit margin.

The following are some of the factors which reduce the financial resources which an acquirer would have available to continue operating a recently acquired business which becomes unprofitable due to depressed market conditions:

1. The new owner of a business often finds that the capital investment needs of that business for the next 12 months will be significantly higher than was anticipated based upon its annual capital expenditures for the past 2 years. The reason for this unpleasant surprise is that once the former owners decided that they would probably be selling their business they became less willing to make capital investments which might be important over the long term but would reduce near-term profits. Examples of the types of capital expenditures which may require a higher funding level than was being provided by the former owners over the past year or two include:

   a. New product development
   b. Executive recruitment and training
   c. Advertising and promotion
   d. Plant modernization

2. The purchaser of the business (e.g., your company) usually finances a substantial portion of the purchase price by obtaining loans secured by the tangible assets of the acquired company and most of its expected earnings. As a result a newly acquired business is usually burdened by a significantly higher amount of debt and debt service (loan payment) requirements than it had prior to the change in ownership.
3. The purchaser funds the portion of the purchase price, which cannot be obtained by borrowing against the assets and earnings of the newly acquired business, by using a portion of its own surplus cash and unused borrowing capacity. As a result the acquiring company is usuallly burdened with more debt than it had prior to making the acquisition.

4. The acquiring company will usually incur substantial legal and accounting expenses prior to completing its acquisition. Once the acquisition is made, it will incur numerous expenses associated with integrating the management, administration, and operations of its preacquisition businesses and its newly acquired business. These expenditures will absorb a portion of the acquiring company's surplus cash and unused borrowing capacity.

Internal growth projects will also reduce the financial resources which your company would have available to continue operating if its new venture (e.g., developing and marketing a new product line) became unprofitable due to depressed market conditions. However, the following factors tend to make this approach less risky than making an acquisition to achieve the same type of corporate growth objective:

1. The dollar amount of your initial investment is generally much lower.

2. Your investment is spread out over a longer period.

3. You can usually slow down or postpone further investment in response to uncertain market conditions.

4. Legal and accounting expenses associated with internal investment projects are usually lower than those required for an acquisition and are spread over a longer time period.

After you have owned a business for 12 months and it has been operating profitably during this period, depressed market conditions are much less likely to endanger your acquisition investment. This is because the following factors will usually have helped to rebuild your pool of financial resources which can be used to continue operating a business which then becomes unprofitable due to depressed market conditions in its industry segment or geographic market:

1. Approximately 15% to 20% of the debts secured by the assets and earning power of the acquired business will have been repaid. The unused borrowing capacity of that business is now increased by that amount.

2. Cost savings and other benefits obtained by combining the acquired business and your preacquisition business will begin to be reflected in higher profit margins.

3. The number of postacquisition management problems and the cost of dealing with them will be significantly lower than it was during the first 12 months following your acquisition.

4. The latest 12 months of earnings from your preacquisition business will have restored some of the financial resources (surplus cash and unused borrowing capacity) which your company used to fund the cash portion of the acquisition purchase price ("cash portion" refers to the portion of the purchase price which could not be borrowed using the assets and expected cash flow of the acquired business).

There is no way to eliminate the risk that a business which you purchase will become unprofitable during the first 12 months that you own it due to depressed market conditions in its industry segment or geographic market. However, you are more likely to be aware of circumstances which give early warning that market conditions may become less favorable in industries and geographic markets in which you already operate. Some of these circumstances which might alert you to an increased likelihood that market conditions might become depressed over the next 12 months include:

1. Increased import competition.
2. Delays in the receipt of expected new orders.
3. Customers requiring more time to pay their bills.
4. The number of competitors increasing more rapidly than the growth in industry revenues.
5. Increased price competition.
6. In a particular geographic market, indications that a growth cycle may be entering its final phase. These indications include:

   a. A decline in hotel occupancy rates
   b. Poorly managed businesses are rapidly expanding.
   c. A sharp increase in the number of help wanted ads seeking salespeople (this indicates that companies' sales are not growing as rapidly as expected)

When your company looks at the business prospects of industries and geographic markets in which you do not currently operate, there is a much greater likelihood that you will fail to spot indications that the risk of depressed market conditions occurring over the next 12 months has increased. The reasons why only companies which operate in the same industry and geographic markets are usually aware that the potential for depressed market conditions has increased may be obvious to you. However since this is not always the case, here is a brief explanation:

Companies which operate in a particular industry and geographic market generally become aware of potential problems (e.g., increased import competition) 6 to 12 months before these problems either begin to have a significant adverse impact on market conditions or turn out to only have a minor impact. It is in the best interests of these companies not to publicize such potential problems since this would make it more difficult or expensive to obtain bank loans, equity financing, skilled labor, credit from suppliers, and other resources needed by their businesses. It would also reduce the prices which they could obtain if they sold their businesses. Even when deteriorating market conditions begin to reduce their monthly revenues, companies tell the media and their bankers (and often themselves) that this is due to temporary short-term circumstances. This veil of silence and optimism is informal and unplanned, but highly effective. As a general rule informed industry observers such as trade association executives, management consultants, and securities analysts do not become aware that market conditions have deteriorated until public companies begin reporting lower quarterly revenues and earnings. The business press rarely notices that market conditions have become depressed until this condition has existed for at least six months.

FOUR POTENTIAL BENEFITS TO CONSIDER WHEN ANALYZING ALTERNATIVE ACQUISITION STRATEGIES

Business diversification

Business diversification means owning different types of businesses. For acquisition planning purposes "business diversification" is defined more narrowly to mean "owning businesses which are likely to follow different economic cycles and trends." This reduces the risk that most of your company's products and services will simultaneously encounter a prolonged period of depressed market conditions. The primary method of achieving this business diversification benefit is to diversify the industry segments to which you sell and the geographic markets in which these customers are located.

Business diversification can improve your company's ability to survive over the long term because your businesses which remain profitable will help your company meet its financial obligations (e.g., loan payments) during periods when depressed market conditions make your other businesses unprofitable. This also helps your company to be able to operate an unprofitable business for a longer period. This is important because if you can "hold on" long enough, an unprofitable business will often become quite profitable and valuable. This return to profitability occurs when either market demand revives, or competition diminishes as weaker competitors withdraw from your industry segment and geographic market.

Although business diversification generally improves your ability to survive over the long term, there is also a disadvantage to becoming more diversified. During periods when none of your company's businesses are encountering depressed market conditions, operating different types of businesses tends to reduce your company's profitability. Some of the reasons why diversified companies are often less profitable than undiversified companies are:

1. It is more difficult and expensive to monitor, manage, and administer unrelated businesses.
2. Dividing scarce management and financial resources among unrelated businesses can result in none of the businesses receiving sufficient resources to maximize their profitability.
3. The least successful businesses which a company owns often absorb a disproportionately large share of senior management's time and attention.

Businesses in different industries which operate in different geographic markets are less likely to be selling their goods and services to the same industry segment. Therefore, a common approach to seeking the benefits of business diversification is to purchase a business which operates in a different industry or a different geographic market than the acquirer's present business. You should be aware, however, that purchasing a business which operates in a different industry or geographic market does not always achieve this business diversification objective of selling to different industry segments. Sometimes it is even possible to achieve business diversification by purchasing a business which is in the same industry and operates in the same geographic market as your present business. The following two examples illustrate these distinctions.

1. A Michigan single-family home builder acquires a manufacturer of automobile door handles located in Ohio. Though the two businesses are in different industries and geographic locations this does not achieve the benefit of business diversification because the two businesses follow the same economic cycles. They are both likely to face sharply reduced demand for their products if the automobile industry becomes depressed.
2. A company which operates a chain of travel agencies in the Boston area acquires a Boston company which produces package tours of New England for non–English-speaking tourists. Though both businesses are in the same industry and the same geographic location, this combination will achieve the business diversification benefit. This is because the two businesses sell their services to different types of customers and therefore serve markets which do not follow the same economic trends and cycles.

Improved growth potential

A company can use acquisitions to improve its growth potential by acquiring a business which has better growth prospects than the company's present business. These "higher growth" businesses usually serve industries, types of customers, or geographic markets which are growing at a more rapid rate than those served by the company's present business. Most customer extension, geographic market extension (distant markets), vertical integration, and diversification–type acquisitions are motivated at least in part by a desire to achieve this potential acquisition benefit.

Operating efficiencies (synergies)

Two businesses which operate in the same industry segment and the same or nearby geographic markets are likely to have personnel and facilities performing similar functions. The two businesses are likely also to be purchasing similar goods and services. Combining two such businesses can produce significant cost savings by eliminating or consolidating duplicate functions and facilities. Combining the purchasing power of the two companies can produce significant cost savings by enabling them to obtain quantity discounts from suppliers. In some industries companies can also obtain significant cost savings in the form of reduced inventory levels and marketing expenses by operating in more than one industry segment. An example would be a lumber producer which also owns a network of lumber distributors.

Your company increases its likelihood of achieving this acquisition benefit (operating synergies) by acquiring businesses in the same industry and geographic markets in which it now operates.

Marketing effectiveness (synergy)

Each company has its own customer base and marketing strengths. Two businesses which operate in the same industry segment can generally use their marketing resources to sell some of each other's products and services, thereby increasing their combined sales. This type of synergy also occurs when two companies in the same segment (e.g., wholesaling) of different industries (e.g., cosmetics and pharmaceuticals) are selling the same to types of customers (e.g., drugstores). Your company increases its potential to obtain this type of acquisition benefit (marketing synergy) by choosing an acquisition strategy which is implemented by acquiring companies in the same industry segment which it now operates in or a company in a different industry which sells its products or services to types of customers which are potential purchasers of the products and services produced by both businesses.

EXAMINING THE ALTERNATIVE ACQUISITION STRATEGIES

The concluding section of this chapter will describe some of the key characteristics, benefits, and potential problems associated with each of the acquisition strategies which your company might use.

THE MARKET INTENSIFICATION ACQUISITION STRATEGY

Description

Market intensification means acquiring a competitor. A competitor is defined as a business which produces products or services which are the same or similar to those which your company produces and sells them in the same market area, and to the same types of customers to which your company sells.

Examples of market intensification

The following are some examples of market intensification–type acquisitions:

1. A fuel oil distributor which operates throughout Connecticut acquires a fuel oil distributor in New Haven.
2. A bank which operates branches in the Philadelphia area acquires a bank which also operates branches in the Philadelphia area.
3. The publisher of a daily newspaper in Washington, DC, acquires another Washington, DC, daily newspaper.
4. A small plumbing contractor in Atlanta acquires a larger Atlanta plumbing contractor.

Potential benefits

The potential benefits of using a market intensification acquisition strategy include:

1. Increasing your market share more rapidly than is usually possible using internal investment projects (e.g., increased advertising).
2. Obtaining significant cost savings (operating synergies) by consolidating managements, staffs, and facilities, and by combining their purchasing power.
3. Since your business and the selling company's business are similar, the likelihood of fewer postacquisition management problems.
4. Since your management already understands the selling company's business, and is located nearby, the likelihood that your executives will be able to handle postacquisition management problems when they do occur.

A potential problem

The assets of a selling company tend to be worth less to a competitor than they are to other prospective acquirers. The reason is that many of the selling company's intangible assets and some of its tangible assets will duplicate assets which the competitor already owns. Examples of such assets might include:

- Accounting and administrative systems
- Established sources of supply
- Industry knowledge
- Management personnel and expertise
- Manufacturing operations
- Distribution facilities

Companies often find that when they attempt to purchase a competitor's business they are outbid by other acquirers who need, and are prepared to pay for, these assets.

Comments

Market intensification is the safest acquisition strategy which your company can use. The failure rate for market intensification–type acquisitions is significantly lower than it is for other types of acquisitions. Market intensification helps a company to add market share quickly and is likely to produce cost savings for the combined businesses. However, the other alternative acquisition strategies each have the potential to yield more long-term benefits for your company (e.g., business diversification).

THE MARKET EXTENSION ACQUISITION STRATEGY (NEARBY MARKETS)

Description

Market extension means acquiring a company which operates a business which is similar to your present business, but serves a different geographic market. A geographic market is considered to be "nearby" when it is close enough to your present market to utilize the same facilities (e.g., warehouses), personnel, or marketing efforts (e.g., advertising).

Examples of market extension (nearby markets)

The following are some examples of market extension (nearby markets)–type acquisitions:

1. A New York City bank acquires a Long Island bank.
2. A ceramic tile distributor which serves the Atlanta area acquires a ceramic tile distributor in Savannah.
3. A book printing company in Philadelphia acquires a book printing business in Baltimore.
4. A chain of furniture stores in the Boston area acquires a chain of furniture stores in Rhode Island.
5. A Miami company which exports used cars to South America acquires a Miami company which exports used cars to Central America.

Potential benefits

Potential benefits using a market extension (nearby markets) acquisition strategy include:

1. Obtaining a larger market share in a new geographic market more rapidly than is usually possible using internal investment projects (e.g., opening a branch office).
2. Starting off with a profitable level of sales in a new market area.
3. Obtaining cost savings for the combined businesses by utilizing the same facilities (e.g., a regional warehouse), personnel (e.g., accounting staffs), or marketing efforts (e.g., advertising).
4. Obtaining better prices from suppliers by combining the purchasing power of the two businesses.
5. Improving the effectiveness of your marketing efforts. For example:

   a. Newspaper advertisements will now include the locations of both businesses.
   b. The ability to utilize more effective, but more expensive advertising techniques (e.g., cable television) because a larger portion of the audience is now within your market area.
   c. Eliminating overlapping sales efforts and redirecting these resources (e.g., salespeople) to other potential customers.

6. Your executives already manage a similar business and they are located near your newly acquired business. As a result it will be less difficult and expensive for them to handle postacquisition management problems at your newly acquired business.

7. Your knowledge of your own industry and markets helps you to analyze more accurately the risk that the acquired business would encounter depressed market conditions over the next 12 months.

When there are indications that market conditions may be more likely to become depressed you should delay making market extension–type acquisitions until either the potential problems fail to have a significant impact or until the depressed market conditions have persisted for at least 12 months. In the latter case, your risk is reduced because you will be able to make acquisitions at bargain prices, and an upturn in market demand or a decline in competition is more likely to occur over the following 12 months.

Potential problem

Businesses in the same industry segment, and different but nearby market areas are affected by many of the same economic problems and trends. Therefore, although you would be operating in a different market area, both your present business and the acquired business are likely to encounter depressed market conditions at approximately the same time.

Comments

The market extension (nearby markets) acquisition strategy is an excellent moderate risk strategy for most prospective acquirers. However, acquisition candidates which would permit your company to implement this strategy may become available infrequently. Companies which use this acquisition strategy effectively overcome this problem by searching for market extension (nearby markets)–type acquisition candidates continuously for periods as long as two years.

THE MARKET EXTENSION (DISTANT MARKETS) ACQUISITION STRATEGY

This acquisition strategy involves acquiring a company which operates a business which is similar to your present business, but serves a distant geographic market. A geographic market is considered to be "distant" when it is too far away from your present market area for your company, and a similar business in this distant market to obtain significant cost savings by using each others facilities or personnel.

A company should consider using this strategy, in spite of its low potential to produce cost savings when that distant geographic market either:

- Has better growth prospects than nearby markets which the company could expand into.
- Is affected by different economic trends (thereby reducing the risk that both businesses would encounter depressed market conditions at the same time).

Examples

1. A Kansas oil producer acquires a Texas oil producer.
2. A New Jersey bank acquires a bank in Florida.
3. A large plumbing contractor in Chicago acquires a large plumbing contractor in Atlanta.
4. A newspaper publisher in Denver acquires a newspaper publisher in Dallas.
5. A company which operates nine Burger King fast-food restaurants in the New York area purchases six Burger King restaurants in Kentucky.

Potential benefits

1. It is often less expensive for a company to acquire a similar, already profitable business, in a distant geographic market than it would be to start up a new business and build it up to the same level of profitability.
2. You will often start off with a larger market share than you could obtain in three years by starting your own operation in that distant market area.
3. When your company's business operates in a distant geographic market, it is less likely to encounter depressed market conditions at the same time as your present business. Even when depressed market conditions affect an entire industry, they tend to start and end at different times in different regional markets.
4. Though two similar businesses operate in distant market areas, they are sometimes able to increase each other's sales revenues. This benefit is called marketing synergy. The following is an example of how a marketing extension (distant markets)–type acquisition generated marketing synergy benefits:

A book printing company located in northern New Jersey had as its principal customers several large book publishers headquartered in the New York area. Three of these book publishers also had publishing subsidiaries located in California. The New Jersey book printing company acquired a small book printing business located in Los Angeles.

The California company had not been able to obtain printing contracts from the California subsidiaries of these New York–based publishing companies, though it did good work at competitive prices. The reason was that these large publishers preferred to deal with larger printing companies.

Some New York publishers require that a book printing company deliver a portion of their order directly to their West Coast distributors. The New Jersey book printing company had been unable to obtain this business because transportation costs made their bids higher than those of competitors which also operated printing plants close to the West Coast.

Following its acquisition by the New Jersey book printing company, the Los Angeles book printing company became eligible ("qualified") to bid on printing contracts awarded by the California subsidiaries of its parent company's New York customers.

Following the acquisition, the New Jersey book printing company bid successfully for printing contracts which required that a portion of the order be delivered directly to the publishers' West Coast distributors.

5. Companies which now operate in geographic markets which have poor to average growth prospects are often able to use this strategy to expand into geographic markets which have better growth prospects.

6. Though you are likely to encounter numerous postacquisition management problems, your executives' familiarity with the selling company's business will help them handle these problems.

Potential problem

Market extension (distant markets)–type acquisitions have a higher failure rate than do the four other types of acquisitions which you can use to expand your present business. The reason is that it is difficult and expensive to deal with postacquisition management problems at a newly acquired business which is not located near your present business.

THE PRODUCT EXTENSION ACQUISITION STRATEGY

Description

Product extension means expanding your company's present business by adding additional products or services. The product extension acquisition strategy refers to acquiring a business which is similar to your present business (it is in the same industry segment) but which produces different, though related, products and services and sells them to the same potential customer base to which you now market.

Examples

1. A private-label manufacturer of shampoos and related hair care products acquires a private-label manufacturer of face creams and other skin care products. Both companies sell their products to supermarket and drugstore chains in the eastern United States.

2. A wholesale grocery distributor acquires a gourmet food importer. Both businesses supply food stores located in California.

3. A New York–area bank which specializes in import/export financing acquires a New York area bank which specializes in construction lending.

4. A fuel oil distributor which serves Maryland and Virginia purchases a propane distributor located in Waldorf, Maryland.

5. A manufacturer of nonferrous eyelets acquires a manufacturer of stainless steel eyelets. Both businesses sell these small metal parts to New England manufacturing companies.

Potential benefits

1. Expanding your product line more rapidly than if you developed your own new products or services.

2. Obtaining cost savings (operating synergies) by combining facilities and consolidating personnel in areas such as management, administration, and marketing.

3. Increasing sales of your company's present products and services by adding some of them to those distributed and marketed by the selling company. Increasing sales of the acquired company's products and services by adding some of their product or services to your product line (marketing synergy benefits).

4. The executives of the acquiring company will understand many (though not all) aspects of the selling company's business. This makes them better able to handle postacquisition management problems.

5. Companies which produce products or services which have poor to average growth prospects are often able to use this strategy to improve the company's growth prospects by adding products or services which have more attractive growth prospects. An example would be a manufacturer of electro-mechanical cash registers which acquires a manufacturer of electronic cash registers.

Potential problems

1. A company may find that there are few companies in its general marketing area whose primary business is producing products or services which it would like to add to its present product line, or which could significantly increase the sales of the acquiring company's present business by adding some of that company's products or services to the selling company's existing product line.

2. Acquirers frequently underestimate the difficulty of having two marketing organizations successfully cross-sell each other's products or services. Product extension–type acquisitions often produce fewer marketing synergy benefits than were anticipated by the executives of both the acquiring company and the selling business.

3. Since both businesses market their products or services to the same types of customers in the same or nearby market areas, they are both likely to encounter depressed market conditions at approximately the same time.

4. The purchase price of the selling business will include assets which will be of limited value to the acquirer because they duplicate assets which the acquiring company already has. For more detailed discussion of this potential problem, refer back to the section of the market intensification acquisition strategy.

Comments

Joint ventures, licensing agreements, and distribution arrangements usually offer a less expensive means of expanding a company's product line than making product extension–type acquisitions. However few companies have been satisfied with the long-term results produced by these cooperative arrangements. One problem is that no single management has sufficient control over product development, production, marketing, and customer service to respond quickly to changing market and competitive conditions. Disagreements over an "equitable" sharing of profits are another reason why cooperative arrangements tend to fail over the longer term.

THE CUSTOMER EXTENSION ACQUISITION STRATEGY

Description

Similar products or services may be sold by different companies to different types of customers. For example, one company may sell a line of cleansers to hardware stores (for sale to homeowners) while another company may sell a similar product line to janitorial supply houses, while a third company may sell a similar product line directly to school systems and hospitals. Customer extension is when one company acquires a business which sells similar products or services but to a different type of customer than the acquiring company now sells to. Both businesses operate in the same general market area (e.g., both businesses serve customers in northern New Jersey).

Examples of customer extension

1. A cosmetics manufacturer, which sells its products to supermarket chains and other mass merchandisers, acquires a cosmetics manufacturer which sells similar products using direct mail.

2. An accounting firm which primarily serves small manufacturing firms acquires an accounting firm which primarily serves companies in the real estate industry.

3. An auto parts distributor supplies garages and service stations which repair automobiles. It acquires an auto parts distributor which supplies retail stores which serve the do-it-yourself market.

4. A French restaurant acquires a catering firm which provides French-style food for weddings and large parties.

5. A fuel oil distributor which serves commercial accounts (apartment houses, schools, and factories) purchases a fuel oil distributor which supplies homeowners in the same market area.

Potential benefits

1. Different types of customers are often affected by different economic trends. Therefore the customer extension acquisition strategy can help a company to achieve business diversification benefits.

2. It is difficult for a business which serves one type of customer to market its products or services successfully to a different type of customer. This is because each type of customer (e.g., pharmacies) usually feels that it has "special needs and requirements" which would not be properly addressed by a supplier which did not specialize in serving its type of business. Acquiring a business which is already an established supplier to a type of customer which your company does not now serve can often enable you to become an "accepted" supplier to that new type of customer much more rapidly than if you set up a new marketing organization to concentrate on serving those potential customers.

3. Two similar businesses which serve different types of customers can usually obtain significant cost savings by consolidating nonmarketing facilities and functions (e.g., manufacturing) and by combining their purchasing power.

4. Since both businesses operate in the same industry segment, postacquisition management problems will be somewhat easier for the executives of the acquiring company to handle.

Potential problems

1. Many companies find that there are few companies in their industry segment and general market area whose primary business is serving a type of customer to which it would like to sell, but does not already serve.

2. The newly acquired business may be unable to retain key customers. The reasons are:

    a. There is likely to be a loss of senior executives and marketing personnel at the acquired business. Customers who have long-standing personal relationships with these individuals may transfer some or all of their business to competitors who subsequently employ these executives and salespeople.

    b. There is a tendency for the executives at the acquiring company to fail to appreciate the subtle differences which made the acquired business successful at serving a different type of customer.

3. The purchase price of the selling business will often include assets (e.g., operating systems, manufacturing facilities, supplier relationships) which are of limited value to an acquiring company which already operates in the same industry segment and geographic markets. Therefore an acquirer who uses this strategy is generally paying a premium price to obtain the selling company's customer base. This premium can be a good investment, but only if the acquirer is able to retain the seller's customer base following the acquisition.

Comments

Market extension–type acquisitions are more likely to be good investments when the acquired business is relatively large in size. The reason is that the key customers of larger companies are more likely to have a relationship with the "company" rather than with the particular executive or salesman who is servicing their account. Therefore, these customers are less likely to change suppliers when there is a change in the particular individual servicing their account. (Due to high management and salesperson turnover at an acquired business, there are usually changes in the individuals responsible for servicing many of the acquired company's customers.)

THE VERTICAL INTEGRATION ACQUISITION STRATEGY

Description

A vertically integrated company is one which owns a business which produced goods or services which it sells to another business owned by the same company. Usually these businesses are in different segments of the same industry. The vertical integration acquisition strategy refers to a company acquiring a business in a different segment of the same industry (e.g., the petroleum industry).

Examples

1. A carpet manufacturer acquires a regional carpet distributor.
2. A pharmaceuticals manufacturer acquires a manufacturer of fine chemicals (the raw materials used to make pharmaceuticals).
3. A bank acquires an equipment leasing company.
4. A single-family home builder acquires an electrical contractor.
5. An oil producer acquires an oil refinery.

Potential benefits of vertical integration–type acquisitions

1. More dependable sources of supply for the acquirer or for the newly acquired business.
2. A guaranteed market for a portion of the production of the acquirer of the newly acquired business.
3. Cost savings (e.g., reduced inventory levels and marketing expense).
4. Improved market response time (i.e., earlier recognition of changes in customer wants and needs).
5. Having an established *profitable* business operating a different segment of its industry several years sooner than if it started a new business in that segment of its industry.

Potential problems

1. It is very difficult to manage a business successfully which operates in different segments of an industry. The management, administration, and marketing styles, systems, and skills which make a company successful operating in one segment of its industry are not applicable to other segments of that same industry.
2. Vertical acquisition–type acquisitions are the most likely to produce a large number of postacquisition management problems. One of the reasons is that the executives in different segments of the same industry generally come from different socioeconomic groups, have different educational backgrounds, and use a different vocabulary (e.g, the same words have different meanings).
3. Once a company owns one business which supplies another business which it owns, it loses its ability to switch suppliers when it becomes dissatisfied with the quality or pricing of the goods or services it is receiving from its captive supplier.
4. Once a company owns one business which purchases the production from another business which it owns it loses the ability to divert production to other customers which may represent better long-term markets for its production.

Comments

Vertical integration–type acquisitions tend to be exceptionally profitable investments when they are successful. However the failure rate among vertical integration–type acquisitions is higher than for most other types of acquisition which a company might make.

The following are some actual examples of vertical-type acquisitions and the outcome of these investments:

1. A New Jersey gasoline wholesaler acquired a chain of gasoline service stations in its market area. This provided a guaranteed sales volume, which protected the wholesaler's subsequent investment in an expensive new automated port-side gasoline storage facility. This facility enabled the company to purchase tanker loads of gasoline directly from refineries anywhere along the Atlantic and Gulf coasts. The cost savings increased the wholesaler's gross profit margins by over 25%.

2. An oil/gas producer acquired a drilling contractor in order to obtain an assured supply of drilling rigs and crews in case there was a shortage. The oil/gas-producing company anticipated that its own drilling needs would utilize most of the drilling contractor's capacity. In 1983 the oil/gas producer was unable to sell its drilling program to investors and therefore developed only 30% of the number of wells which it developed in 1982. The drilling contractor did not begin seeking business from other oil/gas producers until August 1983 because it was reserving its crews and rigs for its parent company's planned 1983–1984 drilling needs. By this time most of the drilling contracts from other potential customers had already been awarded. The drilling contractor operated at only 50% of capacity from July 1983 to April 1984. This was insufficient to generate the cash flow needed to make the loan payments on debt which it had incurred to purchase new drilling rigs in 1980, 1981, 1982, and 1983. The bank foreclosed on the rigs and the drilling contractor went out of business. The loss of its investment in the drilling contractor contributed to the parent oil/gas company's inability to meet its own financial obligations in 1985, at which time it too went out of business.

3. A company operates a large chain of nursing homes which employ a large number of assistant nurses and other semiskilled medical personnel. There is a high turnover among these personnel because low government nursing care cost reimbursement rates limit salary levels for these positions and working conditions are unpleasant. The government, however, requires that the individuals who fill these positions be graduates of approved vocational training programs. The nursing home operator purchase three vocational schools which graduated several hundred allied health workers each year. This provided a captive supply of qualified workers for its nursing homes. The schools were able to attract a larger number of tuition-paying students because they were able to offer guaranteed employment for successful graduates, in their parent company's nursing homes.

4. A mortgage company merged with a large builder of single-family homes. The mortgage company wanted a captive market for its construction lending customers (e.g., savings and loans) and its single-family home mortgage origination business. The home builder wanted to have better access to construction and home buyer financing if credit markets tightened (credit became less readily available). Following the merger, competing home builders which had been customers of the mortgage company, began directing their business and that of their home buyers, to competing mortgage companies. This sharply reduced the mortgage company's profitability.

THE DIVERSIFICATION ACQUISITION STRATEGY

Description

Diversification means the acquisition of a business which operates in a different industry from that in which your company now operates. Most diversification-type acquisitions are of businesses which are not related to the acquiring company's present business. There are, however, two types of diversification acquisitions which are somewhat related to the acquiring company's present business. These are:

1. *Diversification (product extension).*
    The acquiring company and the selling business both sell to the same type of customers in the same market area. Therefore, there is the possibility that the two businesses might be able to sell some of each other's products or services to its customers.
2. *Diversification (vertical integration).*
    The selling company's business is either a supplier or a customer of the acquiring company's business.

When referring to the more common type of diversification acquisition, which is unrelated to the acquiring company's present business, this is referred to in this section as diversification (unrelated).

Examples—Diversification (product extension)

1. A plumbing contractor acquires an electrical contractor which operates in the same general market area.

2. A distributor of paint and wallpaper acquires a distributor of electrical hardware. Both businesses sell to hardware stores and home centers.

3. A manufacturer of wooden office furniture acquires a manufacturer of office desk lamps.

4. A music publishing company acquires a manufacturer of musical instruments.

5. A computer service bureau is acquired by an accounting firm. Both businesses serve financial institutions located in California.

Examples—Diversification (vertical integration)

1. A steel manufacturer acquires a company which mines coal used by steel mills.

2. A bank acquires a data processing business which serves financial institutions in its region.

3. A large department store chain acquires a women's clothing manufacturer.

4. A furniture manufacturer in North Carolina acquires an interstate trucking company headquartered in Charlotte, North Carolina.

Examples—Diversification (unrelated)

1. A plumbing contractor acquires a toy manufacturer.

2. A wallpaper distributor acquires a travel agency.

3. A department store chain purchases a nursing home.

4. A trucking company acquires a motion picture studio.

5. A company which operates a chain of dry cleaners purchases a garden supply store.

Potential benefits

1. Diversification (product extension)–type acquisitions can produce marketing synergy benefits similar to those produced by the product extension acquisition strategy.

2. Diversification (vertical integration)–type acquisitions can produce similar benefits to those produced by vertical integration type acquisitions in the acquiring company's present industry.

3. Diversification (unrelated)–type acquisitions are usually of businesses which have better growth prospects than the acquiring company's present business.

CHAPTER ONE

Potential problems

Diversification-type acquisitions have a higher failure rate than do other types of acquisitions which your company might make. The reasons are:

1. They almost always produce numerous postacquisition management problems.
2. The executives of the acquiring company are rarely expert at the management of businesses in the acquired company's industry. Therefore, they are less able to deal effectively with postacquisition management problems at the acquired business.
3. The acquirer's executives are unlikely to be aware of potential economic problems which have not yet produced lower sales in the selling company's industry or geographic markets, but may do so over the next 12 months.
4. A company which operates in more than one industry is very difficult to manage successfully. Few companies have the management skills and systems necessary to overcome these difficulties.

Comments

1. These few companies which successfully operate businesses in different industries use a holding company management structure. The two key characteristics of a holding company management structure are:

   a. Management is highly decentralized. Each business operates almost as though it were an independent company.
   b. Sophisticated management information, financial control, and business planning systems are used to permit senior management to monitor and control the holding company's portfolio of unrelated businesses.

2. These holding company management structures are not suitable for a company which is rapidly expanding its present business. The reason is that holding company organizations must employ extra executives and staff personnel to operate their sophisticated management information, financial control, and business planning systems. The cost of these additional personnel is substantial. A company whose present business is growing rapidly needs all of its executive labor talent and capital to handle the problems and opportunities created by the growth of its present business.

3. Though diversification-type acquisitions should be avoided by most companies due to their high risk of failure, there is an exception to this guideline. This is when your company's present business is in an industry segment which has low

profitability, intense price competition, and poor growth prospects. Since your present business may not survive, and in any case you would not want to invest to expand it, the risk of diversifying into a different industry is usually justified. The following are examples of the types of companies that may be in this position:

a. Oil field service companies operating in areas where few new wells are being drilled.

b. Metal fastener manufacturers whose products are being replaced by chemical adhesives and plastic fasteners.

c. Small local retail store chains which are unable to compete effectively with large national chains which are beginning to enter their markets.

d. Coal mining companies which sell their production to the domestic steel industry. (Due to technological change decreasing amounts of coal are required to produce a ton of steel.)

e. Tax shelter syndicators which specialized in the oil/gas and equipment leasing investment areas.

COMPARING ALTERNATIVE ACQUISITION STRATEGIES

Each acquisition strategy offers a unique combination of potential benefits and problems. The following section of this chapter will present charts which indicate how the acquisition strategies differ from each other in terms of these potential benefits and problems.

The potential benefits were described earlier in this chapter. They are:

- Cost savings (operating synergies)
- Marketing synergy
- Growth potential improvement
- Business diversification

The following potential problems are referred to on these chart presentations. They include the two principal risks which make acquisitions have a higher failure rate than internal investments used to pursue similar growth strategies. They are:

- Postacquisition management problems
- Near-term depressed market conditions

They also include potential problems which are more likely to occur when a company uses a particular acquisition strategy. They are:

- *Search difficulty*—a likely shortage of suitable acquisition candidates to implement that strategy.
- *Synergy achievement*—expected difficulty in realizing anticipated cost savings or marketing synergies.
- *Purchase price premium*—the value of an acquisition candidate to your company is likely to be lower than its value to competing acquirers. Therefore you are more likely to be forced to pay "extra" in order to implement that acquisition strategy.

ACQUISITION STRATEGY	POTENTIAL BENEFITS				RISK OF FAILURE
	COST SAVINGS	MARKETING SYNERGY	GROWTH IMPROVEMENT	BUSINESS DIVERSIFICATION	
Market intensification	X				Very low
Market extension (nearby)	X	X			Low
Market extension (distant)			X	X	Moderate
Product extension		X	X		Moderate
Customer extension	X		X	X	Moderate
Vertical integration	X*				High
Diversification (product extension)		X		X	Very high
Diversification (vertical integration)	X			X	Very high
Diversification (unrelated)			X	X	Very high

*Vertical integration also has the potential to strengthen significantly a company's competitive position.

| ACQUISITION STRATEGY | POST-ACQUISITION MANAGEMENT PROBLEMS | POTENTIAL PROBLEMS | | | |
		DEPRESSED MARKET CONDITIONS	SEARCH DIFFICULTY	SYNERGY ACHIEVEMENT	PURCHASE PRICE PREMIUM
Market intensification					X
Market extension (nearby			X		X
Market extension (distant)	X	X			
Product extension			X	X	X
Customer extension		X	X	X	
Vertical integration	XX			X	
Diversification	XX	XX			

XX = severe problem.
 X = moderate problem.

C·H·A·P·T·E·R T·W·O

OBTAINING AND USING INFORMATION ABOUT THE SELLING COMPANY MARKETPLACE

A CRITICAL FACTOR MAKES THE SELLING COMPANY MARKETPLACE UNIQUE

Most of the information which you will need to make good acquisitions is hidden. Key examples of this "hidden" information are:

1. The identities of the companies which are for sale. Most companies which are receptive to being acquired keep this a secret.
2. The amount of money which an owner will accept for his company. Many sellers will not quote an asking price. Those sellers who do quote an asking price usually ask much more than they really expect to receive for their companies.
3. The prices that were paid to acquire companies in your target industry. The purchase prices paid for privately owned companies are rarely disclosed.

WHAT IT WILL BE LIKE TO OPERATE IN THIS SELLING COMPANY MARKETPLACE

Initially, it will be very frustrating. After all, how can you decide what to buy or how much to pay if you don't know what companies are for sale or how much it would cost to purchase them?

HOW MOST COMPANY MANAGEMENTS REACT TO THE DIFFICULTY OF OPERATING IN THE ACQUISITION MARKETPLACE

First, they become angry. The anger comes from a feeling of inadequacy. They don't realize that other prospective acquirers are experiencing the same frustrations that they are.

Then they become fearful. The fear which accompanies any large corporate investment is heightened by the lack of comparative price information for sales of companies.

Then they become disillusioned. Most prospective acquirers never progress beyond looking at acquisition opportunities brought to their attention by brokers. For various reasons, which are discussed later in this chapter, these tend to be companies which are overpriced or have serious problems.

WHY THIS CREATES A SPLENDID OPPORTUNITY FOR YOUR COMPANY

There isn't very much competition for most acquisitions. Any company which devotes the necessary time and effort can make excellent, reasonably priced acquisitions in almost any industry. The exceptions are a few glamour industries (e.g., television broadcasting, pharmaceuticals, newspaper publishing) where intense buyer competition has inflated company selling prices.

ACQUISITION MARKET INFORMATION THAT HELPS YOUR COMPANY DEVELOP AN EFFECTIVE ACQUISITION PROGRAM

1. Knowing why profitable companies are sold. This helps you identify potential acquisition candidates, discover hidden problems, and negotiate more effectively with the selling company's owners.

2. Knowing what types of companies are available to be purchased. Ths enables you to develop realistic selection criteria. For example, in the electronics instrument manufacturing industry there are hardly any acquisition candidates located in the Southeastern states. Therefore, you would not want to make a southeast location one of your acquisition requirements for this industry segment.

3. Knowing how much acquisition candidates in your target industry are likely to sell for. This permits you to determine how large a company you could afford to

purchase. It also helps you analyze whether making an acquisition would be more attractive or less attractive than investing in internal growth projects such as new product development.

4. Knowing how many acquisition candidates there are likely to be in your target industry, which meet your size, location, and purchase price criteria, indicates whether or not your proposed acquisition program is likely to be successful. Generally, you will need to find at least five suitable acquisition candidates in order to have a 50–50 chance of completing one acquisition.

THREE TECHNIQUES YOU CAN USE TO FIND ACQUISITION MARKET INFORMATION

1. *Search and learn.*

Develop a set of general acquisition suitability criteria and start looking for acquisition candidates which fit these criteria. As you analyze acquisition candidates and negotiate with their owners, you will become familiar with acquisition market conditions in your target industry and the psychology of the selling company owners.

This process takes about six months. It would work well if managements recognized that the time and effort they invested during this six-month period was designed to prepare them to launch a successful acquisition program at the end of this period. Unfortunately, most prospective acquirers who use this approach become frustrated and give up just when their market knowledge and acquisition skills have reached the level necessary to conduct a successful acquisition program.

2. *Seller motivation analysis.*

Over the years hundreds of corporate executives and acquisition experts have written articles and books which described their experiences dealing with acquisition candidates. Even though these accounts covered different industries, and different economic environments, the authors almost always reported that the same personal and financial factors motivated the owners of profitable companies to consider selling their businesses.

Once you understand the personal and financial factors which frequently cause owners of profitable companies to sell their companies, you can use this knowledge in the following ways:

a. To identify companies which are likely to be available for purchase.

b. To guide your investigation and analysis of acquisition candidates.

c. To improve the effectiveness of your negotiations with selling company owners.

d. To analyze and compare the techniques you can use to find selling companies.

3. *Statistical analysis.*

   Even though you cannot identify most acquisition candidates before you launch your search program, you can predict the type, number, and selling prices of the acquisition candidates you will find. The statistical analysis techniques used to make these predictions are discussed later in this chapter. The rationale for this statistical approach is:

a. The number of selling companies is a relatively stable percentage of the total number of companies which exist. This relationship also applies within industry segments. Thus, if there are 200 electronics distributors and 100 electronic instrument manufacturers there will be approximately twice as many electronics distributors who would consider selling as there are electronic instrument manufacturers who would consider selling their companies.

b. Using industry and state directories you can estimate the number of companies which exist in a particular industry, along with their size and geographic distribution. Then you can use this information to predict the number of companies in this target group which are likely to be "for sale."

c. The average net worth and profitability of companies in a particular industry can be estimated once you know their approximate size. Thus you can develop financial profiles of typical acquisition candidates in your target industry, without the time and expense required to conduct a search program. Later you will learn how to use these financial profiles to plan your acquisition program. The industry ratios of net worth to sales, and earnings to sales, are found in publications such as *Robert Morris Statement Studies*, U.S. business census reports and published market surveys. Comparisons with similar public companies can also help you develop this information.

d. The selling price of acquisition candidates in a particular industry segment is influenced by the amount and type of buyer demand. This buyer demand can be predicted based upon current economic conditions, interest rates, and examining public companies in that industry segment.

WHY YOU WANT TO UNDERSTAND THE PSYCHOLOGY OF SELLING COMPANY OWNERS

1. It provides clues which will help you identify companies which are likely to be available for purchase.

2. It helps you spot the hidden financial factors which made the owners of an acquisition candidate consider selling at this time.

3. It can help you develop a better rapport with the owners of the selling company. This is important because the owners of a selling company choose which prospective acquirer they will begin serious discussions with.

THE FIRST THREE FACTORS WHICH SELLERS LOOK FOR IN A PROSPECTIVE ACQUIRER

1. *Financial eligibility.*

The sellers want to avoid wasting time with prospective acquirers who seem too small or unprofitable to pay a fair price for their company.

2. *Logical combination.*

The sellers recognize that unless there is a logical reason for combining their company and the prospective acquirer's company they are unlikely to receive an attractive price offer.

3. *Comfort level.*

The sellers want the new owners of their business to be a company which they like and respect.

THE PURCHASE PRICE FACTOR COMES LATER

The factor which is the most important to the seller is, of course, finding the purchaser who will pay the highest price for their business. However, a prospective buyer will not make a price offer until after the buyer has had an opportunity to study the selling business. Therefore, the seller must decide whether to disclose their confidential financial information and commence serious discussions with a prospective purchaser without first knowing how much that company will offer to purchase their business. Your objective is to have the seller provide you with their confidential financial information and commence serious discussions with your company, rather than with some other prospective acquirer. You do this by establishing your financial eligibility, describing logical reasons for combining your company and the prospective seller's company, and developing a personal rapport with the owners of the selling company.

WHY OWNERS SELL THEIR PROFITABLE COMPANIES

Most profitable companies are sold due to changes in the personal circumstances of the company's owner(s). The following are examples of personal circumstances which frequently cause the owner of a profitable company to consider selling:

- *Aging.* The company's owner(s) and/or its senior managers are reaching retirement age.
- *Health.* The company's owner or its key senior executive is in poor health. The unfortunate high frequency of heart attacks among businessmen in their forties cause many companies to become available for sale even though their principals will not reach retirement age for many years.
- *Second chance.* The principals of a typical company devote most of their waking hours to their business. Divorce, remarriage, the achievement of financial security, and similar circumstances cause many businesspeople in their forties and fifties to reevaluate whether they wish to spend their remaining prime years devoted almost exclusively to their work.
- *No relay team.* Many owners of profitable companies hope that their sons or daughters will join the business and continue it for another generation. However, the children of successful entrepreneur owners frequently prefer to enter fields where there is an opportunity for less single-minded devotion to business survival and success. When the last remaining son or daughter makes this choice (e.g., becomes a doctor, lawyer, scientist, or musician) or demonstrates limited business skill, the owner of a company frequently considers selling.

You will want to look for companies where these personal circumstances are present. The owners of these companies are likely to be receptive to your inquiry regarding the possible sale of their company.

HOW BUSINESS CIRCUMSTANCES CONTRIBUTE TO AN OWNER'S DECISION TO SELL HIS OR HER COMPANY

At various times in the life cycle of a business, new investments must be made to protect the company's long-term viability. The owners of a company must then decide whether to take this risk. It is at this point that the owners of a company usually review their personal circumstances. Thus business circumstances are usually the factor which triggers the owners' recognition that their personal circumstances have changed and they should consider selling their business.

BUSINESS CIRCUMSTANCES THAT MAY
REQUIRE THE OWNER OF A PROFITABLE
BUSINESS TO INVEST NEW CAPITAL
INTO THE COMPANY

1. *Technological changes.* New technologies force a company to develop new or improved products in order to protect its market share. For example, many large companies have been making their assembly lines more highly automated. The smaller manufacturers which produce the components which these large manufacturers assemble must now redesign their products to make them compatible with their customers new assembly equipment.

2. *Price competition.* Increased price competition forces a company to make new investments in equipment and personnel in order to increase its efficiency and preserve its profit margins.

3. *Changes in sales levels.* Rapidly increasing sales frequency require new investments in equipment and personnel which exceed the amount of new investment capital generated by a company's internal cash flow.

   Declining sales also frequently require new investments in equipment and personnel which exceed the amount of new investment capital generated by a company's internal cash flow. These investments are necessary either to reduce the company's break-even point or to capture additional market share.

4. *Inadequate equity capital.* The minimum amount of equity capital necessary to support a company's business, grows larger when market conditions in its industry are depressed. Customers pay their bills more slowly while lenders become less willing to permit the company to increase its borrowings or to defer loan principal payments.

   High interest rates and tight credit markets are other factors which increase the minimum amount of equity capital needed to support a company's business. During periods of high interest rates and tight credit markets, companies which are highly leveraged will be at a competitive disadvantage unless their owners can contribute additional equity capital.

DISCOVERING BUSINESS CIRCUMSTANCES
WHICH HAVE MADE THE OWNERS OF A
PROFITABLE COMPANY RECEPTIVE TO
YOUR ACQUISITION INQUIRY

A profitable company will generally be available for purchase due to the personal circumstances of the owner(s). However, this decision is likely to have been triggered by a business circumstance. You need to find out what that business situation was because you will be faced with it if you acquire the company.

The owners of the selling company will usually give honest answers to your specific questions. Your first job is, therefore, to learn enough about the company's business so that you can later ask specific questions which will uncover the business circumstances which made the owners of the selling business receptive to your acqusition inquiry.

At your initial meeting with the owners of the selling company, you want to learn as much as you can about the company's products and markets. Unless you already have them, you also want to come away with copies of the company's financial statements for the past three years. A good way to start your inquiries is to ask the owners to tell you about the company's history. Some of the other questions you should ask at this initial meeting include:

1. What are the different segments of your market? (For example, a cosmetics manufacturer's market might consist of department stores, mass merchandisers, beauty salons, regional distributors, direct-mail merchandising to consumers, other manufacturers who add the company's products to their own branded product line, and dermatologists.)
2. What is your market share? How has it changed in recent years?
3. What are the current market trends? How are they affecting the company's business?
4. What changes have you made in your product line?
5. What changes have you made in your marketing?
6. Who are your principal customers? What proportion of your sales are made to these customers?
7. Is there much competition from imports?
8. Who are your principal competitors? What is their market share?
9. How would you expand your business if you had more capital?

Prior to your second meeting with the owners of the selling company, you should analyze their financial statements and study published material which describes market conditions and trends in the selling company's industry. Then you will be able to develop specific questions which will give you insights into the business circumstances which are making the company's owners receptive to selling their business at this time.

ITEMS YOU SHOULD LOOK FOR WHEN REVIEWING THE SELLING COMPANY'S FINANCIAL STATEMENTS

- *Profit margin trends.* Declining profit margins may indicate increased price competition.
- *Sales trend comparisons.* Compare the selling company's sales performance with that of similar-sized companies in this industry. When sales decline more rapidly, or increase more slowly than the industry average, this may indicate that the company's product line is becoming obsolete.
- *Investment in plant and equipment.* Compare year-to-year changes in pre-depreciation property, plant, and equipment items shown on the company's balance sheet. If these show no increases, it may indicate that the company's fixed assets are becoming obsolescent or worn out.
- *Leverage ratio comparisons.* Compare the selling company's sales to net worth ratio and its liability to net worth ratio with those of similar-sized companies in its industry. A company which is more highly leveraged than industry standards will usually need an infusion of additional equity capital sometime soon.

WHERE TO LOOK FOR INFORMATION REGARDING MARKET TRENDS IN THE SELLING COMPANY'S INDUSTRY

- Industry trade magazines
- U.S. Department of Commerce business census reports
- Published market studies
- Industry trade associations
- Annual reports of public companies in the same industry

HOW ACQUISITION CANDIDATES HIDE THEIR FINANCIAL DIFFICULTIES

1. *Inadequate disclosure.*

Unless a company has audited financial statements, its financial statements will generally not include a complete "Notes to the financial statement" section. This is the section of an audited financial statement which describes a company's contingent liabilities, loan repayment terms, litigation, and contract disputes.

2. *Asset valuation.*

There are many ways in which a company can overstate the value of the assets shown on its balance sheet. For example, it may not have provided adequate reserves for bad debts or may have failed to write down obsolescent inventory. In some instances fixed assets are shown at their "appraised market value" rather than their initial cost less depreciation.

3. *Revenue and expense timing.*

Theoretically, a company should report its revenues and the expenses incurred to produce those revenues at the same time. It is relatively easy for a company to defer expenses to a later period, thereby increasing current profits. For example:

a. Equipment repairs could be misclassified as investment in manufacturing equipment. Since investments in equipment are depreciated over several years, this would reduce the company's reported operating expenses for the current year and increase its reported income.

b. Switching from LIFO (last-in, first-out) to FIFO (first-in, first-out) inventory accounting will reduce the company's cost of goods sold during periods when prices are increasing. This in turn will increase the company's reported income.

4. *Executive compensation.*

The owners of a struggling company will often pay themselves below market salaries. This is commendable, but it does tend to make the company's business seem more profitable (or less unprofitable) than it really is.

5. *Intercompany transactions.*

Affiliated companies can be used to boost the reported earnings of an acquisition candidate by purchasing goods or services at above-market prices or absorbing costs which were actually incurred by the acquisition candidate.

DEALING WITH THIS PROBLEM

It is unrealistic to assume that the financial statements of every selling company will use *conservative* accounting techniques which would reduce their current reported earnings or their net worth (book value). However, when there are obvious attempts to mislead you, you should drop further consideration of that acquisition candidate. The techniques described in this book will help you understand and analyze financial information provided by the seller. No technique, however, can protect you if you are dealing with sellers who are dishonest. Some of the indications that you are dealing with a dishonest seller are:

1. Fixed assets on the company's balance sheet are shown at "appraised market values," but this is not explained or noted on the selling company's balance sheet.

2. The information provided by the owners does not match the information contained in their Dun & Bradstreet credit report or the company's income tax returns.

3. The company's accountants are unwilling to confirm financial statement information provided by the owners.

4. The owners are reluctant to provide you with the documents you need to confirm the financial statement information which they have provided you. Examples of such documents include the company's income tax returns, contracts with distributors, and monthly sales figures.

5. A significant portion of the company's business is done with, or through, affiliated companies, but the sellers are reluctant to supply you with financial statements for these companies.

EXAMPLES OF QUESTIONS TO ASK AT YOUR SECOND MEETING WITH THE SELLING COMPANY

1. Why have your profit margins been increasing or declining?

2. Why have your sales been increasing or declining? What are your sales projections for the coming year?

3. How will your costs of doing business change over the next three years? For example, Do you need to purchase new equipment? Open new facilities? Replace key personnel? When do your leases expire?

4. How will the changes in industry market conditions (which your research uncovered) affect the company?

5. Who are your key suppliers? What is your relationship with each of these suppliers? Do you have any exclusive purchasing arrangements (e.g., regional distributorships)? Can they be transferred?

6. Who else do your principal customers buy from? Are any of your customers beginning to enter your business?

7. How have acquisitions in your industry effected your business? How have specific acquisitions (which your research uncovered) affected the company's business?

8. How much does the company spend on advertising? research and development? marketing? How does this compare with your competitors?

9. Where do you sell your products/services? Could you expand into other geographic markets? What sort of investment would be required? Why haven't you expanded into specific markets (which your research indicated as being growth areas)?

10. What new products or services have your competitors been introducing? How is this affecting your company's business?

11. How large is your marketing staff? How does the size and structure of your marketing organization compare with that of your principal competitors?

12. What smaller companies would you like to acquire to expand or strengthen your company? How would these acquisitions help your business?

SAVE THESE "TOUGHER" QUESTIONS FOR YOUR SECOND MEETING

Delaying your "tougher" questions until your second meeting with the selling company is important for two reasons:

1. The owners of the selling company are more likely to provide candid answers once they feel that you are a serious buyer. By meeting with them a second time and demonstrating that you have studied the selling company's industry, you give this impression.

2. You want to use your first meeting to develop a rapport with the owners of the selling company. Asking "tough" questions at this first meeting tends to make the owners of the selling company angry and defensive rather than making the sellers want to deal with your company as opposed to other prospective acquirers.

WHAT TO DO AFTER YOU DISCOVER THE BUSINESS PROBLEMS THAT HAVE MADE THE OWNERS RECEPTIVE TO SELLING

The first step is to overcome your disappointment. It is natural (though unrealistic) to hope to find a problem-free acquisition candidate. The reason you are unlikely to find a problem-free acquisition candidate is that there are hardly any problem-free businesses. Those companies which appear to be problem-free have either done an above-average job of hiding them or they are temporarily between problems.

The next step is to analyze how costly it will be to correct the business problem which has made the owner receptive to selling. For example, if the company's manufacturing facility needs to be modernized, how much will this cost?

The final step is to subtract the capital which you would need to invest to maintain the profitability of the seller's business from the maximum purchase price which you would have offered, if no subsequent capital investment had been required. This reduced amount is the maximum price which you should now be willing to pay for the business.

THE TWO TYPES OF ACQUISITION CANDIDATES

1. *Active sellers.*

Active sellers are companies which have listed themselves with a mergers and acquisition intermediary who has prepared a profile on the selling company.

Companies become active sellers for one of the following three reasons:

a. The companies need an infusion of new capital or credit either to survive, or to finance continued growth.

b. Management or partnership disputes.

c. The owners find that an active marketing effort is necessary in order to attract prospective purchasers.

2. *Silent sellers.*

A silent seller is a company which would be receptive to considering an acquisition offer from a legitimate prospective purchaser, but has not disclosed this to an intermediary. Silent sellers will not disclose that they would consider being acquired until they have been approached by a prospective purchaser or the pruchaser's representative.

ADVANTAGES OF DEALING WITH ACTIVE SELLERS

1. An information package has already been prepared on the company.

2. The sellers are serious. You will not waste your time with owners who are not really serious about selling, but enjoy being courted.

3. It is faster and less expensive to find acquisition candidates which are listed with an intermediary.

DISADVANTAGES OF CONCENTRATING ON ACTIVE SELLERS

1. A substantial portion of the active sellers (over 50%) are being sold due to financial difficulties. These financial difficulties may be cleverly hidden.
2. You will be dealing with the seller through the intermediary who has the listing. The business practices of many acquisition intermediaries leave "a lot to be desired."
3. Most of the better companies which you can acquire will not be active sellers. That is, they will not be listed with an intermediary.

HOW TO USE AN ACQUISITION INTERMEDIARY WHEN DEALING WITH ACTIVE SELLERS

The acquisition intermediary influences the seller's choice of which prospective acquirer they begin negotiations with and their reaction to a purchase offer.

A competent intermediary can play a valuable role by acting as an alternative nonadversarial channel of communication between the seller and the prospective buyer. An experienced intermediary can also play a valuable role by providing suggestions which facilitate the acquisition negotiations process. Unfortunately most acquisition intermediaries are amateurs and some are unethical.

HOW AN INEXPERIENCED ACQUISITION INTERMEDIARY MAY INTERFERE WITH THE ACQUISITION PROCESS

1. They fear that they will not receive their fee unless they control the flow of information between the prospective buyer and the seller. This fear is well justified. However, trying to control the information flow simply creates delays and misunderstandings while not improving the collectability of their finder's fee.
2. The intermediaries feel a responsibility to advise the seller. However, unless they are experienced they frequently give bad advice. This is especially true when the seller is using its own accountant or attorney as the intermediary. For example, accountants and attorneys typically advise their selling company clients to insist upon a stock sale for all cash. Unless the selling company is especially attractive, and has audited financial statements, and will accept a significantly lower price, few prospective buyers will have an interest in an all-cash purchase of the selling company's stock.

3. Inexperienced intermediaries frequently give the selling company's owners an impression that their company can be sold for an unrealistically high price. The sellers then assume that a prospective acquirer who offers to pay them the company's fair market value is trying to take advantage of them.

UNDERSTANDING WHY THE BUSINESS ETHICS OF SOME ACQUISITION INTERMEDIARIES MAY CREATE A PROBLEM

An acquisitions intermediary can influence the seller's choice of which prospective acquirer they should begin negotiations with. An intermediary should encourage the seller to deal with a prospective buyer who they feel will pay the highest price for the seller's company. Intermediaries may, however, be influenced by other factors such as:

1. The likelihood that the intermediary will eventually be paid their finder's fee.

2. Whether the intermediary has a business relationship with one of the prospective acquirers. For example, an accounting firm intermediary would prefer to find a purchaser who is already one of their accounting clients.

3. Whether the intermediary expects to be rewarded for encouraging the seller to deal with a particular prospective acquirer.

4. The selling company's accountant or lawyer will lose a valuable client when the company is sold. They would prefer that the business not be sold. When the selling company's accountant or lawyer is acting as the merger/acquisition intermediary, they are often overly critical of a prospective buyer's acquisition proposals. The lawyer or accountant will rationalize that they are "looking after their client's best interest."

HOW TO DEAL WITH MERGER/ACQUISITION INTERMEDIARIES

Encourage cooperation

1. When the intermediary is a finder/broker (not an attorney, accountant, or consultant retained by the seller), give the intermediary a finder's fee agreement which provides that you will pay his or her fee, unless he or she is paid by the seller. This will make the finder/broker feel more secure and encourage him or her to influence the seller to enter into negotiations with your company. You should also inform the selling company that your company's policy is to pay any finder's fees due intermediaries. The owners of the selling company will find this attractive even though in the end it won't change the amount they will receive for their company. You will reduce your purchase price offer by the amount of the finder's fee you would be paying.

2. When the intermediary is the selling company's lawyer or accountant (or other retained professional) encourage the intermediary to feel that your company will be a source of future business for them. This is actually a reasonable prospect since you will need competent local professionals after you have purchased the acquisition candidate.

Improve performance

1. Make the intermediary familiar with your company and its growth plans. This will help the intermediary to encourage the seller to negotiate with your company. When the intermediary is a finder/broker, it is worthwhile to have them visit your company.

2. Explain the rationale behind your initial purchase price offer to the intermediary. This will help him to make the sellers less angry and to encourage the sellers to make a counter proposal. The sellers' anger is due to their inflated view of their company's market value and their fear that they are being taken advantage of.

3. Tell the intermediary whenever you discover anything negative about the company (e.g., obsolescent inventory). He can then use this to encourage the sellers to become more realistic in their price expectations.

4. Never discuss with an intermediary how you plan to finance the acquisition. Simply tell them that you have the money available from your banks. Intermediaries become very nervous when they think that their finder's fee might be in jeopardy because you may be unable to obtain acquisition financing. This nervousness is then passed through to the owners of the selling company, who are already afraid that they may be making a mistake in choosing your company to negotiate with.

WHY MOST SELLING COMPANIES ARE "SILENT SELLERS" RATHER THAN "ACTIVE SELLERS"

Once it becomes known that a company is going to be sold, there is a significant negative impact on the company's business. This is due to the following factors:

1. The company's executives and salespeople become nervous about their job and their future role in the company. They become receptive to employment offers from the company's competitors and/or consider going into business for themselves. This creates a high turnover of key employees and makes it difficult for the company to recruit replacements.

2. The company's customers become nervous that the company may no longer be there to handle their service needs and that there may be a deterioration in the company's quality controls. Rumors will develop that the company is encountering severe financial difficulties. To be on the "safe side," customers will begin shifting some of their business to alternative suppliers.

3. The company's suppliers become nervous that they may lose the company's future business if it changes ownership. They also become concerned that the company may be having financial problems and will not pay its bills. Suppliers begin giving the company lower delivery priority and become less willing to extend trade credit.

HOW SILENT SELLERS REACT TO ACQUISITION INQUIRIES

Silent sellers will generally not indicate their willingness to discuss being acquired until they are reasonably certain that there is a bona fide purchaser who has a sound business reason for seeking to acquire their company.

DISCLOSING THE IDENTITY OF THE PROSPECTIVE ACQUIRER

Potential acquirers whose policy is not to disclose their identity until they know that a company is for sale rarely make acquisitions. These companies generally learn of the availability of an ideal acquisition candidate when it is announced that one of their competitors has bought it.

USING STATISTICAL ANALYSIS TO UNCOVER HIDDEN ACQUISITION MARKETPLACE INFORMATION

FACTS ABOUT THE NUMBER OF COMPANIES WHICH ARE ACQUISITION CANDIDATES

Over any six-month period approximately 15% of the companies in the United States would consider being sold to a larger company. For example, Dun & Bradstreet's *Million Dollar Directory* lists 160,000 companies which have a net worth over $500,000. Over the next six months approximately 24,000 of these companies would be willing to discuss being acquired by a larger company in their industry.

The proportion of companies which are acquisition candidates in a particular industry varies from 10% to around 20%.

For example:

PARTICULAR INDUSTRY	APPROXIMATE NUMBER OF COMPANIES (MINIMUM NET WORTH $500,000)	ESTIMATED NUMBER OF ACQUISITION CANDIDATES
Curtain and drapery manufacturers	80	8 to 16
Wood kitchen cabinet manufacturers	90	9 to 18
Commercial printers	450	45 to 90
Wine, beer, and liquor distributors	600	60 to 120
Candy and chocolate manufacturers	90	9 to 18

FACTORS IN A PARTICULAR INDUSTRY THAT INFLUENCE THE PERCENTAGE OF ACQUISITION CANDIDATES

1. Economic conditions
2. Company-size distribution
3. Acquisition price levels

HOW THESE FACTORS AFFECT THE AVAILABILITY OF ACQUISITION CANDIDATES IN A PARTICULAR INDUSTRY

1. Depressed economic conditions (e.g., reduced earnings levels) in an industry increase the number of companies which would consider being acquired. Examples of depressed industries include oil field services, coal mining, and electronic component manufacturing.

2. Large companies are less likely to consider being acquired than are small and medium-sized companies. Examples of Industries in which most of the companies are large include electric utilities, television set manufacturing, and plate glass manufacturing.

3. High acquisition price levels in an industry increase the number of companies which would consider being acquired. Examples of industries where acquisition prices are high relative to annual earnings are television stations, newspaper publishing, and banking.

HOW TO ESTIMATE THE NUMBER OF ACQUISITION CANDIDATES AMONG A GROUP OF COMPANIES

Multiply the number of companies by 15%. This will give you a reasonable approximation of the number of acquisition candidates which are likely to exist among that group of companies. When the factors outlined in the preceding paragraph apply to your target industry, you can add or subtract 20% from the number of selling companies you estimated by multiplying the number of target companies times 15%.

ESTIMATING THE NUMBER OF SELLING COMPANIES IS A VALUABLE TECHNIQUE FOR A PROSPECTIVE ACQUIRER

Earlier in this chapter we discussed the difficulty of operating in the acquisition marketplace due to the lack of key information. In conjunction with your analysis of a target industry, you can use your estimate of the number of selling companies to fill in a great deal of missing information. Specifically, you will be able to:

1. Describe the acquisition candidates you are likely to find.
2. Predict the likelihood that your acquisition program will be successful.
3. Select a cost-effective combination of acquisition search techniques.

Example:

A New Jersey–based electronic instrument manufacturer with sales of $20 million seeks to acquire other similar companies with sales of $2 million to $15 million. Using industry directories, this potential acquirer has identified 80 electronic instrument manufacturers with sales of $2 million to $15 million. Thirty of these companies are located on the West Coast while 50 are located in the East. As we will soon learn, contracting acquisition finder/brokers is likely to uncover one-third of the acquisition candidates while other more time-consuming search techniques would be required to find the other acquisition candidates. The New Jersey company next estimates the number of acquisition candidates it is likely to find in each geographic area, and how many of these are likely to be active sellers and silent sellers:

TYPES OF COMPANIES	NUMBER OF COMPANIES	ACQUISITION AVAILABILITY	NUMBER OF SELLING COMPANIES
West Coast companies	30	15%	4 to 5
Companies in the East	50	15	7 to 8
All companies	80	15	12
	WEST COAST	EAST	COMBINED
Active sellers (listed with brokers)	1 to 2	2 to 3	4
Silent sellers (not listed with brokers)	3	5	8
Total number of selling companies	4 to 5	7 to 8	12

THE NUMBER OF SUITABLE ACQUISITION CANDIDATES PREDICTS THE SUCCESS OR FAILURE OF A PROPOSED ACQUISITION PROGRAM

1. The minimum number of acquisition candidates which you need to find in order to have a 50–50 chance of concluding a successful acquisition is 5. Since acquisition programs are somewhat expensive and very time consuming, it is not cost effective to launch an acquisition program which has less than a 50% chance of being successful. Generally, a company which cannot expect at least a 50% chance of success will be better off concentrating its management time and resources on internal growth projects such as market expansion and product development.

2. A company which is prepared to pay the market price for acquisition candidates has better than an 80% chance of concluding a successful acquisition transaction if it can find ten suitable acquisition candidates.

USING THESE STANDARDS TO DESIGN ITS ACQUISITION PROGRAM

1. To have a 50% chance of success, the company needs to find five acquisition candidates. In our example only four such companies are likely to be listed with brokers. Therefore, the company would also need to use additional acquisition search techniques (e.g., direct mail, advertising, telephone solicitation) to find the selling companies which are not listed with brokers. These are called silent sellers.

2. To have at least an 80% chance of success the company would need to find at least ten acquisition candidates. The company would therefore, need to search for acquisition candidates located both on the West Coast and in the East. The New Jersey company could however limit its search to either the West Coast or the East if it is prepared to accept a 50% chance of success for its acquisition program.

ALTERNATIVES WHEN YOUR ANALYSIS INDICATES THAT THERE WILL BE FEWER THAN FIVE SUITABLE ACQUISITION CANDIDATES

1. Examine the size and geographic distribution of companies in your target industry. Determine why your suitability criteria eliminated so many com-

panies from your target company population. Then consider broadening your industry segment, size, or geographic criteria in a way which will increase the number of target companies. In the New Jersey electronic instrument manufacturer example, the company might consider changing its suitability criteria in the following ways:

a. Including electronic instrument manufacturing companies located in Canada

b. Including electronic instrument manufacturers with annual sales of $1 million to $2 million

c. Including companies which distribute and service electronic instruments

2. Keep your acquisition suitability requirements unchanged, but don't devote too much time or effort to your acquisition program since your chances of success are low.

HOW TO USE PUBLICATIONS SUCH AS DUN & BRADSTREET'S *MILLION DOLLAR DIRECTORY* TO DEVELOP YOUR STATISTICAL ANALYSIS

One of your first objectives is to estimate the approximate size (sales volume) of the acquisition candidates you are likely to find in your target industry. This analysis technique involves first computing the number of companies in your target industry which fall within various size ranges. Once you have this company-size distribution you can pick out those company-size ranges which a significant portion (e.g., 25%) of your target companies fall in. The final step is to compute the average size of the companies which fall within these size ranges.

The following is the size distribution for 73 electronic instrument manufacturing companies listed in the Dun & Bradstreet *Million Dollar Directory* with annual sales of $1 million to $20 million.

SALES	NUMBER OF COMPANIES
$ 1 million	9
$ 2 million	6
$ 3 million	12
$ 4 million	9
$ 5 million	7
$ 6 million	2
$ 7 million	7

SALES	NUMBER OF COMPANIES
$ 8 million	2
$ 9 million	3
$10 million	2
$11 million	2
$12 million	1
$13 million	4
$14 million	1
$15 million	2
$16 million	2
$17 million	1
$18 million	1
Total	73

Looking at this size distribution you will notice that 37% of the target companies have sales of $1 million to $3 million, and 42% of the target companies have sales of $4 million to $10 million. Therefore, it is likely that most of the available acquisition candidates will fall within one of these two size ranges. We can now generate two examples of typical size acquisition candidates. The formula used to make this computation is

$$\frac{\text{Sales} \times \text{number of companies}}{\text{Total number of companies}}$$

For **our two** selected size ranges the computations are as follows:

NUMBER OF COMPANIES	SALES RANGE ($1 TO $3 MILLION) SALES LEVEL		
9	×	$1 million	=	$ 9 million
6	×	$2 million	=	12 million
12	×	$3 million	=	36 million
27		Totals		$57 million

Average size company $= \dfrac{\$ 57 \text{ million}}{27 \text{ companies}} = \$2,110,000$, rounded to $2 million

| | | **SALES RANGE ($4 TO $10 MILLION)** | | |
NUMBER OF COMPANIES		SALES LEVEL		
9	×	$4 million	=	$36 million
7	×	$5 million	=	35 million
2	×	$6 million	=	12 million
7	×	$7 million	=	49 million
2	×	$8 million	=	16 million
3	×	$9 million	=	27 million
2	×	$10 million	=	20 million
32		Totals		$195 million

Average size company $\dfrac{= \$195 \text{ million}}{32 \text{ companies}} = \$6,090,000$, rounded to $6 million

HOW SIZE INDICATIONS OF ACQUISITION CANDIDATES CAN HELP YOU

1. You can estimate how a typical acquisition would effect your own company's size (sales volume).

2. Using the techniques discussed in the following sections of this chapter you will be able to develop profiles of typical acquisition candidates in your target industry. These profiles will include the estimated sales, net income, book value, and selling price of typical acquisition candidates which you are likely to find in your target industry.

WHERE TO LOOK FOR COMPANY SIZE AND LOCATION INFORMATION FOR YOUR TARGET INDUSTRY

1. *Multi-industry directories*
   Dun & Bradstreet's Million Dollar Directory
      Dun & Bradstreet, Inc.
      99 Church Street
      New York, NY 10007

   Register of American Manufacturers
      Thomas Publishing Company
      One Penn Plaza
      New York, NY 10001

State industrial directories (various states)
State Industrial Directories Corporation
Two Penn Plaza
New York, NY 10004

Ward's Business Directory, Volumes 1 and 2
Information Access Company
11 Davis Drive
Belmont, CA 94002

2. *Industry directories*

To find whether there is a company directory for your target industry consult the following publications.

Directory Information Service
Gale Research Company
Book Tower
Detroit, MI 48226

Encyclopedia of Business Information
Gale Research Company
Book Tower
Detroit, MI 48226

3. *Industry statistics*

Census of Manufacturers
U.S. Printing Office
Superintendent of Documents
Washington, DC 20402

Statistics Sources
Gale Research Company
Book Tower
Detroit, MI 48226

4. *Trade associations*

Trade associations frequently compile statistical information for companies in their industry. Consult the following publications to find the trade association for your target industry.

Encyclopedia of Associations
Gale Research Company
Book Tower
Detroit, MI 48226

National Trade & Professional Associations
Columbia Books, Inc.
777 14th Street, NW
Washington, DC 20005

5. *Industry market studies*

Companies which compile and publish a large number of market research studies include:

Predicasts, Inc.
Industry Surveys Department
1101 Cedar Avenue
Cleveland, OH 44106

Find/SVP
Information Clearing House
500 Fifth Avenue
New York, NY 10036

Frost & Sullivan
106 Fulton Street
New York, NY 10038

Morton Research
1745 Merrick Avenue
Merrick, NY 11566

The following directories list the market research studies available from several hundred research publishers:

The Directory of U.S. and Canadian Marketing Surveys
C.H. Kline & Co., Inc.
330 Passaic Avenue
Fairfield, NJ 07006

Findex
Information Clearing House
500 Fifth Avenue
New York, NY 10036

International Directory of Published Market Research
Undine Corporation
230 West 55th Street
New York, NY 10019

6. *Industry Periodicals*

Many industry periodicals have an annual review which contains company size and location data for the industry which that periodical serves. One of the most comprehensive directories of industry periodicals is:

Business Publications Rates and Data
Standard Rate and Data Service
5201 Old Orchard Road
Skokie, IL 60077

7. *Mailing List Compilers*

Companies which compile mailing lists of companies in your target industry can sometimes give you a statistical breakdown by company size and location. To find the companies which compile mailing lists in your target industry, consult the following publication:

Direct Mail List Rates and Data
Standard Rate and Data Service
5201 Old Orchard Road
Skokie, IL 60077

USING THE NUMBER OF EMPLOYEES TO ESTIMATE A COMPANY'S SALES

Many directories and compilations of industry statistics give company size data in terms of number of employees rather than sales volume. In order to estimate the sales volume of these companies you multiply the number of employees that a company has, times the average sales per employee for companies in that industry. For example, if a company has 40 employees and the average sales volume for similarly sized companies is $200,000 per employee, then you would estimate the company's annual sales to be $8,000,000.

OTHER ACQUISITION MARKETPLACE INFORMATION WHICH WILL HELP YOU DEVELOP YOUR ACQUISITION PROGRAM

Using the techniques described in the previous section of this chapter you now have a good idea of the number, size, and geographic distribution of the acquisition candidates in your target industry segment. It would also be helpful to have some idea of what a typical acquisition candidate's earnings, cash flow, and net worth are likely to be.

For acquirers which are public companies, the earnings of an acquisition candidate are especially important because their stock price tends to be a multiple of their earnings. Therefore, they need to be able to see how adding the selling company's earnings would affect their own earnings, after deducting the interest on the money they would borrow to make the acquisition.

For privately owned acquirers, cash flow is especially important because this is the money which the selling business generates which would be available for repaying the loans used to make the acquisition, and providing compensation to the new owners for the money which they invest from their existing business.

For both public and privately owned acquirers, the seller's net worth gives an indication of its liquidation value. Liquidation value is the amount of money which would be left over after selling off the acquired company's assets and repaying its liabilities. Since the selling price of a business is usually greater than its liquidation value, this difference represents an estimate of the amount which a purchaser would lose if it decided to close down the business due to inadequate earnings and cash flow after it owned it.

DEFINING THE CASH FLOW OF A SELLING BUSINESS

There are many definitions of cash flow. The ideal definition for an acquirer would be the amount of cash generated by a selling business which will be available to repay loans used to make the acquisition and to provide a return on the cash taken out of the acquirer's existing business and used to make the acquisition. At this stage in your analysis you will not have sufficient information to determine how much of the cash generated by a selling business would need to be reinvested in that business to maintain its operations and its profitability. Therefore, a simplified accounting definition will be used. This is to take pretax earnings and add to them the noncash depreciation and amortization expenses which were deducted for tax purposes in order to determine the taxable earnings of the business.

DEFINING THE NET WORTH (BOOK VALUE) OF A SELLING BUSINESS

Net worth or book value are defined as the assets of the selling business less its liabilities. The fixed assets (e.g., property, plant, and equipment) are shown on the balance sheet of a business at their cost less accumulated depreciation. Since these fixed assets are not adjusted for inflation there is a tendency for their values on a selling company's balance sheet to be lower than the fair market value of these assets. This undervaluation tends to be greatest when the selling business is privately owned because the owners frequently have reduced their annual corporate income taxes by classifying capital expenditures as current expenses and taking the maximum depreciation permitted by the Internal Revenue Service. In spite of these limitations, net worth (book value) does give some indication of the liquidation value of a selling business.

HOW YOU CAN ESTIMATE THE CASH FLOW, EARNINGS, AND NET WORTH OF THE ACQUISITION CANDIDATES YOU ARE LIKELY TO FIND IN YOUR TARGET INDUSTRY

Various publications provide comparative financial statement data for various-sized companies in different industries and industry segments. One of the best of these publications is a business ratio handbook entitled, *Robert Morris Statement Studies*. Although this is produced to meet the needs of bank credit and loan officers, anyone may purchase a copy from Robert Morris Associates (The National Association of Bank Loan Officers), 1616 Philadelphia National Bank Building, Philadelphia, PA 19107.

Using comparative financial statement data, you are able to compute the net income/sales, cash flow/sales, and net worth/sales ratios for the size categories that would include your target acquisition candidates. For example, assume that the comparative financial statement data for electronics instrument manufacturers is as follows:

Size (sales range)	$1 to 3 million	$5 to 10 million
Number of companies in sample	30	20
Average sales	$2,500,000	$7,000,000
Average net income	$ 150,000	$ 350,000
Average cash flow	$ 175,000	$ 450,000
Average net worth	$ 325,000	$1,000,000

Using these data we are able to compute the net income/sales, cash flow/sales and net worth/sales for companies in the two company size ranges.

	SIZE (SALES RANGE)	
	$1 TO 3 MILLION	$5 TO 10 MILLION
Net income / Sales	$\dfrac{\$150,000}{\$2,500,000} = 6\%$	$\dfrac{\$350,000}{\$7,000,000} = 5\%$
Cash flow / Sales	$\dfrac{\$175,000}{\$2,500,000} = 7\%$	$\dfrac{\$450,000}{\$7,000,000} = 6\%$
Net worth / Sales	$\dfrac{\$325,000}{\$2,500,000} = 13\%$	$\dfrac{\$1,000,000}{\$7,000,000} = 14\%$

Now we apply these ratios to the average sales volumes for typical companies in our target industry. For electronics instrument manufacturers, the representative company size levels were:

Company A = $2 million annual sales
Company B = $6 million annual sales

When we apply the ratios which we computed to our representative-size electronics instrument companies, we create a financial profile of typical acquisition candidates in this industry:

	COMPANY A	COMPANY B
Sales	$2 million	$6 million
Net income	$120,000 (sales × 6%)	$300,000 (sales × 5%)
Cash flow	$140,000 (sales × 7%)	$360,000 (sales × 6%)
Net worth	$260,000 (sales × 13%)	$840,000 (sales × 14%)

ANALYZING THE BUYER SIDE OF THE SELLING COMPANY MARKETPLACE

Up to this point our discussion has concentrated on understanding the motivations and characteristics of the selling companies in your target industry segment. Now we are ready to examine the two "components" of the buyer side of the marketplace. These two components are:

1. The amount of buyer competition you are likely to encounter when you seek acquisitions in a particular industry segment.

2. The types of acquirers who are likely to be competing with you to acquire businesses in a particular industry segment.

WHY THE AMOUNT OF BUYER COMPETITION IS IMPORTANT TO YOUR COMPANY

1. When there is limited competition among potential purchasers for companies in your target industry you can usually find good candidates by searching for active sellers. It is considerably less expensive to search for active sellers than for silent sellers.

2. When there are likely to be many interested acquirers for companies in your target industry, it is almost useless to search for active sellers. The better acquisition candidates will be picked off before they become active sellers.

3. When there is limited buyer interest for companies in your target industry, the seller may accept an installment sale arrangement rather than insisting on an all-cash sale. An installment sale is when the seller agrees to receive a portion of the selling price in future payments.

4. When there are likely to be many interested acquirers for companies which fit your search criteria it is pointless to make an offer less than book value, or to insist on an installment purchase. In almost every such case, you will lose the company to an "all-cash" buyer who will pay book value. This will occur even if you are well along in the negotiating process and you think you have reached an agreement with the seller.

BUYER DEMAND VERSUS SELLING COMPANY SUPPLY

Like any other marketplace, price levels are determined by the interaction of supply and demand. However, in most industries, the number of selling companies remains fairly constant from year to year. This is because most companies are sold due to the personal circumstances of their owners. In contrast, the number and type of buyers varies from year to year in response to changing economic conditions. Therefore, buyer demand is the principal factor which determines the price levels for acquisitions in a particular industry.

FACTORS WHICH INCREASE OR DECREASE THE AMOUNT OF BUYER COMPETITION FOR PROFITABLE ACQUISITION CANDIDATES

1. *Industry business conditions.* Most companies are sold to other companies in their same industry. When an industry is prosperous, there will be more companies seeking to acquire others within the industry. When an industry has been depressed for longer than 12 months, few companies will seek to acquire others in their own industry.

2. *Size (sales volume).* There tends to be considerable buyer competition for any profitable company with sales of $10 million or more, regardless of what industry it is in. On the other hand, if you are seeking acquisitions of companies with sales of $3 million to $10 million you can expect to find significantly less competition from other prospective purchasers.

3. *Size (book value).* Many individuals and groups of individuals would like to acquire a profitable smaller company. These noncorporate acquirers can typically raise enough money from savings and personal borrowings to acquire a manufacturing company with a book value of up to $1 million or a service company with a book value of up to $500,000. There are, therefore usually many interested acquirers for companies at or below these size levels.

4. *Growth potential/glamour/profitability.* Companies which are in industries which are considered glamorous (e.g., computer software) or especially lucrative (e.g., television stations), or which are growing rapidly (e.g., hazardous waste disposal) attract considerable buyer interest. This high level of buyer interest will apply to even relatively small companies (annual sales of $2 million) in glamorous or rapidly growing industries.

5. *Credit availability.* Most companies and investment groups borrow from financial institutions in order to finance their acquisitions. When lenders make longer-term financing available at attractive interest rates, more companies begin launching acquisition programs. Buyer demand is higher when the prime interest rate has been declining for six months or has dropped below 10% per annum.

6. *Stock market conditions.* There are over 7,000 public companies. These companies tend to become acquisition minded when their stock is selling for more than book value and their current price/earnings ratio is higher than 12 to 1. A company's price/earnings ratio is the market price of its stock divided by its net income per share.

HOW TO PREDICT THE AMOUNT OF BUYER COMPETITION FOR ACQUISITION CANDIDATES IN YOUR TARGET INDUSTRY

Three approaches which help you estimate the amount of buyer competition are:

1. Analyze the amount of reported merger/acquisition activity in your target industry.
2. Examine the current economic conditions in the national economy and in your target industry.
3. Examine the price/earnings levels (market price per share divided by earnings per share) of a large diversified group of public companies. Then compare this

with the average price/earnings level of public companies in your target industry.

HOW TO ANALYZE THE AMOUNT OF REPORTED MERGER/ACQUISITION ACTIVITY IN YOUR TARGET INDUSTRY

The proportion of the companies in an industry which are sold or merged over a recent 12-month period indicates the level of buyer interest in that industry. You can use the following guidelines to make this estimate:

% OF COMPANIES SOLD OR MERGED	INDICATES
3% or higher	Intense buyer competition
2% to 3%	Normal buyer competition
Less than 2%	Low buyer competition

The procedure for computing the percentage of companies in your target industry which were sold consists of the following steps.

1. *Count* the number of companies in your target industry listed in Dun & Bradstreet's *Million Dollar Directory.* Only count those companies whose primary SIC (Standard Industrial Classification Code) number is that of your target industry. Do not count those companies which are listed in the directory under your target industry classification but have a different primary SIC number.

2. *Count* the number of reported acquisitions and mergers in your target industry by consulting one of the publications which compiles this information. Two of these publications are:

    Mergers & Acquisitions (quarterly journal)

    Mergerstat Review (annual)

3. *Divide* the number of reported acquisitions and mergers in your target industry by the number of companies in that industry listed in Dun & Bradstreet's *Million Dollar Directory.* For example, if there were 7 reported acquisitions and mergers in an industry which had 280 companies listed in the Dun & Bradstreet directory, the computation would be 7 ÷ 280 = 2.5%.

WHEN TO AVOID USING THIS APPROACH

The statistics for the number of reported acquisitions and mergers are compiled for a prior period such as the previous calendar year. They will not indicate current merger/acquisition activity levels in your target industry if current economic conditions are now significantly better or worse than they were for the period when the reported acquisition and merger activity occurred. Therefore, you should avoid using this approach when economic conditions in your target industry have been changing over the past 12 months.

HOW TO USE ECONOMIC CONDITIONS TO ESTIMATE THE LEVEL OF BUYER COMPETITION FOR ACQUISITIONS IN YOUR TARGET INDUSTRY

1. First, examine the current status of the national economy. It is necessary to decide only whether the general economy is considered to be in a recession or a nonrecession period.

2. Next examine interest rate levels and note which of the following two categories apply.

   a. The prime interest rate is less than 8%, or it is under 10% and is declining.
   b. The prime interest rate is over 10%, or it is over 8% and increasing.

3. The final step is to classify economic conditions of your target industry in one of the following three categories:

   a. Depressed or declining
   b. Profitable and growing at a similar rate as the national economy
   c. Profitable and growing rapidly

4. Choose Chart A, B, C, or D depending upon national economic conditions and interest rate levels. After making this choice, select the line which indicates the economic conditions in your target industry. Finally read across to find the level of buyer competition.

**A. National economic conditions : depressed
    Interest rates : high or increasing**

TARGET INDUSTRY ECONOMIC CONDITIONS	BUYER COMPETITION
Depressed or declining	Very low
Profitable, average growth rate	Low
Profitable, high growth rate	Moderate

**B. National economic conditions : depressed
    Interest rates : low or declining**

TARGET INDUSTRY ECONOMIC CONDITIONS	BUYER COMPETITION
Depressed or declining	Low
Profitable, average growth rate	Below average
Profitable, high growth rate	Average

**C. National economic conditions : nonrecessionary
    Interest rates : high or increasing**

TARGET INDUSTRY ECONOMIC CONDITIONS	BUYER COMPETITION
Depressed or declining	Low
Profitable, average growth rate	Average
Profitable, high growth rate	Above average

**D. National economic conditions : nonrecessionary
    Interest rates : low or declining**

TARGET INDUSTRY ECONOMIC CONDITIONS	BUYER COMPETITION
Depressed or declining	Low
Profitable, average growth rate	Above average
Profitable, high growth rate	Intense

HOW TO USE STOCK MARKET PRICE/ EARNINGS LEVELS TO PREDICT THE AMOUNT OF BUYER COMPETITION IN YOUR TARGET INDUSTRY

Stock market price levels are influenced by many of the same factors which increase or decrease the amount of buyer competition for acquisition candidates. These factors include:

- The current status and growth prospects of the national economy
- Interest rate levels and trends
- The relative profitablility and growth potential of different industries

You can predict the amount of buyer competition for acquisition candidates in your target industry by examining how the stock market is valuing public companies in that same industry.

1. The first step is to estimate the general level of buyer interest in making acquisitions. You can make this estimate by examining the average price/ earnings ratio for a large group of public companies in a diversified group of industries.

The *Value Line Investment Survey* (found in most public libraries) is a good source of this average price/earnings data. Each week the *Survey* computes the average price/earnings ratio for a group of approximately 1,600 public companies. Based upon the average price/earnings ratio, you can make the following assumptions:

AVERAGE PRICE/EARNINGS RATIO	GENERAL LEVEL OF BUYER COMPETITION
8:1 or lower	Low or average
9:1 to 11:1	Average or above average
11:1 or higher	Above average or high

As indicated, the average price/earnings ratio for public company stocks indicates the range of buyer interest in acquisitions.

2. The next step is to decide which of the two levels of buyer interest within the range indicated by general stock market price/earnings levels should apply to your target industry.

To make this determination you compare the average price/earnings ratio for public companies in your target industry with the average price/earnings ratio for public stocks in all industries. You can find average price/earnings ratios for public companies in specific industries in the *Value Line Investment Survey* and *Standard & Poor's Industry Survey*. When your target industry's average price/earnings ratio is not listed in these, or similar publications, you will have to make the computation yourself. To do this you first make a list of public companies in your target industry. When your company will be seeking to acquire small or medium-sized companies in its target industry, you should select public companies in this size range for your average price/earnings ratio computation. You will find most of the small and medium-sized public companies in your target industry listed and described in *Moody's OTC Manual.* (The larger public companies in your target industry are listed and described in *Moody's Industrial Manual.*) You will find these publications in the business reference section of most public libraries.

3. The next step is to find the annual earnings per share for the public companies on your list and their recent stock price. You can find their current earnings in *Standard & Poor's Corporation Records* and obtain their stock prices from *The Wall Street Journal.*

4. Now you are ready to compute the price/earnings ratio for each company by dividing their current stock price by their annual reported earnings per share. Disregard those companies which are not profitable because this would distort your computation. The following are examples of how price/earnings ratios are **computed.**

COMPANY	STOCK PRICE	EARNINGS PER SHARE	PRICE ÷ EARNINGS	P/E RATIO
A	$15	$1.50	$15/1.50	10:1
B	40	2.00	40/2.00	20:1
C	7	1.00	7/1.00	7:1
D	20	1.80	20/1.80	11:1

5. The final computation is to average together the price/earnings ratios by adding together the first numbers of the price/earnings ratios and then dividing by the number of companies in your sample. The following illustrates this computation.

COMPANY	FIRST NUMBER OF P/E RATIO
A	10
B	20
C	7
D	11

Total 48 ÷ 4 companies = 12 to 1 average
P/E ratio

You now have two average price/earnings ratios. One is for a large number of public companies in a diversified group of industries while the second is for a group of public companies in your target industry. By comparing these ratios you can see how attractive your industry is to investors and prospective company acquirers. Take the first number of the price/earnings ratio for public companies in your industry and divide it by the first number of the price/earnings ratio for a large number of companies in a diversified group of industries. For example, assume that the average price/earnings ratio for the approximately 1,600 stocks in the *Value Line Investment Survey* is 12 to 1 and the average price/earnings ratios for different industries are as follows:

INDUSTRY	INDUSTRY P/E RATIO	STOCK MARKET P/E RATIO	INDUSTRY ATTRACTIVENESS QUOTIENT
A	15:1	12:1	15 ÷ 12 = 125%
B	11:1	12:1	11 ÷ 12 = 92%
C	8:1	12:1	8 ÷ 12 = 67%

When an industry has an industry attractiveness quotient of 90% to 110%, its attractiveness to acquirers is average. A quotient below 90% indicates that companies in that industry have below-average attractiveness relative to companies in other industries while a quotient over 110% indicates an above-average attractiveness. Now we are ready to estimate the level of buyer competition in your target industry by combining the general level of buyer interest in acquisitions with the relative attractiveness of your target industry.

Buyer Interest in Acquisitions

INDUSTRY ATTRACTIVENESS QUOTIENT	AVERAGE PRICE/EARNINGS LEVEL FOR PUBLIC COMPANIES		
	8:1 OR LOWER	9:1 TO 11:1	11:1 OR HIGHER
90% or lower	Low	Low	Average
90% to 110%	Average	Average	Above average
110% or higher	Above average	Above average	High

TWO USEFUL OBSERVATIONS INDICATED BY THIS CHART

1. There will be a considerable amount of buyer competition for acquisitions in industries which investors consider to be especially attractive due to their superior earnings and growth prospects. This will be true even when poor economic conditions and high interest rates have caused stock market prices to be at low levels relative to company earnings.

2. There will be limited buyer competition for acquisitions in industries which are depressed even when prosperous economic conditions and low or declining interest rates have caused average stock market prices to be at high levels relative to company earnings.

THE ADVANTAGE OF ESTIMATING BUYER DEMAND FOR ACQUISITIONS BASED UPON AN EXAMINATION OF PRICE/ EARNINGS LEVELS FOR PUBLIC COMPANIES

Stock market price/earnings ratios anticipate economic conditions and interest rates over the next 6 to 12 months. This approach, therefore, gives an indication of the future level of buyer competition for acquisition search programs which you plan to begin over the next 6 months. The other two approaches tend to reflect current acquisition market conditions. They are, therefore, more useful for estimating buyer competition when you have already launched your acquisition search program.

WHY YOU WANT TO EXAMINE THE TYPES OF ACQUIRERS LIKELY TO BE SEEKING TO PURCHASE BUSINESSES IN YOUR TARGET INDUSTRY

Each of the four types of acquirers which seek to purchase businesses value acquisition candidates in a different manner. Once you determine the types of acquirers who are likely to be competing with you to make acquisitions in your target industry segment, you can develop a rough estimate of how much you would need to pay to acquire a typical selling company in that industry segment.

THE FOUR TYPES OF COMPANY PURCHASERS

Most purchasers of selling companies fall into one of the following four categories:

1. Asset buyers (bargain hunters).
2. Privately owned companies in the same industry as the selling company.
3. Public companies in the same industry as the selling company.
4. Public companies in other industries who wish to enter the selling company's industry.

DEFINING THE ASSET BUYER (BARGAIN HUNTER) SEGMENT OF THE COMPANY ACQUIRER MARKET

This segment of the market consists of companies, entrepreneurs, and private investor groups that will seek to acquire a profitable company if they can borrow most of the purchase price. The terms and cost of acquisition financing is therefore a key factor which influences the amount which this type of purchaser will pay for an acquisition candidate.

HOW THE FOUR TYPES OF COMPANY PURCHASERS VALUE ACQUISITION CANDIDATES

1. *Asset buyers (bargain hunters)* tend to base their valuations on the amount which they can borrow against the selling company's assets and its current cash flow.

2. *Privately owned companies in the same industry* as the selling company tend to base their valuations on a combination of book value and projected cash flow.

3. *Public companies in the same industry* as the selling company are concerned about how an acquisition would effect their own earnings per share. They therefore tend to value an acquisition candidate based upon its current net income.

4. *Public companies which wish to enter the selling company's industry* are usually seeking to improve their own company's growth rate. They, therefore, tend to value an acquisition candidate based upon its projected net income over the next three to five years.

The following chart summarizes these valuation approaches used by the four types of company purchasers:

TYPE OF PURCHASER	VALUATION BASED UPON SELLING COMPANY'S				
	NET WORTH	CURRENT CASH FLOW	PROJECTED CASH FLOW	CURRENT NET INCOME	PROJECTED NET INCOME
Privately owned companies (same industry)	X		X		
Public companies (same industry)				X	
Public companies (different industries)					X
Asset buyers (bargain hunters)	X	X			

HOW TO DETERMINE WHICH TYPE(S) OF PURCHASERS ARE SEEKING ACQUISITIONS IN YOUR TARGET INDUSTRY

One approach is to examine the acquisitions which have been announced over the past 12 months in your target industry and note which type(s) of purchasers have been making these acquisitions. There are several publications which report on current acquisition activity. Two of these are:

National Review of Corporate Acquisitions
   Tweed Publishing Company
   9720 Wilshire Boulevard
   Beverly Hills, CA 90212

Mergers & Acquisitions (quarterly journal)
   229 South 18th Street
   Philadelphia, PA 19103

A difficulty in using these two sources is that they often overlook acquisitions of privately owned companies by other privately owned companies. Therefore, a better, though more time-consuming, technique is to review the acquisitions reported in the principal trade publication for your target industry.

Another approach which is not quite as accurate, but which is satisfactory for planning purposes, is to examine the price/earnings ratios for public companies in your target industry. This approach uses the same price/earnings comparisons that were used to predict the amount of buyer interest for companies in a target industry. We again utilize the average price/earnings ratio for a large diversified group of public companies and the attractiveness quotient for our target industry. Then you use the following chart to predict the type(s) of purchasers who are seeking acquisitions in your target industry.

Projected Types of Purchasers

INDUSTRY ATTRACTIVENESS	AVERAGE PRICE/EARNINGS LEVEL FOR PUBLIC COMPANIES	
	9:1 OR LOWER	10:1 OR HIGHER
Below average	Asset buyers	Asset buyers Private companies (same industry)
Average	Asset buyers Private companies (same industry)	Asset buyers Private companies (same industry) Public companies (same industry)
Above average	Asset buyers Private companies (same industry) Public companies (same industry)	Asset buyers Private companies (same industry) Public companies (same industry) Public companies (other industries)

HOW TO ESTIMATE THE AVERAGE SELLING PRICE OF A TYPICAL ACQUISITION CANDIDATE IN YOUR TARGET INDUSTRY SEGMENT

The actual selling price of a particular selling company will depend upon a wide variety of factors. These include the selling company's size, market position, cash flow, earnings capacity and stability, growth potential, liquidation value, and how anxious its owners are to sell its business. In spite of these limitations it is possible to develop a rough estimate of the average selling prices of typical acquisition candidates in a particular industry segment.

The first step is to use the techniques described earlier in this chapter to determine the size (sales), earnings, cash flow, and net worth (book value) of a typical acquisition candidate in your target industry segment.

The next step is to use the techniques described in the previous section to predict the types of acquirers which are likely to be seeking acquisitions in your target industry segment.

The final step is to use the following guidelines to estimate the selling price of this typical acquisition candidate.

GUIDELINES FOR ESTIMATING THE AVERAGE SELLING PRICE OF A TYPICAL ACQUISITION CANDIDATE IN YOUR TARGET INDUSTRY SEGMENT

1. Asset purchasers will typically pay 10% to 15% more than the amount which they can borrow against the net worth and cash flow of the selling business. The amount which they can borrow is generally three to three and a half times the cash flow of the selling business, but not more than 100% to 150% of the selling company's net worth. This percentage of net worth is lowest for service companies and wholesalers, because they are less likely to have undervalued assets, and highest for manufacturers and other types of companies which are likely to own undervalued assets.

2. Privately owned companies in the same industry as the selling business can usually expect to achieve some cost savings or other synergies after the two companies are combined. Therefore, they are usually prepared to pay a little more for a company than would an asset purchaser. These privately owned acquirers in the same industry as the selling company often pay the amount which they expect the selling company to be able to repay over the next five years out of its projected cash flow. This amount tends to be approximately four to five times the current flow of the selling business. Though privately owned companies in the same industry focus primarily on cash flow, they rarely pay more than 200% of net worth because this would make it too difficult to arrange financing.

3. Public companies seeking acquisitions in a particular industry segment tend to focus on earnings rather than cash flow. The average stock price to pretax earnings ratio for public companies in an industry segment gives a rough estimate of how much public company acquirers would pay for acquisition candidates in that industry segment.

AN EXAMPLE OF HOW TO DEVELOP A SELLING PRICE ESTIMATE FOR A TYPICAL ACQUISITION CANDIDATE IN YOUR TARGET INDUSTRY SEGMENT

Alpha Electronics, Inc., is considering acquiring a company which manufactures electronic instruments. Using the techniques described earlier in this chapter, they developed the following financial profiles for typical acquisition candidates in the two size ranges in which most of the acquisition candidates are likely to be found.

SIZE RANGE	COMPANY A: $1 TO 3 MILLION SALES	COMPANY B: $4 TO 10 MILLION SALES
Annual sales	$2,000,000	$6,000,000
Pretax income	120,000	300,000
Cash flow	140,000	360,000
Net worth	260,000	840,000

Alpha studied the acquisitions of electronic instrument companies which were reported in the trade publication for this industry. It determined that most of the acquisitions of the smaller companies ($1 million to $3 million sales) had been made by asset purchasers, while most of the acquisition of the larger companies had been made by privately owned electronic instrument manufacturers. They, therefore, used the following guidelines to develop their selling price estimates:

- *Company A:* Selling price will be the lesser of 3.5 times cash flow or 150% of net worth (book value).
- *Company B:* Selling price will be the lesser of 4.5 times cash flow or 200% of net worth (book value).

For Company A these computations were:

3.5 times cash flow =
3.5 × $140,000 = $490,000

150% × net worth =
150% × $260,000 = $390,000

The lesser of $490,000 and $390,000 is $390,000. Therefore, the estimated selling price is $390,000.

For Company B the computations were:

4.5 times cash flow =
4.5 × $360,000 = $1,620,000

$$2 \text{ times net worth } =$$
$$2 \times \$840,000 = \$1,680,000$$

The lesser of $1,620,000 and $1,680,000 is $1,620,000. Therefore, the estimated selling price is $1,620,000.

THE RATIONALE FOR DEVELOPING AND ANALYZING SAMPLE ACQUISITION CANDIDATES IN YOUR TARGET INDUSTRY

Acquisition search programs are expensive and time consuming. Therefore, a company should examine acquisition market conditions in its target industry before developing its acquisition program. The easiest way to do this would be to examine a group of suitable acquisition candidates. However, few acquisition candidates are listed, and their asking prices do not reflect the prices at which they will be sold. Creating representative sample acquisition candidates provides a way for your company to examine acquisition market conditions in your target industry without the expense of finding and negotiating with real acquisition candidates.

C·H·A·P·T·E·R T·H·R·E·E

HOW TO PREPARE AN ACQUISITION SEARCH PROGRAM

ACQUISITION SEARCH PROGRAMS

An acquisition search program is the process which a company uses to identify and find suitable acquisition candidates.

The acquisition search program is comprised of three elements. These are:

1. *Prospecting*—the search for selling companies (acquisition candidates). Some of the techniques which are used to find selling companies include:

   a. Utilizing merger/acquisition intermediaries
   b. Advertising
   c. Direct-mail solicitation

2. *Screening*—the analysis of companies or acquisition candidates to determine whether they meet the prospective acquirer's minimum acquisition suitability criteria. These are called screening criteria. Examples of typical screening criteria are:

   a. Industry segment (type of business)
   b. Company size
   c. Geographic location

3. *Selecting*—the selection of companies with which to begin acquisition negotiations. These are generally companies which have indicated that they are willing to consider being acquired. However, sometimes a prospective acquirer will first identify the companies it would like to own before finding out whether they would consider being acquired. This latter arrangement is called the research approach. Examples of factors which a prospective acquirer might use to help decide which companies it should begin acquisition negotiations with include:

a. Profitability
b. Market share
c. Growth potential
d. Management quality

THE KEY TO A SUCCESSFUL ACQUISITION SEARCH PROGRAM

A successful search program is one which produces at least ten selling businesses which your company would like to own. Commencing negotiations with this many selling companies usually produces at least one completed acquisition for your company.

THE IMPORTANCE OF NEGOTIATING WITH TEN SUITABLE ACQUISITION CANDIDATES IN ORDER TO COMPLETE JUST ONE OR TWO ACQUISITIONS

There are many circumstances which occur during the negotiation process which will prevent you from acquiring 80% to 90% of the acquisition candidates you are pursuing. For example:

1. Many owners think they want to sell but then change their minds.when they get a serious offer. This is because many owners develop a strong emotional attachment to their companies and are unable to face the prospect of giving up their business.

2. During the negotiating process you will learn many new facts about each selling company. Some of the candidates which initially appeared to be attractive to your company will no longer justify the cost and risk of your acquiring them at this time.

3. Some sellers will be unwilling to accept the purchase price or payment terms which your company is prepared to offer.

DEFINING A SUITABLE ACQUISITION CANDIDATE

There are over 600,000 companies in the United States. Approximately 6% to 7% of the 50,000 largest of these companies are sold each year. Since smaller companies are more likely to be sold than are larger companies, a conservative estimate would be that over 50,000 U.S. companies will be sold over the next 12 months. A similar number of companies will enter into discussions to be acquired but will not be sold over this 12-month period. Thus the total number of potential acquisition candidates appearing over the next 12 months is likely to exceed 80,000 companies.

Though we estimate that there will be over 80,000 potential acquisition candidates which will become available over the next 12 months, most of these acquisition candidates will not be of interest to your company because they do not match your needs, requirements, and preferences. The term "unsuitable" will be used to define this larger group of acquisition candidates which you would have no interest in acquiring. The term "suitable" will be used to define those acquisition candidates which your company would have an interest in purchasing. For the purpose of developing an acquisition program this definition of "suitable" acquisition candidates is further refined to mean acquisition candidates which are of sufficient interest to justify your investing the time and effort to investigate and analyze their business, so that you can make an initial purchase price offer. The characteristics which define the types of acquisition candidates which would be "suitable" for your company are called your acquisition suitability criteria. Examples of acquisition suitability criteria include:

1. Industry segment (e.g., hand tool manufacturing)
2. Size (sales volume)
3. Geographic location
4. Profitability
5. Reputation
6. Growth potential
7. Market share
8. Management quality

Successful acquirers develop their suitability criteria in two stages. First they develop suitability criteria to help them screen companies. Later they develop criteria to help them select which acquisition candidates to begin negotiating with.

TWO TYPES OF ACQUISITION SUITABILITY CRITERIA

Screening criteria

These are your minimum criteria for evaluating companies. They should be used in the following ways:

1. To select companies which should be contacted to learn whether they would consider selling.
2. To screen out unsuitable acquisition candidates.
3. To provide guidance to merger/acquisition intermediaries who have listings of selling companies.

A company should develop separate screening criteria for each type of business it is considering acquiring. For example, a residential fuel oil distributor located on Long Island might have the following acquisition screening criteria:

Industry segment	Residential fuel oil distributors
Size	Sales $1 million to $5 million
Geographic location	Northeast United States
Industry segment	Industrial fuel oil distributors
Size	Sales $5 million to $15 million
Geographic location	New York, New Jersey, or Connecticut
Facilities	Own or lease a waterfront tank farm
Industry segment	Gasoline distributors
Size	Sales $7 million to $15 million
Geographic location	Within 60 miles of New York City
Suppliers	Established relationship with a large U.S. oil company which has refineries in the northeast
Industry segment	Propane distributors
Size	Sales $3 million to $10 million
Geographic location	Eastern United States
Management	Must be willing to remain for at least three years

Selection criteria

These are the criteria you use to select the acquisition candidates with whom you should begin price negotiations (while continuing to investigate and analyze their business). Four examples of selection criteria are:

1. Profitability
2. Market share
3. Growth potential
4. Management quality

HOW SCREENING CRITERIA SAVES YOU TIME AND MONEY

It is expensive and time consuming to determine whether a company is willing to consider being acquired by your company. Therefore, you want to avoid pursuing companies which would not meet your minimum suitability criteria. For planning purposes, you can assume that it will cost an average of $25 and take three executive labor hours to determine whether a target company is willing to *consider* being acquired by your company. (However, you won't know whether the owners of a company are really serious about selling until you meet with them at least once.)

It is very expensive and time consuming to gather and analyze the information you need to value a selling company. Usually this will require at least one meeting with the selling company. Therefore, you want to screen out unsuitable acquisition candidates before you incur this time and expense. For planning purposes you can assume that gathering the information you need to begin to estimate the value of a selling company will require 12 executive labor hours and $300 in out-of-pocket expenses.

Intermediaries (e.g., acquisition finders and brokers) can be a useful source of acquisition opportunities for your company. However, unless you provide them with your screening criteria you are likely to encounter two problems. These are:

1. The intermediaries will send you all the acquisition opportunities they don't know what to do with. You will be swamped with hundreds of acquisition profiles which you have neither the time nor the staff to review and analyze. By the time you identify those few acquisition profiles which you find attractive, the selling companies will probably already be negotiating with someone else.
2. The intermediaries will not give your company priority when they obtain new listings of selling companies. This is because intermediaries realize that they are more likely to earn a commission if they send their new listings to a

prospective acquirer which already had indicated an interest in the type of business which is being sold.

THE IMPORTANCE OF DEVELOPING EFFECTIVE SCREENING CRITERIA

Effective screening criteria enable a prospective acquirer quickly to screen out companies and acquisition candidates which it would not want to own. At the same time they permit the prospective acquirer to focus its limited executive resources on those few target companies and acquisition candidates which are the most likely to still be of interest after they are investigated and analyzed.

The principal reason why companies fail to make acquisitions is their failure to reduce, and then manage, the work load associated with their acquisition search programs. Managing your acquisition work load is discussed in Chapter 9, Staffing and Managing Your Acquisition Program.

WHY SCREENING CRITERIA DEVELOPED BY MANY PROSPECTIVE ACQUIRERS ARE INEFFECTIVE

1. Their screening criteria require types of information about a selling company which can be obtained only by meeting with the owners of the selling company. They are then unable to use their screening criteria to decide which companies they should meet with.

2. They use the same company size and location criteria for different types of businesses which they are interested in acquiring. In order to avoid screening out suitable acquisition opportunities they must then make their size and location screening criteria very broad (unrestrictive). For example, if our Long Island residential fuel oil distributor used a single set of size and location criteria their screening criteria might be:

Industry	Petroleum product distributors
Minimum size	$1 million annual sales
Location	Eastern United States

When the company applied these criteria it, would find itself pursuing many acquisition opportunities which were in the wrong locations or were too small. You will recall that this Long Island company was interested only in acquiring gasoline distributors if they had minimum sales of $7 million and were located within 60 miles of New York City. However, if it used this more restrictive set of criteria for every target industry segment, it would then find themselves screening out many of the propane distributors which they were interested in acquiring.

3. Many prospective acquirers develop their screening criteria in the wrong order. That is, they start with their size criteria instead of first selecting their target industry segments. This is equivalent to selecting minimum educational and experience requirements for a new executive position without first deciding what functions that executive would be expected to perform.

4. Many prospective acquirers develop each of their acquisition screening criteria (e.g., industry segment, minimum company size, and geographic location) separately. Though each of the criteria seems logical, when they are combined, they screen out almost all the potential acquisition candidates. For example, assume that there are 1,000 plumbing wholesalers and that they are segmented in the following manner:

SIZE

SALES	NUMBER OF COMPANIES
$1 to $3 million	500
$3 to $7 million	300
$7 to $10 million	100
Over $10 million	100
Total	1,000

LOCATION

GEOGRAPHIC AREA	NUMBER OF COMPANIES
Northeast	200
Mid-Atlantic	200
Southeast	200
Midwest	200
Southwest	100
West coast	100
Total	1,000

Next assume that 10% of these companies would consider being acquired.

Professional Supply Co. is a typical acquirer seeking to purchase plumbing wholesalers. Professional Supply is a plumbing wholesaler serving the Mid-Atlantic region. The company's annual sales are around $50 million. Professional Supply's senior executives meet one morning to discuss what acquisition criteria they should use. They decide to seek to acquire plumbing wholesalers with sales over $7 million. This is an appropriate minimum size for an acquirer with sales of $50 million and they know that there are lots of plumbing wholesalers who meet this size criterion.

They then decide to seek to acquire a plumbing wholesaler located in the Southeast because this is a good growth area and it is adjacent to their existing market area. Once again this is a logical location criterion for this company to use.

Using probability analysis, we can estimate number of plumbing wholesalers with sales over $7 million which are located in the Southeast. To make this computation, we first multiply the probabilities of a company meeting each of the two criteria:

Probability of sales over $7 million

×

Probability of location in Southeast

$$\frac{200 \text{ companies with sales over } \$7 \text{ million}}{1,000 \text{ companies}}$$

×

$$\frac{200 \text{ companies in the Southeast}}{1,000 \text{ companies}}$$

$$1/5 \times 1/5 = 1/25$$

Then multiply this probability (1/25) times the number of plumbing wholesalers (1,000 companies)

$$1/25 \times 1,000 = 40 \text{ companies which meet both criteria}$$

Using our assumption that 10% of the plumbing wholesalers would consider selling, we find that there are likely to be only four suitable acquisition candidates which will meet Professional Supply's screening criteria. Even if Professional Supply found all four acquisition candidates, this is too few acquisition candidates to assure the successful acquisition of at least one company.

GUIDELINES TO FOLLOW WHEN SELECTING COMPANY CHARACTERISTICS FOR USE AS SCREENING CRITERIA

1. The information you need to apply your screening criteria should be available from published sources or from information easily obtained from a company (e.g., product brochures). Examples are:

   a. Size (number of employees or sales)
   b. Location

c. Industry

d. Number of years in business

2. Unless you are searching for public companies to acquire you will rarely have access to their financial statements. Therefore, avoid using criteria such as:

a. Profitability

b. Profit margins

c. Net worth

d. Growth rate

3. Never use the seller's asking price as a screening criterion. The seller's asking price has little or no relation to how much a company is actually sold for. Often the asking price is 1 1/2 to 2 1/2 times what the seller actually expects to get for his company.

4. Never use the reason the company is for sale as a screening criterion. Even if you get an explanation from the seller, it will probably be either incomplete or untrue.

5. You can supplement your basic screening criteria with additional screening criteria which you can apply after your initial phone conversation with the selling company or their representative. These criteria should relate to simple questions which the seller is likely to be willing to answer over the telephone. For example:

a. Are you unionized?

b. Will management stay?

c. What proportion of your sales are to the military?

Most sucessful acquirers use three basic screening criteria. We refer to them as "standard screening criteria." They are:

a. Industry segment (type of business)

b. Company size (annual sales)

c. Geographic location.

HOW TO START DEVELOPING YOUR ACQUISITION SCREENING CRITERIA

The first step is to select the industry segments in which you will seek to make acquisitions. The industry segment(s) which you select are referred to as your target industry segments.

WHAT IS AN INDUSTRY SEGMENT?

For acquisition purposes, an industry segment consists of a group of companies which handle the same products (e.g., wooden office furniture) or services (e.g., life insurance), perform the same function (e.g., wholesaling, manufacturing, mining, processing, retailing), and sell to the same types of customers (e.g., consumers, retailers, original equipment manufacturers). The following are some examples of industry segments:

1. Fruit and vegetable wholesalers which supply restaurants
2. Office furniture retailers
3. Savings banks
4. Auto parts manufacturers which sell to the automobile manufacturers (OEM market)

DEFINE YOUR TARGET INDUSTRY SEGMENT

1. A target industry segment should be narrow enough to screen out most of the types of businesses you would not be interested in acquiring. For example, if your company was interested in acquiring plumbing wholesalers, you should not define your target industry segment as building supply wholesalers.
2. A target industry segment should be broad enough to permit you to utilize published industry information such as company lists and comparative financial data. Your target industry should also be defined broadly enough to be readily understandable to merger/acquisition intermediaries. For example, assume that your company was primarily interested in acquiring companies which manufactured specialty chemicals sold to the food processing, textile, or metal working industries. You could define your target industrial segments as:

   a. Manufacturers of specialty chemicals used in the food processing industry
   b. Manufacturers of specialty chemicals used in the textile industry
   c. Manufacturers of specialty chemicals used in the metal working industry

These target industry segments are, however, too narrow to be used as your screening criteria. It would be better to define your target industry segment as industrial specialty chemical manufacturers.

THREE FACTORS YOU SHOULD CONSIDER BEFORE SELECTING THE TARGET INDUSTRY SEGMENTS(S) FOR YOUR COMPANY'S SCREENING CRITERIA

1. The alternative growth strategies which your company could use to strengthen, expand, or diversify its current businesses.
2. The advantages and disadvantages of using acquisitions to accomplish these alternative growth strategies.
3. The likelihood that you will be able to find a sufficient number of acquisition candidates, within your price range, which would accomplish these alternative growth strategies.

HOW TO ANALYZE USING ACQUISITIONS TO ACHIEVE YOUR GROWTH STRATEGIES

The preferred approach is to use an acquisition planning system such as the one presented in Chapter 5.

TWO IMPORTANT ADVANTAGES OF USING AN ACQUISITION PLANNING SYSTEM

1. It helps your management to consider the full range of alternative growth strategies which your company could accomplish using acquisitions. Companies which do not use an acquisition planning system frequently overlook those attractive alternative growth strategies which they could only implement by using acquisitions. This is because conventional corporate planning focuses on internal growth opportunities.
2. It helps your management to recognize how your company's own strengths and weaknesses would affect the attractiveness and risks of owning different types of selling companies.

HOW TO BEGIN DEVELOPING YOUR SCREENING CRITERIA

1. Select your target industry segments. Unless you already know the type of business you would like to own, it is wise to use an acquisition planning system

to help your management analyze how acquiring different types of businesses would affect your company.

2. Gather the information you will need to develop your geographic location criteria for each target industry segment. This information consists of the number of companies in a target industry segment which are located in each region, state, and major metropolitan area.

HOW TO ESTIMATE THE NUMBER OF COMPANIES IN A PARTICULAR INDUSTRY SEGMENT WITHIN EACH GEOGRAPHIC AREA

1. Determine the approximate number of companies in a target industry segment by using one or more of the following information sources:

a. Industry directories

b. U.S. Department of Commerce business census reports

c. Trade association executives

d. Published market studies

e. Contacting mailing list compilers (e.g., Dun & Bradstreet)

f. Articles in industry trade periodicals

For example, assume that you determine that there are approximately 900 mortgage brokerage firms.

2. Next find a directory or mailing list which lists the names and addresses of companies in your target industry segment. Determine the geographic distribution of these companies. For example, assume that you are interested in acquiring a mortgage brokerage firm. You find a trade association directory which lists 120 of the 900 mortgage brokerage firms. Their geographic distribution is on the next page.

3. Compute the percentage of companies located in each geographic area. For example, if the directory listed 120 mortgage brokerage firms and 6 were located in Texas, the percentage for Texas would be $6/120 = 5\%$.

4. Multiply the percentage for each geographic area times the number of companies in the industry segment. For example, if there are estimated to be 900 mortgage companies in the United States you can assume that 45 ($5\% \times 90 = 45$) are located in Texas. The reason you can make this assumption is that the companies which are not listed in the directory tend to have the same geographic distribution as those which are listed.

GEOGRAPHIC LOCATION		NUMBER OF COMPANIES
New England region		16
Massachusetts	7	
Connecticut	4	
New Hampshire	3	
Rhode Island	1	
Vermont	1	
Northeast region		20
Pennsylvania	7	
New Jersey	7	
New York	6	
Mid-Atlantic states		10
Delaware	1	
Virginia	4	
Maryland	5	
Southeast region	3	18
North Carolina		
South Carolina	1	
Georgia	3	
Florida	9	
Alabama	1	
Mississippi	1	
Midwest region		20
Illinois	6	
Ohio	4	
Indiana	3	
Kentucky	1	
Tennessee	3	
Michigan	3	
Southwest region		12
Texas	6	
Oklahoma	2	
Arizona	3	
New Mexico	1	
Western region		24
California	20	
Colorado	3	
Nevada	1	

THREE FACTORS YOU SHOULD CONSIDER BEFORE SELECTING YOUR GEOGRAPHIC SCREENING CRITERIA FOR A TARGET INDUSTRY SEGMENT

1. *Risk increases with distance.* The farther away an acquisition candidate is from your company, the more difficult it will be to operate it successfully after you own it. Unless your company is already set up to operate geographically dispersed operations you should generally avoid acquiring companies located further than two hours' traveling time from your headquarters.

2. *Risk increases with diversity.* That is, it is riskier to own a company which is in a business different from the one you now operate than it is to acquire a company in the same business. It is therefore important to reduce your geographic risk when you are seeking acquisitions outside your present line of business. The following computation illustrates this concept.

3. Acquiring companies in growing markets tends to reduce the risk of owning such companies. The reason is that profit margins are higher and it is easier for these companies to add or regain sales volume than is the case for companies competing in markets which are stable or declining. Therefore a prospective acquirer should include distant locations which are high-growth markets if it feels that it has or can develop the ability to manage a geographically distant business.

HOW TO GO ABOUT SELECTING YOUR GEOGRAPHIC LOCATION SCREENING CRITERIA FOR A TARGET INDUSTRY SEGMENT

1. For each target industry segment your management should complete the following two statements:

    a. "We would *prefer* to acquire a company which is located in one of the following geographic areas."

    b. "We would *not* consider acquiring a company which was located in the following geographic areas."

2. Then make a list of preferred and acceptable geographic locations for each target industry segment. The acceptable geographic locations are those which were neither preferred (see statement 1) nor excluded (see statement 2). Here is an example of how this works:

The management of a large commercial bank headquartered in Boston seeks to acquire a mortgage brokerage firm. Its geographic location statements were:

- "We would *prefer* to acquire mortgage brokerage companies located in Connecticut."

- "We would *not* consider acquiring mortgage brokerage companies located outside New England."

Based upon these statements, this company's preferred and acceptable geographic locations are:

PREFERRED LOCATIONS	ACCEPTABLE LOCATIONS
Connecticut	Massachusetts
	Rhode Island
	Vermont
	Maine
	New Hampshire

3. Next estimate how many companies in the target industry segment would meet your preferred and acceptable location criteria. Using our mortgage brokerage firm example this location distribution was:

LOCATION	NUMBER OF COMPANIES
Connecticut	30
Massachusetts	53
Rhode Island	7
Vermont	7
New Hampshire	23
Total New England	120

4. Your preliminary location screening criteria for a target industry segment should include at least 100 companies. Start with your preferred geographic location and then add acceptable geographic locations if there are not likely to be enough companies located in your preferred geographic location. In our mortgage broker example, there were not enough companies located in Connecticut. Therefore, our prospective acquirer should expand its geographic location screening criteria to include other New England states.

5. Later you will examine how many companies are likely to meet both your size and geographic location criteria. Then further adjustments may be necessary to broaden or narrow these two types of screening criteria.

HOW A PROSPECTIVE ACQUIRER DEFINES ITS COMPANY-SIZE SCREENING CRITERIA

1. Company-size screening criteria are the minimum and maximum sales of companies you would consider acquiring in a particular industry segment.

2. A minimum and maximum number of employees is sometimes used as a substitute for minimum and maximum annual sales.

In some industry segments, published information sources such as industry directories give the number of company employees but do not provide sales estimates for each company. In these instances a prospective acquirer sets company employment levels which are comparable to its preferred sales level. For example, assume that the average annual sales in a particular industry segment are $30,000 per employee and the prospective acquirer seeks to acquire only companies in that industry segment with annual sales over $5 million. By dividing $5 million by $30,000 we find that companies with over 167 employees ($5 million/$30,000 per employee = 166.7 employees) are likely to meet its minimum size criteria.

FACTORS TO CONSIDER WHEN DETERMINING YOUR PREFERRED SIZE RANGE FOR COMPANIES IN A SELECTED TARGET INDUSTRY SEGMENT

1. The principal reason for acquiring a company in the same business you are already in is to grow more rapidly. Since acquisitions are generally riskier than internal growth investments (e.g., adding salespeople), you should use them to expand your present business when they would add more sales than your company expects to add through internal growth over the next two years. As a general rule you should seek to acquire companies in your present line of business which would add at least 20% to your present annual sales volume.

2. When you acquire a company in a business different from the one you are already in, it is important to acquire a company which is large enough to support a team of professional salaried managers. This is because there tends to be a high turnover of senior executives in the first 12 months after a company changes ownership. As a general rule a company with annual net income of over $150,000 is large enough to support a professional management team should it be necessary to replace the former owner/managers. In order to estimate the equivalent sales level for such a company you divide $150,000 by the average profitability ratio (net income/sales) for companies in that industry segment. For example, assume that companies in the target industry segment generate average net income equal to 3% of their annual sales. The computation would be:

$$\frac{\$150,000 \text{ net income}}{3\% \text{ of sales}} = \$5 \text{ million minimum annual sales}$$

DEVELOPING ACQUISITION-SIZE SCREENING CRITERIA

Your acquisition-size screening criteria should set a maximum and a minimum company size for each industry segment in which you are seeking acquisition opportunities. Each of the size ranges should be broad enough to include at least 100 existing companies.

DETERMINING THE MAXIMUM COMPANY SIZE TO USE FOR YOUR ACQUISITION SCREENING CRITERIA

The first step in developing your maximum company-size screening criteria for a particular target industry is to determine the maximum-size company which it would be *realistic* for your company to consider purchasing. There are two factors which limit how large a company it would be realistic for your company to acquire, own, and operate. These are:

1. The ability of your executives to understand and use the management techniques and systems appropriate for a company of that size.
2. The amount of investment capital which your company is prepared to use to purchase a business. Your investment capital consists of the cash and unused borrowing capacity not needed to operate your present business.

DIFFERENT COMPANY-SIZE CATEGORIES REQUIRE DIFFERENT MANAGEMENT KNOWLEDGE AND EXPERIENCE

1. Local companies. Generally, these are small companies which operate in one or two local markets. An example of a local market would be the Denver metropolitan area.
2. Regional companies. Generally, these are medium-sized companies which operate in a regional market. An example of a regional market would be the New England states.
3. National companies. Generally these are larger companies which operate in several regional markets.

Different management techniques and systems are used by companies in each of these three company-size categories. For example, national companies require formal information systems to keep their senior executives informed of current market conditions.

HOW TO DETERMINE YOUR COMPANY'S ABILITY TO HANDLE ACQUISITIONS IN A LARGER SIZE CATEGORY

The prior management experience of your senior executives determines your company's ability to handle acquisitions in a larger size category. When your executives' careers have included management positions with companies in a larger size category than your company's present size category, they will be sufficiently familiar with the management techniques and systems used by companies in a larger size category for your company to acquire a business in a larger size category. It is not necessary however for all of your senior executives to have previously filled management positions in a company in a larger size category. Generally, it is sufficient that your senior marketing and your senior production executive have had this prior experience.

HOW TO OFFSET YOUR EXECUTIVES LACK OF PRIOR EXPERIENCE WITH COMPANIES IN LARGER SIZE CATEGORIES

The safest way to handle this problem is to seek acquisition candidates which are in the same company-size category which your company is in, or which are in a smaller company size category.

When your company does not wish to follow this approach, your strategy should be to select businesses in larger size categories which are less likely to need to utilize your own executives management talents and expertise. These will be acquisition candidates which are managed by salaried, nonowner senior executives, and which are well staffed with midlevel managers. Nonowner executives are more likely to stay longer and remain productive than former owner/managers following the acquisition. There will still be a higher than normal loss of senior executives at the new acquired business following the change in ownership. However, if the newly acquired company has good management depth, its midlevel executives generally can move up to fill the vacant senior executive positions and often perform surprisingly well.

WHY THE AMOUNT WHICH YOU HAVE AVAILABLE TO INVEST LIMITS THE ACQUISITION SELLING PRICE WHICH YOU CAN AFFORD TO PAY

The selling price of a business is usually 20% to 40% higher than the amount which can be financed by using the seller's unused borrowing capacity and liquidating its surplus assets. In order to pay this premium, you will need to use your own company's investment capital. For example, assume that companies in your target industry segment generally sell for 20% more than an acquirer could finance by utilizing the sellers unused borrowing capacity and liquidating its surplus assets. A typical acquisition candidate which you could acquire for $1,000,000 would then require you to use $200,000 (20% × $1,000,000) of your own company's investment capital.

WHY YOU SHOULD NOT SEEK TO FIND ACQUISITION CANDIDATES WHICH ARE LARGER THAN YOU CAN AFFORD TO BUY

Acquisition programs absorb a great deal of your executives' limited time, energy, and enthusiasm. Therefore you cannot afford to waste this valuable, scarce resource pursuing acquisition candidates which you will probably be unable to purchase because they would require more of your own company's investment capital than you are prepared to use for an acquisition.

DEFINING A LEVERAGED BUYOUT

A leveraged buyout is an acquisition which requires a smaller than usual proportion of the acquirer's own investment capital to pay the sellng price of the acquisition candidate. An alternative way of saying this is that a higher than normal proportion of the purchase price can be financed by utilizing the unused borrowing capacity of the selling business and liquidating its surplus or underutilized assets. Theoretically, this would enable a company to acquire a business which is larger than it could normally expect to acquire using its own limited investment capital.

WHY LEVERAGED BUYOUTS ARE RARELY A USEFUL STRATEGY FOR YOUR COMPANY TO PURSUE

1. There are very few leveraged buyout opportunities. The wide publicity given to those few instances in which a smaller company acquires a much larger company have, however, given the impression that leverage buyout opportunities exist in greater numbers than is actually the case.

2. Leveraged buyouts are a high-risk strategy. In many of those instances in which a small company acquired a much larger company, the ultimate result has been both businesses had to be sold or liquidated several years later. The reason for this high failure rate is that the acquirer overcame its lack of sufficient investment capital by taking on a larger amount of expensive debt financing. Then the combined businesses were unable to make their debt service payments when there was a temporary downturn in their earnings and cash flow due to depressed economic conditions or increased price competition in their industry. A successful leveraged buyout is usually dependent upon both businesses maintaining their profitability and not requiring additional outside financing for the three years following the leveraged buyout.

HOW TO ESTIMATE HOW LARGE A COMPANY YOU CAN AFFORD TO ACQUIRE

1. Determine the amount of cash and unused borrowing capacity which your company has available to finance expansion projects such as increasing your production capacity and making acquisitions. This cash and unused borrowing capacity is your investment capital. For publicly owned acquirers, available investment capital also includes:

   a. The amount of additional equity which they would be willing and able to obtain by selling additional stock

   b. The amount of stock which they would be prepared to pay to the owners of a selling business

The analysis of how the issuance of additional registered or unregistered stock will affect the future earnings and stock price of a public company acquirer is beyond the scope of this book. However, it is worth noting that stock issued to make acquisitions is generally valued at 15% to 25% less than the current public market value of that stock. This is because:

a. To market a new public stock issue, the shares must usually be sold at a discount.

b. The legal and underwriting expenses of a new public stock issue reduce the net proceeds per share realized by the public company.

c. The resale of unregistered stock which has been issued to the owners of a selling business is restricted. Therefore, the sellers will value it at a discount relative to its current public market value.

2. Determine the amount of your investment capital which you are prepared to use for acquisitions. This is your acquisition investment capital budget. In deciding how much of your investment capital to allocate to making acquisitions you should keep in mind that the investment capital which you allocate to your acquisition budget reduces the amount of capital available to maintain or increase the profitability of your company's present business.

3. Once you have determined your acquisition investment budget you are ready to estimate the maximum purchase price which your acquisition investment capital budget would permit you to pay for companies in each of your target industry segments. You can generally assume that you can leverage your acquisition investment capital 5 to 1 for target industry segments in which companies tend to have substantial fixed assets (e.g., manufacturing). For other target industry segments you can generally assume that you could leverage your acquisition investment budget 4 to 1. For example, if your company wished to acquire an office supply manufacturer and had an acquisition investment capital budget of $1.5 million you would estimate the maximum purchase price which you could afford to pay by multiplying $1.5 million times 5. This would yield an estimated maximum purchase price of $7.5 million for office supply manufacturing companies.

4. Next you estimate the annual sales to acquisition selling price ratio for companies in each of your target industry segments. To do this you compute the average sales to public market value ratio for a group of profitable public companies in each of your target industry segments. This average annual sales to public market value ratio is roughly equivalent to the sales to company selling price ratio for companies in that industry segment. When you select public companies in an industry segment to average together, look for profitable companies which have public market values which are approximately the same as the maximum purchase price which you estimated that you could afford to pay for companies in that industry segment. The public market

value of a company is its total number of shares outstanding times the current selling price of a share of its stock.

5. The final step is to estimate how large a company (maximum annual sales) you could afford to purchase in a particular industry segment. To do this you multiply your estimated maximum purchase price times the average sales to public market value ratio for companies in that target industry segment. For example, assume that your maximum purchase price for an offices supplies manufacturing company is $7.5 million and the average sales to public market value ratio is 2 to 1. Then the maximum size office supply manufacturing company which you could afford to purchase would have annual sales of $15 million ($7.5 million times 2 equals $15 million).

HOW TO SET YOUR MINIMUM COMPANY-SIZE CRITERIA

1. Start off by using a percentage of your own company's sales as your minimum size criteria. The following formulas can be used for planning purposes:

INDUSTRY SEGMENT	PERCENTAGE OF ACQUIRER'S SALES
Same business as acquiring company	20%
Different business from that of acquiring company	30%

2. Once you have set your initial size range for each target industry segment, estimate the number of companies which fall within this size range. Increase or decrease the minimum size until you have at least 100 companies which fall within your size range. For example, assume that a company seeking acquisitions in its present industry has annual sales of $15 million and estimates that it could afford to purchase a company in its industry with sales of up to $6 million. The company initially uses 20% of its own sales ($3 million) as its minimum size criteria. It then examines company size statistics in its target industry segment and finds the following size distribution:

ANNUAL SALES	NUMBER OF COMPANIES
Under $1 million	400
$1 to $2 million	87
$2 to $3 million	59
$3 to $4 million	43
$4 to $5 million	27
$5 to $6 million	19

In this example the prospective acquirer finds that it should adjust its minimum size criteria downward (e.g., from $3 million to $2 million) in order to include a minimum of 100 companies in its preferred company size range.

HOW TO DETERMINE THE EFFECT OF COMBINING YOUR PRELIMINARY SIZE AND GEOGRAPHIC LOCATION SCREENING CRITERIA

1. Compute the proportion of the companies in your target industry segment which meet your preliminary geographic location criteria. For example, if there are 600 companies in the target industry segment and 120 meet your preliminary geographic location criteria, the computation is 120/600 = 20%.

2. Compute the proportion of the companies in your target industry segment which fall within your target size range. For example, if there are 600 companies in the industry segment and 150 meet your preliminary size criteria, the computation is 150/600 = 25%.

3. Multiply the proportion of the companies which meet your preliminary location criteria times the proportion of the companies which meet your preliminary size criteria. In our example this computation would be 20% × 25% = 5%. This is the proportion of the companies in the target industry segment which are likely to meet both criteria.

4. Multiply the proportion of companies which are likely to meet both your size and geographic criteria times the estimated number of companies in that industry segment. In our example, this computation is 5% × 600 companies = 30 companies. This is the number of companies which are likely to meet both your preliminary size and location criteria.

5. For planning purposes you can assume that 10% of the companies which meet both your preliminary size and location screening criteria are acquisition candidates. In our example there are likely to be only three acquisition candidates which will meet both criteria (10% × 30 companies = 3 acquisition candidates).

HOW TO USE THIS INFORMATION TO ITS FULLEST ADVANTAGE

Once you have estimated the number of companies which meet your preliminary size and geographic location screening criteria for each target industry segment, you can predict the likelihood that your acquisition research program will be successful. To do this, you first add up the number of companies in each target industry segment which met the preliminary location and size screening criteria you used for that industry segment. For example, assume that the Long Island fuel distributor discussed on page 87 found that the likely results of using its preliminary screening criteria would be as follows:

INDUSTRY SEGMENT	NUMBER OF COMPANIES THAT MEET BOTH SIZE AND LOCATION CRITERIA
Residential fuel oil distributors	70
Industrial fuel oil distributors	12
Gasoline distributors	9
Propane distributors	30
Total	121

Use the following guidelines to estimate the likelihood of making a successful acquisition.

NUMBER OF COMPANIES THAT MEET THE ACQUIRER'S SCREENING CRITERIA	ESTIMATED PROBABILITY OF SUCCESS
25	10%
50	25
75	40
100	50
125	60
150	70
175	80
200	90

Using our Long Island fuel oil distributor example you can see that they have a reasonable likelihood (60% probability) of making an acquisition.

WHAT TO DO IF YOUR ACQUISITION SEARCH PROGRAM APPEARS TO HAVE TOO FEW COMPANIES WHICH MEET YOUR PRELIMINARY CRITERIA

1. The most common weakness in companies' acquisition screening criteria is that they set their minimum-size criterion a little too high. Therefore, for each of your target industry segments analyze whether a modest reduction in your minimum company-size criterion would significantly increase the number of qualifying companies. For example, if your company size range for a particular target industry segment was annual sales of $3 to $6 million, examine how many additional companies would qualify if you used $2 million in sales as your minimum sales level.

2. Companies in particular industry segments tend to be concentrated in a limited number of metropolitan areas or geographic regions. Many acquirers inadvertently exclude large numbers of companies in their target industry segment by not including key geographic areas which seem too distant, but are actually convenient in terms of travel time. For example, a food-processing company located in New England might initially define its geographic criterion as the northeastern United States. By thereby excluding St. Louis, the company would screen out numerous food-processing companies which are actually closer in terms of travel times than many Northeastern food-processing companies which are located in rural areas of the Northeast. The next step after you review your minimum-size criterion is, therefore, to analyze whether a modest change in your geographic location criterion might significantly increase the number of companies which meet your criterion.

3. Sometimes you will find that there simply aren't very many companies in your target industry segments in the right locations which are large enough to be attractive but small enough for your company to afford to acquire. When this occurs you should go back and analyze whether there are additional target industry segments which your company should consider for its acquisition program.

WHEN COMPANIES DEVELOP THEIR ACQUISITION SCREENING CRITERIA

The most popular approach is for a company to develop its acquisition screening criteria before it begins looking for acquisition candidates. Some companies, however, choose to develop their screening criteria as they go along. They do this by starting with very general screening criteria. As they reveiw acquisition candidates which meet these general criteria, their managements narrow their screening criteria. After a few months they finally wind up with a good set of screening criteria which define their target industry segments and their size and location screening criteria for each target industry segment. Here is an example of the general screening criteria which such a prospective acquirer might start with:

Industry	Financial services
Size	Annual revenues $5 million to $20 million
Location	Eastern United States

Companies which begin searching for acquisition candidates, and then complete the development of their screening criteria are using an acquisition search program format called the Opportunistic Approach.

Companies which start by developing their standard screening criteria (target industry segment, minimum size, and geographic location) and then search for acquisition candidates which meet these criteria are using an acquisition search program format called the Standard Approach.

Companies may also develop their standard screening criteria, and then proceed to develop their selection criteria before beginning to search for acquisition candidates. This acquisition search program format is called the Research Approach.

Later in this chapter we will compare these three approaches in greater detail.

THE KEY DISADVANTAGE OF DEVELOPING YOUR SCREENING CRITERIA BEFORE YOUR COMPANY BEGINS SEARCHING FOR ACQUISITION CANDIDATES

It is more difficult for a company's management to define their acquisition preferences in the abstract than it would be if they were examining some acquisition candidates. For example, a commercial bank may think that it should acquire a consumer finance company. However, when it examines some actual consumer finance acquisition opportunities its management might decide that this isn't really the type of business they should acquire. On the other hand, this same commercial bank might have placed a low priority on acquiring residential mortgage bankers. Then when their management has the opportunity to examine some actual mortgage banking companies they may decide that this is the type of business they should acquire.

As explained earlier in this chapter, it is very expensive and time consuming for a company to carry out an acquisition search program unless it first develops its standard screening criteria (industry segment, company size, and geographic location). Less than 5% of the companies which use the Opportunistic Approach ever make an acquisition. They usually give up after a few months because the executive labor power requirements of the acquisition search program begin to divert management resources from the prospective acquirer's ongoing business.

A USEFUL TECHNIQUE TO HELP MANAGEMENT EVALUATE ITS ACQUISITION PREFERENCES WHILE STILL USING THE STANDARD APPROACH FORMAT

After your company develops its acquisition screening criteria, prepare profiles on actual public companies which meet these criteria and public companies which almost meet your screening criteria. Then have your senior executives review these company profiles as though they were actual acquisition candidates.

For example, assume that a British publisher of business periodicals seeks to acquire similar companies in the United States and has developed the following screening criteria.

Industry segment	Business publishing
Size	Annual sales $5 to $10 million
Location	Northeastern United States

The public companies to be profiled might include:

- A business magazine publisher located in New York City with annual sales of $7 million

- A business magazine publisher located in Boston with annual sales of $15 million

- A publisher of business books, magazines and newsletters located in New York City which has annual sales of $25 million

- A business book publisher located in Philadelphia which has annual sales of $7 million

- A highly profitable business newsletter publisher located in New York City which has sales of $3 million

- A business market research firm located in Washington, DC, which has sales of $10 million

- An unprofitable business periodical and book publisher located in Texas which has annual sales of $50 million

After your management has decided what they liked and disliked about each of these sample companies, revise your screening criteria to reflect these preferences.

This technique for testing and improving a company's screening criteria was developed by Salomon Brothers, a large New York investment banking firm. One of the important side benefits of using this technique is that it helps a company's senior executives to develop a consensus regarding its own company's acquisition preferences.

DEVELOP SELECTION CRITERIA FOR ACQUISITION SUITABILITY

These are the criteria which your company will use to help decide with which acquisition candidates (which met your screening criteria) you should begin negotiations. The following are examples of selection criteria which you might use:

- Growth potential
- Management quality
- Profitability
- Minimum gross profit margins
- Cost competitiveness
- Market share
- Company reputation
- Modern manufacturing facilities
- Vulnerability to import competition
- Product quality
- Manufacturing capacity
- Marketing skill
- Marketing resources
- Patent protection
- Technical expertise
- Product development capability

THREE FACTORS TO CONSIDER WHEN CHOOSING YOUR SELECTION CRITERIA

Your selection criteria should be business characteristics of a selling company which would help you achieve one of the following three objectives:

1. *Improve the selling company's ability to survive and prosper after you own it.* For example, strong product lines and modern manufacturing facilities are factors which could help the selling company to continue to compete successfully after you owned it.

2. *Utilize your own company's strengths.* For example, assume that a prospective acquirer has a strong marketing network. This company might use "compatibility of the acquisition candidate's product line with our marketing network" as one of its selection criteria.

3. *Offset your own company's weaknesses.* For example, if a company has limited new product development capabilities it might use as one of its selection criteria "strong new product development skills."

HOW ACQUISITION PLANNING HELPS A COMPANY TO DEVELOP ITS SELECTION CRITERIA RANKING SYSTEM

The relative importance of different selling company business characteristics depends upon how they would affect your company after you owned the acquisition candidate. For example, if your company has good management depth, and the acquisition candidates are in the same line of business in which you already operate, you would not choose to use acquisition candidate management depth as one of your selection criteria since this would duplicate your own area of strength. On the other hand, if your company has limited growth potential because it serves mature markets, this factor would make an acquisition candidate which served a growing market more attractive for your company. You could then incorporate this into your acquisition strategy by using growth potential as one of your selection criteria and assigning it a high weighting factor value (e.g., "3" on a three-point scale).

To predict how the characteristics of an acquisition candidate would interact with your own company's strengths and weaknesses, you must first develop an objective assessment of your own company's strengths and weaknesses. An acquisition planning system like the one described in Chapter 5 enables your management to determine your company's strengths and weaknesses.

USING YOUR SELECTION CRITERIA FOR BEST RESULTS

Your selection criteria are used to create rating systems for ranking the acquisition candidates in a target industry segment which met your other screening criteria (e.g., size and location). For example, if your company were seeking to acquire office furniture manufacturers and commercial floor covering distributors, you would select separate selection criteria for each of these two types of businesses.

Once you have chosen your selection criteria for a particular target industry segment, the next step is to assign numerical values to each individual selection criterion item. These numerical values represent the relative importance of each individual selection criterion. Assign a value to each of your selection criteria using the following three-point scale.

> 1 = somewhat important
> 2 = important
> 3 = very important

The following example shows the selection criteria and ratings which were developed by a British business publisher which sought to acquire U.S. business newsletter publishers with annual sales of over $1 million.

SELECTION CRITERIA	VALUE (WEIGHT FACTOR)
Growth potential	3 (very important)
Management quality	1 (somewhat important)
Product reputation	3 (very important)
Market share	2 (important)
Profitability	1 (somewhat important)
Export sales potential	3 (very important)

The British company then compared three business newsletter publisher acquisition candidates using its selection criteria.

	COMPANY A	COMPANY B	COMPANY C
Growth potential	Poor	Good	Excellent
Management quality	Good	Excellent	Poor
Product reputation	Excellent	Good	Good
Market share	High	Low	Medium
Profitability	Excellent	Average	Poor
Export sales potential	Low	Low	High

The final step was to assign numerical ratings based on how well each target company met each criterion. An acquisition candidate which fully met a particular selection criterion was assigned 100% of its weighting factor value, an acquisition candidate which partially met a particular selection criterion was assigned 50% of its weighting factor value, and an acquisition candidate which did not meet a particular selection criterion was assigned 0% of its weighting value factor.

	COMPANY A	COMPANY B	COMPANY C
Growth potential	0% × 3 = 0	50% × 3 = 1.5	100 × 3 = 3.0
Management quality	50% × 1 − 0.5	100% × 1 = 1.0	0% × 1 = 0
Product reputation	100% × 3 − 3.0	50% × 3 = 1.5	50% × 3 = 1.5
Market share	100% × 2 = 2.0	0% × 2 = 0	50% × 2 = 1.0
Profitability	100% × 1 = 1.0	50% × 1 = 0.5	0% × 1 = 0
Export sales potential	0% × 3 = 0	0% × 3 = 0	100% × 3 = 3.0
Total rating	6.5	4.5	8.5

In this case the British company decided to commence price negotiations only with Company C.

FIVE REASONS FOR YOUR COMPANY TO DEVELOP A SELECTION CRITERIA RANKING SYSTEM

1. It is expensive and time consuming to value and to negotiate to purchase an acquisition candidate. Therefore, you need to concentrate on those acquisition candidates which would have the greatest value to your company if you owned them.

2. A successful acquisition search program will produce more acquisition candidates which meet your screening criteria than you have the time or management resources to follow up with. Therefore, it is important to have a mechanism which enables your company to select which acquisition candidates you should concentrate on.

3. Each acquisition candidate which meets your screening criteria is a unique combination of business characteristics. This diversity makes it very difficult, confusing, and time consuming for your management to evaluate them in an objective way. A selection criteria ranking system reduces the time, effort, and difficulty involved in evaluating acquisition candidates and increases the objectivity of your decision making.

4. The success of a company after you own it is dependent upon the enthusiastic support and involvement of your company's key executives. This requires that these executives reach a consensus regarding the characteristics which a suitable acquisition candidate should exhibit. Another problem is the surfacing of personality conflicts when management attempts to evaluate acquisition candidates which are attractive to some of your executives but are disliked by some of your other executives. Developing a selection criteria ranking system helps your executives reach a consensus while also reducing the potential for personality conflicts.

5. In order to maintain good relations with a selling company it is essential to give its owners a preliminary indication of your level of interest within one week after you have your initial meeting with them. Delays in providing this response will alienate both the companies you decide to negotiate with, and those which you are not prepared to pursue at this time but may later wish to reconsider. A selection criteria ranking system helps you to analyze quickly the relative attractiveness of selling companies so that you can give the owners of a selling company a response within two weeks after your initial meeting with them.

HOW A COMPANY SHOULD ASSIGN COMPARATIVE VALUES (WEIGHTING FACTORS) TO ITS SELECTION CRITERIA FOR A TARGET INDUSTRY SEGMENT

A prospective acquirer should wait until its management has an opportunity to analyze and compare at least six companies in the target industry segment which meet its screening criteria. This is because it is very difficult for a company's executives to determine the relative importance of different selection criteria unless they can compare actual companies. There are three ways in which a company can obtain profiles of companies in a target industry segment which meet its screening criteria. These are:

1. Identify public companies in its target industry segment which meet its screening criteria. Then use the information contained in their annual reports and Form 10-K's (filed with the SEC) to develop a profile similar to that which would be prepared if the public companies were being sold. This technique works best in industries where there are a large number of public companies to choose from, such as banking, pharmaceutical manufacturing, and electronics manufacturing.

2. Research and investigate the companies in a particular industry segment. Surprisingly complete company profiles can be developed by consultants who specialize in this type of business research. This technique is used primarily by companies which are using the Research Approach format.

3. Find six or more acquisition candidates which meet your screening criteria before deciding the relative importance (weighting factors) of your selection criteria.

THREE APPROACHES A COMPANY CAN USE WHEN ORGANIZING ITS ACQUISITION SEARCH PROGRAM

1. *The Opportunistic Approach.* The company begins looking at acquisition candidates and then decides what type of company it should seek to acquire.

2. *The Research Approach.* The company decides which individual companies it would like to own. Then it contacts these companies to learn whether they would consider selling.

3. *The Standard Approach.* The company decides which types of companies it would consider acquiring. Then it searches for selling companies which meet these screening criteria (industry segment, size, location, etc.). This approach is called the Standard Approach because it is the one used by most prospective acquirers.

The following table shows the sequence in which the three elements of an acquisition search program are applied for each alternative approach:

OPPORTUNISTIC APPROACH	RESEARCH APPROACH	STANDARD APPROACH
1. Prospecting	1. Screening	1. Screening
2. Screening	2. Selection	2. Prospecting
3. Selection	3. Prospecting	3. Selection

WHO SHOULD USE THE OPPORTUNISTIC APPROACH

Companies unsure of what types of businesses to acquire should use the Opportunistic Approach. There are two good reasons why a company may be unable to define its standard screening criteria before it begins looking at acquisition candidates. These are:

1. The company wants to diversify into a new type of business which is unrelated to its current line of business. Looking at actual acquisition candidates in different businesses helps the company's management to understand the advantages and disadvantages of operating in different industries.

2. The company seeks to acquire profitable companies which can be paid for with loans secured by the selling company's assets and cash flow. These leveraged buyout opportunities occur infrequently. Therefore, a company which seeks to find them cannot use standard screening criteria because they would screen out too many acquisition opportunities. It must instead solicit a large number of acquisition opportunities by using relatively broad screening criteria.

HOW TO USE THE OPPORTUNISTIC APPROACH

1. Make a list of the types of businesses you would not want to own (e.g., employment agencies, steel mills, oil/gas producers, banks).
2. Make a list of the geographic locations where you would not want to operate (e.g., Europe, California, New York City).
3. Decide how small a company you would be willing to purchase.
4. Using the preceding preferences as your guide, develop a general set of screening criteria. For example,

Industry	Light manufacturing
Size	Annual sales over $5 million
Location	Eastern United States

5. Solicit acquisition opportunities by contacting merger/acquisition intermediaries who have listings of selling companies. This is the easiest way to review quickly a large number of acquisition opportunities because the intermediaries will generally have prepared an information package on the selling companies.
6. Review 30 to 40 acquisition opportunities, and then, based upon your reactions, narrow your screening criteria. For example, a company which started looking for light manufacturing companies, located in the east, might decide to concentrate on electronic manufacturers located in the Northeast. Narrowing your criteria produces a better response rate from intermediaries because they feel that you are more likely to be a serious acquirer. It also makes it easier for your own executives to screen out unacceptable acquisition opportunities.

A DISADVANTAGE IN USING THE OPPORTUNISTIC APPROACH

The Opportunistic Approach is very time consuming. Companies which have made a successful acquisition using the Opportunistic Approach find that they have reviewed 150 to 200 acquisition opportunities. This requires that one company executive devote full time, or two executives devote half their time, for seven to nine months in order to produce ten acquisition candidates which the prospective acquirer will want to begin negotiating to acquire. As discussed earlier in this chapter, a prospective acquirer which begins negotiating with ten companies which it thinks it would like to own will usually complete at least one acquisition.

Why do most companies which use the Opportunistic Approach fail to make an acquisition? They give up after three or four months because they are overwhelmed by the work load and are frustrated by the high proportion of acquisition candidates (over 90%) which they find unattractive. Failure to anticipate the time and effort required to find suitable acquisition opportunities is the principal reason why most companies which launch acquisition programs fail to make an acquisition. This problem, however, tends to be more severe for companies which use the Opportunistic Approach for the following reasons:

1. The Opportunistic Approach requires more executive labor hours (1,000 to 1,300 hours) than the Standard Approach (700 executive labor hours) or the Research Approach (300 executive labor hours).
2. Managements which choose the Opportunistic Approach tend to be less committed to making an acquisition. They frequently choose the Opportunistic Approach because they are not willing to spend the time required to develop standard screening criteria.

WHO SHOULD USE THE STANDARD APPROACH

Companies which have selected the types of companies they would consider acquiring but are not prepared to concentrate their search on a single type of company (industry segment) should use the Standard Approach. For these companies, the Standard Approach is preferable to the Opportunistic Approach because it saves time and executive labor hours. A typical company using effective screening criteria (see page 91) will devote about 700 executive labor hours in order to find ten acquisition candidates which it will want to begin negotiating to acquire. These 700 executive labor hours include the time required to develop and test the company's standard screening criteria. Assuming the company employs one executive working full time on its acquisition program, or two executives devoting half their time, its acquisition search program will be completed in four to five months. This compares with seven to nine months for a company using the Opportunistic Approach.

For companies which are not prepared to concentrate their search on a single type of company (industry segment), the Standard Approach is preferable to the Research Approach, though it requires more executive labor hours (700 executive labor hours versus 300 executive labor hours for the Research Approach). The reason is that most companies which use the Research Approach must employ outside market research consultants. The cost of employing these consultants is proportional to the number of target industry segments which are to be investigated. Therefore, the cost of using the Research Approach is usually greater than the cost of the 400 additional executive labor hours required by users of the Standard Approach when the prospective acquirer is searching for acquisition opportunities in more than one target industry segment.

ACQUISITION SEARCH TECHNIQUES GENERALLY USED BY COMPANIES SELECTING THE STANDARD APPROACH

Companies which select the Standard Approach usually locate suitable acquisition candidates by contacting intermediaries who have listings of selling companies and by writing letters to the chief executives of companies which appear to meet their standard screening criteria. These techniques typically find most of the active sellers and half of the silent sellers which meet the prospective acquirer's screening criteria. In order to find 10 acquisition candidates which the prospective acquirer would want to begin negotiating to acquire, the company will need to find 20 to 30 acquisition candidates which meet its selection criteria. Generally this goal can be achieved if there exists at least 300 companies which meet its acquisition screening criteria. When a prospective acquirer estimates that there are fewer than 100 companies which will meet its screening criteria, it should consider using the Research Approach even though it is more expensive. The Research Approach enables a prospective acquirer to identify more of the acquisition candidates which meet its screening criteria by finding a greater proportion of these companies which are silent sellers.

PROCEDURE FOR A COMPANY USING THE STANDARD APPROACH

1. Develop a set of standard screening criteria for each industry segment in which the company will seek acquisition opportunities.
2. Estimate the number of companies which exist which meet these screening criteria.
3. When the number of companies which meet your screening criteria is less than 300, consider broadening your screening criteria. When this number is less than 100, consider using the Research Approach rather than the Standard Approach.

4. Select the acquisition search techniques which you will use to find selling companies. These are discussed in Chapter 4.

5. Begin searching for acquisition candidates which meet your screening criteria. Once you have found at least six such companies, develop your selection criteria and your numerical ranking system for comparing acquisition candidates. This system will make it easier to decide with which acquisition candidates you should begin negotiating. It also tends to make the acquisition candidate evaluation process more objective.

HOW A COMPANY USES THE RESEARCH APPROACH

The prospective acquirer develops screening criteria in the same manner as companies which use the Standard Approach. However, once it develops these screening criteria, the prospective acquirer does not begin looking for acquisition candidates. Instead the acquirer employs market research consultants to perform three functions. These are:

1. Prepare to study the target industry.
2. Find all the companies, and the subsidiaries and divisions of companies, which meet its screening criteria.
3. Investigate these companies, subsidiaries and divisions and prepare a profile describing each one.

Then the prospective acquirer studies these profiles, develops its selection criteria ranking system, and decides which companies that it would like to own. Unlike companies using Opportunistic and the Standard Approaches, companies using the Research Approach complete the target company selection process before finding out which companies would be willing to discuss being acquired. The final stage of Research Approach is to find out which of the selected target companies would consider being acquired.

Companies which choose the Research Approach attempt to meet with each of the companies they believe they would like to own. They or their consultants contact these target companies by letter, telephone, and telegram. They seek to be introduced to the owners of those companies which fail to respond to this direct solicitation.

The market research experts may be paid either a straight consulting fee or a retainer plus a success fee.

TWO ADVANTAGES OF THE RESEARCH APPROACH

1. It increases the likelihood that a prospective acquirer will make a successful completed acquisition. You will recall that the key factor was finding at least 10 acquisition candidates which the prospective acquirer would like to own. Companies which use the Research Approach can generally find 10 acquisition candidates which they would like to own if there exists 100 to 150 companies which meet their screening criteria. In contrast a company using the Standard Approach can generally find 10 acquisition candidates which they would like to own if there exist 300 companies which meet their screening criteria.

2. It reduces the time required to carry out an acquisition search program. Companies using the Research Approach can generally complete their acquisition search program in three months. This compares with four to five months for companies using the Standard Approach and seven to nine months for companies using the Opportunistic Approach.

KEY DISADVANTAGE OF USING THE RESEARCH APPROACH

The prospective acquirer must usually employ market research experts to investigate the target industry segment and the companies in that segment. The cost of employing these experts averages $40,000 to $60,000 per target industry segment.

WHEN TO CONSIDER USING THE RESEARCH APPROACH

There are three circumstances in which the Research Approach is preferable to the Standard Approach. These are:

1. The prospective acquirer has selected one industry segment in which it strongly desires to make an acquisition.

2. The prospective acquirer finds that there are fewer than 100 companies which meet its screening criteria. Therefore, if they choose the Standard Approach they will have less than a 50% chance of completing a successful acquisition.

3. The prospective acquirer has already tried using the Standard Approach but has failed to make an acquisition because it found too few suitable acquisition opportunities.

COMPARE THE COSTS OF THE THREE ALTERNATIVE ACQUISITION SEARCH PROGRAM APPROACHES

The Research Approach is the most expensive of the three approaches for companies which fail to make an acquisition. It is, however, often less expensive than the Opportunistic and the Standard Approaches for companies which complete an acquisition. The following presentation examines the cost structure of the three different approaches:

Assumptions

1. The prospective acquirer seeks to make an acquisition in a single industry segment (e.g., housewares manufacturers).

2. The likelihood that the acquirer will need to pay a finders fee to an intermediary is 100% for companies using the Opportunistic Approach, 70% for companies using the Standard Approach, and 20% for companies using the Research Approach.

3. The finder's fee paid to an intermediary who arranges a completed acquisition averages $100,000.

4. The company's own executives who work on the acquisition search program are paid an average of $50 per hour, which includes benefits and travel expenses.

5. The consultants employed when the Research Approach is used are paid $50,000 in fees and expense reimbursements.

    A.   **Estimated cost if no acquisition is made**

        1. Opportunistic Approach

1,000 executive labor hours × $50	$50,000
Finder's fees	none
Total cost	$50,000

        2. Standard Approach

700 executive labor hours × $50	$35,000
Finder's fees	none
Total cost	$35,000

        3. Research Approach

300 executive labor hours × $50	$15,000
Consultants fees and expenses	60,000
Finder's fees	none
Total cost	$65,000

B. Estimated cost if one company is acquired

1. *Opportunistic Approach*

1,000 executive labor hours × $50	$ 50,000
Finder's fee $100,000 × 100% probability	100,000
Total cost	$150,000

2. *Standard Approach*

700 executive manhours × $50	$ 35,000
Finder's fees $100,000 × 70% probability	70,000
Total cost	$105,000

3. *Research Approach*

300 executive manhours × $50	$ 15,000
Consultants' fees and expenses	50,000
Finder's fees $100,000 × 20% probability	20,000
Total cost	$ 85,000

C. Summary

	NO ACQUISITION MADE	ONE COMPLETED ACQUISITION
Opportunistic Approach	$50,000	$150,000
Standard Approach	35,000	105,000
Research Approach	65,000	85,000

The number of target industry segments in which the prospective acquirer seeks to find suitable acquisition candidates is an important consideration. The estimated cost of using consultants is $40,000 to $60,000 for each target industry segment. Therefore, the Research Approach is much more expensive to use if the prospective acquirer seeks acquisitions in more than one industry segment.

HOW YOUR COMPANY SHOULD DECIDE WHICH APPROACH TO USE

1. Use the Opportunistic Approach only if your company is unable to develop its standard screening criteria. The Opportunistic Approach is always more time consuming than the Research and Standard approaches. It is also the most expensive approach unless you fail to make an acquisition.

2. After you develop your screening criteria, estimate the number of companies which exist which meet your criteria. When the number of companies is over 300, or you seek acquisition in more than one industry segment, use the Standard Approach. When the number of companies is fewer than 100 and

you seek acquisitions in only one industry segment, the Research Approach is preferable. When there are 100 to 300 companies which meet your screening criteria, use the Research Approach if you seek acquisitions in one industry segment or two closely related industry segments. Otherwise, start with the Standard Approach and then switch to the Research Approach if you don't find at least 5 acquisition candidates which you would like to try to acquire.

HOW TO FIND THE SELLING COMPANIES

EIGHT TECHNIQUES FOR FINDING ACQUISITION CANDIDATES

The following are the principal acquisition search techniques. They may be used by a company directly or by brokers and consultants whom the company employs.

1. *Intermediaries who have listings of acquisition candidates.* The primary sources of these listings are acquisition finder/brokers. Secondary sources are invest-ment bankers, the acquistion departments of commercial banks and account-ing firms, and industry trade associations.

2. *"Targeted" direct-mail solicitation.* This refers to letters sent to the owners (usually the chief executive) of companies which meet a prospective acquirer's screening criteria. Generally, these mailings are to a small number of companies (e.g., 10 to 30).

3. *"Semitargeted" direct-mail solicitation.* This refers to letters sent to the owners of companies which *may* meet a prospective acquirer's screening criteria. Typically, a prospective acquirer eliminates those companies which clearly do not meet its screening criteria and writes to all the others. Mailings of this type are generally made to 100 to 300 companies.

4. *Target telephone solicitation.* This refers to telephone calls to the owners (usually the chief executive) of companies which meet your screening criteria. Generally, this involves 20 to 30 companies.

5. *Semitargeted telephone solicitation.* This refers to telephone calls to the owners of companies which may meet your screening criteria. Generally, this involves contacting a large number of companies (sometimes as many as 300).

6. *Advertising.* Advertisements seeking acquisitions are generally placed in the classified sections of *The Wall Street Journal* and industry trade journals.

7. *Internal public relations.* Publicizing your growth plans and acquisition criteria among your own employees and quasi-employees (e.g., your outside accountants, lawyers, and lenders). This technique is used to identify companies which are likely to be receptive to being contacted by letter or telephone due to the personal circumstances of their owners/managers or financial problems. For example, the president of one of your competitors may have mentioned to your sales manager that he wants to retire.

8. *External public relations.* Using the media (e.g., industry publications) to publicize your company's growth plans and acquisition criteria. This technique encourages the owners of acquisition candidates to contact you directly. It also encourages intermediaries who have suitable listings to contact you. The publicity will also strengthen your marketing and employee recruitment programs.

A SELECTIVE RESEARCH TECHNIQUE SAVES TIME

A "selective" search technique is one which produces a high proportion of acquisition candidates which meet your screening criteria. Selectivity is important because it takes an average of two hours of an executive's time to review each new acquisition candidate that is submitted for your consideration. It will become very time consuming and expensive if you have to review large numbers of acquisition candidates in order to find only a few which meet your screening criteria. An example of a selective search technique would be writing to the owners of companies which appear to meet your screening criteria.

A PRODUCTIVE SEARCH TECHNIQUE OFFERS MANY CANDIDATES

A "productive" search technique is one which generates large numbers of acquisition candidates for your consideration. Unless your company is one of the few which uses the research approach, you want to be able to look at a significant number of acquisition candidates (e.g., 40 to 60 companies). Therefore, you cannot limit your choice of search techniques to those which are only likely to produce a small number of acquisition candidates. An example of a search technique which produces small numbers of candidates would be contacting the executive secretary of your trade association. An example of a search technique which is more "productive" would be contacting 20 acquisition finder/brokers.

HOW TO USE THESE SELECTIVITY AND PRODUCTIVITY CHARACTERISTICS TO CHOOSE ACQUISITION SEARCH TECHNIQUES

Each prospective acquirer's target market is different. The results generated by the search technique you start with provide you with the information you need to choose your next search technique. When your initial search technique produces too few responses, you should consider using a more productive technique. When your initial search technique produces a very low percentage of responses which meet your screening criteria, you should consider using a more selective search technique. The following examples illustrate this concept:

A company contacts 5 finder/brokers. It receives 20 acquisition candidate submittals, but none of them meets its screening criteria. This company should next use one of the more selective search techniques such as direct-mail solicitation.

A company writes to the owners of 10 companies which meet its screening criteria. There are over 2,000 companies which *might* meet its screening criteria. However, the company cannot gather enough information inexpensively to determine whether the other 1,990 companies meet its screening criteria. The 10 letters produce 2 positive responses. However, the company's management wants to look at more acquisition opportunities before making a decision whether it should commence serious negotiations. This company should next use one of the more productive search techniques such as contacting finder/brokers or making a larger, less selective, direct-mail solicitation.

A company contacts 2 finder/brokers. It receives 10 acquisition candidate submittals. Five of the 10 candidates meet its screening criteria. This company should consider contacting more finder/brokers since this search technique seems to be working.

RELATIVE SELECTIVITY AND PRODUCTIVITY
OF THE EIGHT SEARCH TECHNIQUES

TECHNIQUE	SELECTIVITY	PRODUCTIVITY
Contacting intermediaries	Low	High
Targeted direct mail	High	Low
Semitargeted direct mail	Average	Average
Targeted telephone solicitation	High	Below average
Semitargeted telephone solicitation	Average	Above average
Advertising	Variable	Variable
Internal public relations	High	Low
External public relations	Average	Below average

FACTORS THAT SHOULD INFLUENCE YOUR
CHOICE OF ACQUISITION SEARCH
TECHNIQUES

1. *Your choice of an acquisition search strategy.* The following chart indicates the
   search techniques that are likely to be the most effective with each of the three
   alternative strategies. The standard approach has been subdivided into two
   strategies because different search techniques are appropriate after you have
   completed your review of the first group of acquisition candidates and
   narrowed your screening criteria.

ACQUISITION SEARCH STRATEGY	PRIMARY SEARCH TECHNIQUES	SECONDARY SEARCH TECHNIQUES
Opportunistic	Contacting intermediaries	Advertising External public relations
Research	Targeted direct mail Targeted telephone solicitation	Internal public relations
Standard (1st stage)	Contacting intermediaries	Advertising Semitargeted direct mail External public relations
Standard (2nd stage)	Semitargeted direct mail	Semitargeted telephone solicitation Internal public relations

2. *Your willingness and ability to pay consulting fees or retainers.*

Most smaller companies will need to employ an acquisition search specialist to carry out direct-mail or telephone solicitation search techniques. Acquisition search specialists who are experienced in the use of these techniques are generally paid on a consulting or retainer basis rather than on straight commission.

USING INTERMEDIARIES TO FIND SELLING COMPANIES

The most popular acquisition search technique is to contact intermediaries who have listings of acquisition candidates. The two principal types of intermediaries are:

a. Acquisition finder/brokers
b. Investment bankers

ROLE OF ACQUISITION FINDERS AND BROKERS

The primary role of acquisition finders and brokers is to represent active sellers and to seek suitable active seller listings for prospective purchasers by exchanging listing information with other finders and brokers.

The secondary role of acquisition finders and brokers is to contact company owners/managements, on behalf of a prospective purchaser, to learn whether they are silent sellers. The better finder/brokers are very good at finding silent sellers. They will, however, rarely perform this function unless they are either granted an exclusive or are paid a retainer by the prospective acquirer.

THE DIFFERENCE BETWEEN A FINDER AND A BROKER

In actual practice there is no difference. Most intermediaries perform the work of a broker (they represent either a buyer or a seller); however, most intermediaries use a commission agreement that provides that they be paid for their work as a "finder." This arrangement is designed to make it easier for the intermediary to collect his fee because the only legal responsibility for a finder is making a bona fide introduction.

HOW MERGER/ACQUISITION FINDERS AND BROKERS ARE COMPENSATED

Most finders and brokers work on a commission basis. In some cases the finder/broker is paid a retainer which is then deducted from the commission when a transaction, which they arranged, is consummated. A retainer fee is justified if a finder/broker is being employed to search for silent sellers.

HOW THE COMMISSION IS COMPUTED

Finders and brokers are usually paid a commission based upon the purchase price of the acquired company. The most commonly used arrangement is a sliding scale called the Lehman formula. The Lehman formula is 5% of the first $1 million, plus 4% of the second $1 million, plus 3% of the third $1 million, plus 2% of the fourth $1 million, plus 1% of everything over $4 million. On acquisitions which are under $1 million, the Lehman sliding scale is 10% of the first $100,000, 9% of the second $100,000, 8% of the third $100,000, and so on. It is also common on small transactions for a finder/broker to be paid a flat commission of 6% to 10% of the purchase price rather than using the Lehman formula.

WHO PAYS THE COMMISSION

The agreement to pay a finder/broker may either be with the purchaser or the seller or both. However, ultimately the acquirer winds up paying the commission since sellers will simply increase their selling price if they are paying the commission.

THE PREFERRED ARRANGEMENT FOR A PROSPECTIVE ACQUIRER

The prospective acquirer should insist on having a finder's fee agreement with the broker for the following reasons:

1. Even though a broker may have a finder's fee agreement with the seller, he will give preferential consideration to a prospective acquirer with whom he also has a finder's fee agreement. This is because the double agreement increases the likelihood that he will be paid by someone. It should not, however, increase his compensation. Your finder's fee agreement should always provide that the commission you owe will be offset by any commission paid by the seller.

2. Your finder's fee agreement will provide you with protection against unwarranted or duplicate claims for broker fees.

3. You have greater psychological control over the broker when you are the one who will be paying him or her.

WHERE TO GET ADDITIONAL INFORMATION ON FINDER'S FEE AGREEMENTS

There are several multivolume handbooks on mergers and acquisitions which are written for attorneys. These contain a discussion of finder compensation and finder's agreements. Following are two of these sources.

Corporate Acquisition and Mergers
Byron E. Fox and Eleanor M. Fox
Matthew Binder, New York, NY
1983, see Volume 3, Chapter 30.

Business Acquisitions
edited by John W. Herz and Charles H. Baller
Practicing Law Institute
New York, NY
see Volume 1, Chapter 3, and Volume 2, Forms No. 29 and 30

HOW TO CHOOSE THE MERGER/ACQUISITION FINDERS AND BROKERS WITH WHOM TO WORK

Try to select experienced, reputable finders and brokers who specialize in the industry in which you seek to make acquisitions. When this is impractical, you should seek experienced, reputable finders and brokers who specialize in the geographic area where you seek to find acquisition opportunities. The executive secretary of the appropriate trade association can usually provide you with the names of some good finder/brokers who specialize in your target industry.

There is no comprehensive directory for merger/acquisition finders and brokers but some of the larger, more reputable firms are listed in *Who's Who of Corporate Acquisition.* This directory is published by Capitol Publishing Corporation, 2 Laurel Avenue, Wellesley Hills, MA 02181.

There is no trade association for merger/acquisition finders and brokers, however, some of the better finders and brokers are members of the Association for Corporate Growth. Many corporation executives who are responsible for their company's merger/acquisition activities are also members of this trade association.

The association's headquarters are at 5940 W. Touhy Avenue, Suite 300, Chicago, IL 60648.

A key obstacle confronts the smaller company which wants to use finders and brokers. It is difficult for smaller acquirers to attract the time and attention of the better acquisition finders and brokers.

HOW A SMALLER COMPANY CAN MOTIVATE FINDERS AND BROKERS TO WORK ON ITS BEHALF

1. Make their job easier:

    a. Develop a good set of screening criteria.

    b. Provide a list of companies that meet these criteria. This will help the finder/broker to understand your screening criteria.

2. Show that you are a serious buyer:

    a. Arrange for the finder/broker to meet your key people and tour your facilities.

    b. Respond quickly to the acquisition proposals the finder/broker presents. Explain what you liked or did not like about the selling company.

    c. Have one of your executives go out and meet with any sellers that look interesting.

3. Reduce the finder/broker's financial risk:

    a. Reimburse the finder/broker for their travel expenses and advertising costs (if any).

    b. Grant the finder/broker an exclusive four month finder's fee agreement.

    c. Agree to pay a minimum commission (e.g., $50,000) on small deals (e.g., under $1 million).

HOW TO HANDLE INQUIRIES FROM FINDER/ BROKERS

1. Request the finder/broker to send you his or her references and a list of the transactions he or she has arranged. This will help to weed out the amateurs who have never done a deal and are never likely to.

2. Once you have confirmed that you are dealing with an experienced, successful, finder/broker, send him or her your company profile and your finder's fee agreement. It is best if you refrain from accepting acquisition candidate referrals from a finder/broker until you have received back the executed finder's fee agreement.

3. Keep a log of acquisition candidate submittals. The log should indicate the name and address of the acquisition candidate submittal, the date, and the source. The log is important. You will frequently receive the same acqusition candidate submission from several different intermediaries. Your finder's fee agreement will make it clear that you will only pay the first intermediary who submits a deal and arranges a meeting with the principals of the selling company. However, this protection is lost if you don't keep good records.

4. Whenever you receive a submittal from a finder/broker, check to be sure that you have not received it previously from any other source. If you have, immediately return the entire package with a letter indicating that you cannot accept the submission.

5. When you receive a new acquisiton candidate submission, phone the broker and tell him or her that you have received it.

6. Whenever you decide that an acquisition candidate is not of interest, return the entire package with a short note to the finder/broker. Telephone the finder/ broker and tell him or her why it was not of interest. The quicker you turn down unacceptable transactions and inform the broker, the more likely it is that the broker will contact you before contacting other prospective acquirers when he or she has new listings. This is because a timely response helps the broker to maintain a good relationship with the seller.

THE ACQUISITION ROLE OF INVESTMENT BANKERS

1. Represent public companies which are active sellers.

2. Represent large public companies which seek to sell a subsidiary or a division.

3. Search for public acquisition candidates, by exchanging information with other investment bankers.

4. Structure acquisition transactions in which the owners of the selling company will receive a portion of their compensation in the form of the acquiring company's securities (e.g., stock and debentures).

WHEN A SMALLER COMPANY SHOULD USE AN INVESTMENT BANKER

1. The prospective acquirer is a small public company which intends to use its stock to pay a portion of the purchase price of an acquisition.

2. The prospective acquirer is a private company which wants to own a public company.

3. The prospective acquirer is a private company which wants to become a public company. Merging your company into a public company, which you then take control of, is a cost-effective way to accomplish this objective.

SOME DISADVANTAGES OF ACQUIRING A PUBLIC COMPANY

1. The legal costs are significantly higher than if you acquire an equivalent privately owned company.

2. The purchase price for a public company is generally 20% higher than the purchase price for an equivalent privately owned company.

HOW INVESTMENT BANKERS ARE COMPENSATED

Investment bankers are paid a nonrefundable retainer (e.g., $25,000) which is applied against their commissions if they arrange a completed acquisition. Their commissions are computed using the Lehman formula.

HOW A SMALLER PUBLIC COMPANY SHOULD SELECT ITS INVESTMENT BANKER

The objective is to find a regional investment banking firm which has been successful working with smaller public companies which were either in your industry or which were located in your geographic area.

When a smaller public company selects a large national securities firm to be its investment banker, the results can be less than desired.

1. The smaller company's chief executive and senior officers will meet with, and be entertained by, a senior partner. This will be their final contact with any officer who is 28-years-old or older.

2. The investment banking firm will happily accept the retainer. Investment bankers will never turn down a retainer.

3. The company's acquisition and corporate finance assignments will be assigned to the investment banking firm's youngest, least experienced officer. (Note: The lowest-level position at an investment banking firm is an assistant vice president.)

THE EXPERIENCE OF COMPANIES THAT PLACE ADVERTISEMENTS SEEKING ACQUISITION OPPORTUNITIES

1. They either receive some attractive acquisition candidate submittals or they do not receive any good acquisition opportunities. There appears to be no middle ground.

2. They receive dozens of inquiries from finder/brokers who claim that they have suitable acquisition candidates, but they first need the company to execute a finder's agreement. Some of these finder/brokers may be good sources. Therefore, you should request each one to send you their references and a list of transactions they have arranged.

THE BEST PLACES TO ADVERTISE

1. The classified section of *The Wall Street Journal.*

2. Classified sections of industry publications where you find other merger/acquisition advertising.

SIX GUIDELINES TO FOLLOW WHEN ADVERTISING IN *THE WALL STREET JOURNAL*

1. Place your classified advertisement in all the regional editions. Even though you may only want to buy a company in one area (e.g., the Southwest), the intermediary who has the listing might be somewhere else (e.g., New York, Chicago, Los Angeles).

2. Run your advertisement two different days, two consecutive weeks (a total of two insertions). Do not advertise on Monday or Saturday because the readership is much lower on these days.

3. Have *The Wall Street Journal* set the type. The "real" advertisements are "pub" set. The flaky advertisements are set in special type by advertising agencies.

4. Have a box placed around your advertisement. Pay for an extra line of white space below the headline and below the copy. This will make your advertisement stand out.

5. Do not use a blind box number. Either give your company's name, address, and telephone number or give the name, address and telephone number of your representative (e.g., your lawyer).

6. Insert at the conclusion of your advertisement, "brokers protected." you want to encourage finder/brokers who have suitable listings to contact you. Trying to avoid paying a broker's commission on an acquisition is like trying to find a home to buy without paying a realtor's commission.

HOW PUBLIC RELATIONS IS USED AS AN ACQUISITION SEARCH TECHNIQUE

1. Owners of selling companies, and their representatives, will often contact prospective acquirers who they believe would have an interest in purchasing their company. External public relations is the process encouraging these contacts by making the business community aware of your company's acquisition objectives. The principal external public relations technique is arranging for articles to appear in industry trade publications which describe your company, its growth plans, and its acquisition objectives.

2. A company's own employees and quasi-employees (e.g., the company's lawyer, accountant, banker, and trade association secretary) often become aware of companies which would be receptive to an acquisition inquiry from your company. Internal public relations is the process of encouraging these suggestions by making your own employees and quasi-employees aware of your company's acquisition objectives. Direct-mail or telephone solicitation is then used to follow up on these suggestions.

WHY A SMALLER COMPANY SHOULD LAUNCH AN EXTERNAL PUBLIC RELATIONS PROGRAM

Publicizing a smaller company in the industry trade press produces many benefits such as:

1. Increased morale and productivity among your own employees.
2. New proposals from prospective suppliers, lenders, customers, and joint venture partners.
3. More inquiries from executives, salespeople, and other prospective employees.
4. Increased credibility and stature with your present suppliers, lenders, and customers.
5. A larger number of acquisition proposals from the owners of companies and their representatives.

FIVE OBSTACLES WHICH MAKE IT DIFFICULT FOR MANY SMALLER COMPANIES TO USE EXTERNAL PUBLIC RELATIONS AS AN ACQUISITION SEARCH TECHNIQUE

1. Smaller companies are not likely to be of interest to industry trade publications because a smaller proportion of the publication's readership is likely to be affected by the company's activities.
2. Privately owned companies are less likely to be of interest to industry trade publications than are public companies.
3. Smaller companies rarely have their own internal public relations staff.
4. The larger relations firms will not assign their experienced account officers to work with smaller companies because they cannot afford to pay as much as a larger company.

COMPARING EXTERNAL PUBLIC RELATIONS WITH ADVERTISING AS AN ACQUISITION SEARCH TECHNIQUE

1. Articles in the industry trade press reach a much larger audience than do advertisements in the same publications.
2. It is quick, easy, and relatively inexpensive to place classified advertisements seeking acquisition opportunities. Public relations compaigns are difficult and time consuming to undertake. They generally do not begin to produce results (e.g., articles in trade publications) for six to nine months.

SOME GUIDELINES FOR A SMALLER COMPANY DECIDING TO LAUNCH A PUBLIC RELATIONS CAMPAIGN

1. Start by preparing a profile describing your company.
2. Employ a public relations consultant who is experienced working with smaller companies in your industry.
3. Be patient. Many smaller companies drop their public relations efforts just when they are about to begin producing good results. Don't start a public relations program unless you are prepared to fund it for at least 12 months.

SEARCH TECHNIQUES FOR FINDING SILENT SELLERS

1. Internal public relations
2. Direct-mail solicitation
3. Telephone solicitation

HOW AN INTERNAL PUBLIC RELATIONS PROGRAM CAN FIND SILENT SELLERS

Most silent sellers are companies which became receptive to an acquisition inquiry because of the personal circumstances of their owner/executives. Examples of these personal circumstances include illness, death, estate planning problems, and disagreements among a company's owners. A company's employees and quasi-employees (e.g., the company's lawyer, accountant, banker) who have frequent contact with other companies in your industry will often be aware of companies which are likely to be silent sellers due to the personal circumstances of their owner/executives. An internal public relations program is designed to encourage your employees and quasi-employees to identify these opportunities and bring them to your attention so that you can contact the companies by letter or by telephone.

Surveys of successful acquirers indicate that internal public relations is the most effective, but least used acquisition search technique.

SOME PROBLEMS ASSOCIATED WITH USING AN INTERNAL PUBLIC RELATIONS SEARCH TECHNIQUE

1. Your employees and quasi-employees will become angry and discouraged if you don't respond quickly to their acquisition suggestions.
2. There is a danger that you will be swamped with unsuitable acquisition suggestions from your employees and quasi-employees. This is most likely to occur if your acquisition criteria are not well defined before you launch your internal public relations program.

WHEN TO USE INTERNAL PUBLIC RELATIONS TO SEARCH FOR ACQUISITION OPPORTUNITIES

Internal public relations is one of the most effective search techniques for companies which seek to acquire competitors (market intensification), and similar companies which operate in different geographic markets (geographic extension). When internal public relations is used by companies with other acquisition objectives (e.g., product extension), they tend to be swamped with unsuitable acquisition suggestions.

TARGETS OF YOUR INTERNAL PUBLIC RELATIONS PROGRAM

Your internal public relations program should focus on those executives, key employees, and quasi-employees who are likely to become aware of the personal circumstances of the owner/executives of other companies in your industry. They include:

1. Senior executives
2. Salesmen
3. Truck drivers
4. Technical experts (e.g., engineers, researchers)
5. Outside accountants

6. Outside law firms

7. Advertising agency

8. Management and marketing consultants

9. Trade industry executives

10. Labor union executives

11. Bankers and other lenders

KEY ELEMENTS OF AN EFFECTIVE INTERNAL PUBLIC RELATIONS PROGRAM

1. Prepare a written presentation describing your company acquisition objectives and acquisition candidate screening criteria. Prepare a form for employees and quasi-employees to use for making acquisition suggestions.

2. Set up meetings with selected employees and quasi-employees to brief them on your acquisition objectives and to answer their questions. Then distribute the written materials.

3. Assign one of your executives responsibility for handling and quickly responding to acquisition suggestions from employees and quasi-employees.

4. Set up a system for recognizing and rewarding an employee whose suggestions lead to a meeting with the principals of an acquisition prospect. The reward should be high enough to encourage cooperation, but not so high that it diverts your employees from their primary work responsibility. A bonus payment of around $500 is usually an appropriate amount to pay employees who are not directly involved in your acquisition program. No bonus should be paid to your senior executives and other employees for whom acquisition work is part of their job.

HOW DIRECT-MAIL SOLICITATION CAN FIND SILENT SELLERS

Direct-mail solicitation is a letter-writing campaign directed to companies that you might be interested in purchasing if they were available to be acquired. When preparing a solicitation letter remember these two objectives:

1. You want the company's chief executive to read your letter. He or she is likely to be the only one who knows that the time has come to consider selling the company. If your letter is diverted to another executive, it will "disappear."

This is because the company's other executives view a possible sale of their company as a threat to their job security.

2. You want the recipient of the letter (e.g., the company president) to feel that you selected a limited number of companies to write to, rather than conducted a mass mailing. Most company presidents won't respond if they feel your letter is part of a mass mailing.

EIGHT GUIDELINES TO FOLLOW WHEN PREPARING A SOLICITATION LETTER

1. *Length.* Your letter should be one-page long. Company presidents typically have three-minute attention spans. They frequently will only glance at a letter or document that is longer than one page and then refer it to one of their executives, or to their attorney. The letter then disappears if it suggests a sale of the company.

2. *Paper.* Use good white bond paper. First impressions are important.

3. *Addressee.* Send your letter to the company's chief executive (usually the president for smaller companies). Be sure to include his or her first name, not his or her initials. Do not abbreviate street names or city names. Do not use mailing labels. These items all indicate to a recipient that a letter is part of a mass mailing.

4. *Printing.* Each letter should be individually typed using a standard typeface.

5. *Signature.* The signature should be in blue ink, using a felt-tip pen. This indicates to the recipient that a person (rather than a machine) signed the letter.

6. *Enclosures.* Do not include any enclosures (e.g., your company brochure). Secretaries typically open and redirect letters which have enclosures or are not in a standard size (#10) envelope.

7. *Postage.* Use a postage meter, not postage stamps. A postage stamp indicates that the sender can't afford a postage meter.

8. *Marking.* Type on both the envelope and the top of the letter "Personal and Confidential." This increases the likelihood that the President's secretary will not open it and divert it to another senior executive.

HOW TO COMPOSE AN EFFECTIVE SOLICITATION LETTER

Your letter should be three paragraphs long. The first paragraph tells why you are writing. For example:

Our company (or our client) is a toy manufacturer. We believe that combining our company with another toy manufacturer would enable both companies to be more profitable (or to grow more rapidly).

The second paragraph describes your company, your growth plans, and your acquisition criteria. For example:

Our company is 25-years-old, but has young aggressive management. In 1985 we anticipate that our sales will reach $15 million. We sell primarily to K-Mart and other mass merchandisers. We seek to find a toy manufacturer with sales of over $5 million which could use our marketing and distribution network. The management of your company should be prepared to join the senior management of the new combined company (or should be prepared to continue running your company for at least 12 months).

The third paragraph (the action close) tells the recipient what you want him or her to do. For example:

Please phone me and let us dicuss whether an acquisition or merger could benefit both our companies.

Somewhat surprisingly, your letter will draw a better response if it is sent by your representative rather than directly by your company. The reason is that the recipient will be curious regarding your company's identity and therefore is more likely to respond if he or she doesn't know who the prospective buyer is.

EXPECTED RESULTS

Most silent sellers will respond that they are not for sale, but wouldn't mind getting together to talk further. This means that they are for sale, but don't want to appear too anxious.

An effective letter-writing campaign should produce a positive response rate of 7% to 14%. If you get less than a 6% positive response rate either your letter needs to be improved or you need to develop a better mailing list.

WHAT TO DO WHEN A COMPANY RESPONDS TO YOUR ACQUISITION SOLICITATION LETTER

1. Order a Dun & Bradstreet credit report on the company. This will give you some background information on the company and its principals.

2. Suggest that you exchange information. Send them the profile you have prepared describing your own company. You hope that they will send you a similar information package and also their financial statements. Then you can decide if it is worthwhile proceeding further. However, keep in mind that it is

often necessary for one of your executives to go out and meet with the principals of a smaller privately owned company before they will provide their financial statements. Nine times out of ten, at the conclusion of this first meeting the prospective selling company will give you their financial statements.

HOW TO PREPARE A LIST OF COMPANIES FOR SOLICITATION LETTERS

There are four types of business information sources used by companies to develop acquisition mailing lists. These are:

1. "Dun's Market Identifier" cards
2. Commercial mailing lists
3. Directories of companies

HOW "DUN'S MARKET IDENTIFIER" CARDS CAN HELP YOU

Dun & Bradstreet (D&B) extracts key information from its data base of company credit reports and presents this information on 3×5 file cards. You can order these cards for companies by industry, geographic location, size category, or a combination of these variables. On each card you will have the company name, address, telephone number, chief executive officer, sales volume, number of employees, and Dun's number. The Dun's number is used when you request the full credit report on the company.

SOME ADVANTAGES AND DISADVANTAGES OF USING D&B MARKETING CARDS TO DEVELOP YOUR MAILING LIST

1. The D & B credit files are sorted by four-digit SIC number. You will not be able to use this source effectively if your target industry is a subgroup within a four-digit SIC number category. Within a four-digit SIC code, however, you can purchase only those cards which are for companies that are the size and location you are looking for.
2. D & B has a full credit report available for each company that they provide a marketing card for. This makes it easy to get additional information on a company which responds favorably to your mail solicitation.

3. The D & B company files leaves out 25% to 50% of the privately owned companies. This varies by industry.

4. The sales volume estimates in D & B's data base are very unreliable. However, the number of employees is relatively accurate. Therefore when ordering cards you should select a minimum and maximum number of employees, rather than setting a minimum and maximum sales volume.

5. The D & B cards are computer generated. The computer abbreviates words by dropping vowels. For example, Henry Robert Smallwood, Chairman, Superior Tool and Manufacturing Company, 137 Henry Wadsworth Highway, New South Brunswick, New Jersey may be listed as:

H. R. Smallwood, Ch.
Superior Tl & Mnfctng C.
137 Hnry Wadsworth Hwy.
New S. Brnswck, NJ

An executive receiving a letter addressed in this fashion would assume that it was a mass mailing.

HOW TO FIND MAILING LISTS OF COMPANY CHIEF EXECUTIVES

The publication describing many of the mailing lists that you can purchase is:

Direct Mail Lists Rates and Data
Standard Rate & Data Service
5201 Old Orchard Road
Skokie, IL 60007

You will find that there are mailing lists available for most types of businesses including very narrow industry segments such as aluminum window screen manufacturers. You can order most company mailing lists by location but not by size. They will not include the company telephone number, which is a disadvantage.

COMPANY DIRECTORIES YOU CAN USE

The principal multi-industry company directories are:

Million Dollar Directory
Dun & Bradstreet, Inc.
99 Church Street
New York, NY 10007

Register of American Manufacturers
   Thomas Publishing Company
   One Penn Plaza
   New York, NY 10001

OTC Industrials Manual
   Moody's Investor Service, Inc.
   99 Church Street
   New York, NY 10007

Standard Directory of Advertisers
   National Register Publishing Company, Inc.
   5201 Old Orchard Road
   Skokie, IL 60077

State Industrial Directories (26 state editions)
   State Industrial Directories Corporation
   2 Penn Plaza
   New York, NY 10001

Metalworking
   Dun & Bradstreet, Inc.
   99 Church Street
   New York, NY 10007

The best directories for specific types of companies are as follows:

1. Industrial products—*Thomas' Register of American Manufacturers*

2. Branded consumer products—*Standard Directory of Advertisers*

3. Within your state—*State Industrial Director*, published by State Industrial Directories Corporation

4. Small public companies—Moody's *OTC Industrials Manual*

5. Small service companies—Dun & Bradstreet's *Million Dollar Directory*

There is an advantage in using a directory prepared for your specific target industry. Directories prepared for a specific industry (e.g., plumbing wholesalers) usually lists a higher proportion of the smaller private companies that you will find listed in the multi-industry directories. The listings are also generally more up to date.

HOW TO FIND OUT WHICH COMPANY DIRECTORIES ARE AVAILABLE IN YOUR TARGET INDUSTRY

1. Obtain the membership directory for the trade association in your target industry. In many cases you will need to join the trade association to get this directory because it is not sold to nonmembers. There are two good directories of trade associations. These are:

Encyclopedia of Associations
   Gale Research Company
   Book Tower
   Detroit, MI 48226

National Trade & Professional Associations
   Columbia Books, Inc.
   777 14th Street, N.W.
   Washington DC 10005

2. There are two reference books which list many of the industry directories which you can purchase. These are:

Directory Information Service
   Gale Research Company
   Book Tower
   Detroit, MI 48226

Encyclopedia of Business Information
   Gale Research Company
   Book Tower
   Detroit, MI 48226

HOW TELEPHONE SOLICITATION CAN FIND SILENT PARTNERS

1. *President-to-president contact (targeted telephone solicitation).* The chief executive of your company telephones the chief executive of a company you would like to acquire. This is the most effective acquisition search technique. However, it will be very embarrassing and cause bad feelings if you use this technique to contact a company, and then decide not to follow up because you learn that the company is less attractive than you thought it was.

2. *Semitargeted telephone solicitation.* One of your junior executives or your representative phones the chief executives of companies which you would consider acquiring if they were willing to sell.

WHEN TO CONSIDER LAUNCHING A SEMITARGETED TELEPHONE SOLICITATION PROGRAM

When your direct-mail program doesn't draw a high enough response rate, consider launching a semitargeted telephone solicitation program. Telephone solicitation is 50% to 100% more effective than direct-mail solicitation. It is also considerably more expensive. It costs about $25 per company president spoken with. This includes salaries and long-distance telephone charges. By comparison, it costs about $5 in direct and indirect costs to contact company presidents using a letter-writing campaign. This $5 includes the cost of purchasing or preparing your mailing list, preparing and sending the letters, and handling the responses.

TWO WAYS TO SELECT A COMBINATION OF SEARCH TECHNIQUES THAT IS RIGHT FOR YOU

1. Start searching for active sellers using a productive search technique such as merger/acquisition intermediaries. Then switch to a more selective search technique (e.g., direct mail) if this doesn't produce satisfactory results.
2. Select an acquisition search strategy and then use the search techniques which are the most effective for implementing that strategy. Acquisition search strategies were discussed in Chapter 3.

C·H·A·P·T·E·R F·I·V·E

ACQUISITION PLANNING SYSTEMS

THE PURPOSE OF ACQUISITION PLANNING

Acquisition planning helps your company choose the two or three types of businesses it should try to acquire. These types of businesses are then used for your acquisition screening criteria. (The development and use of acquisition screening criteria were discussed in chapter 3.)

A DEFINITION OF ACQUISITION PLANNING

There are dozens of different acquisition planning systems which companies have used successfully. Later in this chapter there will be a detailed description of one of these systems which has worked particularly well for companies which had limited previous success making successful acquisitions.

Most (though not all) acquisition planning systems fall into one of the following three categories:

1. Strategic planning systems
2. Growth planning systems
3. "Engineering"-type planning systems

The following sections will describe each of these three types of planning systems.

STRATEGIC-TYPE PLANNING SYSTEMS

Strategic planning systems start with a company's long-term goals. Those goals are broad general statements of what the company would like to look like five years from now. Then the company develops a set of medium-term (e.g., two to five year) corporate objectives which would lead toward its achieving its long-term goals. Next the company selects the strategies which it will employ to attempt to achieve its corporate objectives. Finally, the company selects specific internal growth investments and acquisition investments to implement these strategies. A key characteristic of strategic planning systems is that a company develops its corporate objectives and strategies prior to considering what types of businesses it might acquire or start up.

The long-term goals which a company develops for its strategic plan are sometimes called the company's "mission statement." the following are examples of mission statements which might be developed by a wood office furniture manufacturer:

> "We seek to become one of the five leading national manufacturers of high-quality wood office furniture. Due to the cyclical nature of this industry, we would also like to derive at least one quarter of our reserves and profits from another business which is less cyclical than furniture manufacturing." "We seek to become one of the most profitable medium-sized companies in the office furniture industry."
>
> "We seek to grow more rapidly while continuing to be a North Carolina–based manufacturer."

After a company develops its long-term goals, the company's next planning job is to develop a set of medium-term (e.g., two to five year) objectives based upon its long-term goals. These objectives should generally involve measurable achievement levels. The following are examples of corporate objectives:

- Increase annual sales to $30 million within three years.
- Increase annual pretax income to $2.5 million within two years.
- Increase New England market share to 25% within four years.
- Expand into the Southwest and capture a 15% market share within five years.
- Within three years derive at least 15% of its revenues from a business which is less cyclical than furniture manufacturing.
- Reduce unit manufacturing costs by 5% per year for the next three years in order to become more competitive with imports.

Once senior management has selected its corporate growth objectives, the next step is to decide which parts of its existing business operation it should concentrate on improving (e.g., customer service) or expanding, and which new types of business it should consider expanding into. In order to make these decisions wisely the company should now take the time to examine thoroughly its existing business. Some of the factors which should be considered in this analysis include the company's strengths and weaknesses, its growth prospects and opportunities, competitive market conditions, changes in technology, and industry and market trends.

The next step in a strategic acquisition planning system is to consider the alternative strategies and techniques which the company could use to achieve its corporate objectives. The best way of doing this is to use the corporate growth strategies described in Chapter 1 and then to list under each of these the alternative, techniques which your company could use to implement each strategy. For example, a wood office furniture manufacturer located in North Carolina presently sells its production to wholesalers located along the East Coast. Some of the strategies and techniques which it is considering using might include:

1. Expanding its wood office furniture product line

  a. Setting up a product development department
  b. Purchasing the rights to produce a foreign manufacturer's product line in the United States
  c. Acquiring a company which has a complimentary product line

2. Entering the Midwest office furniture market

  a. Hiring sales representatives to call on Midwest distributors
  b. Acquiring a Midwest office furniture distributor
  c. Setting up a company-owned office furniture distributor to serve the Midwest market

3. Increasing its market share in the New York area

  a. Launching an advertising/promotion campaign
  b. Hiring additional sales representatives
  c. Acquiring a competitor which sells primarily to customers in New York

The final step in the strategic planning process is to select the strategies and techniques which the company will employ to seek to achieve its corporate objectives.

ADVANTAGES OF STRATEGIC ACQUISITION PLANNING SYSTEMS

1. All the company's expansion efforts (internal growth and acquisitions) are concentrated on pursuing the same corporate growth objectives and strategies. This helps the company avoid spreading its limited investment capital and management resources in too many different directions at the same time.

2. The time and effort required to develop a company's acquisition plan is substantially reduced since the company develops a single set of corporate objectives and growth strategies for both its internal growth planning and its acquisition planning.

DISADVANTAGES OF STRATEGIC ACQUISITION PLANNING SYSTEMS

1. The company develops its corporate objectives, and the alternative growth strategies which it will analyze, without first considering the types of businesses which it could acquire.

2. Proposed internal growth techniques and acquisition ideas are usually recommended by the company's executives who manage its existing business units. These executives are unlikely to suggest acquisition ideas which would:

   a. Divert investment capital away from the business which they manage.
   b. Place them under the management of a similar but larger or stronger business which could be acquired by their company.

GROWTH-TYPE ACQUISITION PLANNING SYSTEMS

Growth planning systems are based upon the assumption that a company should invest in businesses and industry segments which have above-average growth prospects. This approach was developed by large corporate consulting firms such as the Boston Consulting Group. The rationale for using this approach is that companies in industry segments which are growing rapidly usually have better profit margins, better earnings, and higher return on investment than did companies in industry segments which are stable, declining, or growing slowly. The primary reasons why companies in high-growth industries perform better are:

1. It is less expensive for these companies to increase their sales. This is because these companies can grow without capturing market share from their competi-

tors. Instead they need merely to maintain their market share as the market grows in size.

2. There is usually less price competition in a rapidly growing industry segment. Therefore, profit margins are usually higher.

Growth planning systems are used primarily by diversified companies and by companies which wish to become more diversified. A company which already operates businesses in several industry segments uses growth planning to help it decide which of these businesses it should concentrate on expanding. Both diversified and undiversified companies use growth planning to help them decide which new industry segments they should enter. Growth planning systems tend to be acquistion oriented. Therefore, for convenience the term growth planning system will be used to mean a growth-type acquisition planning system.

A company prepares to use a growth planning system by examining demographic, economic, and industry trends. Its objective is to provide a knowledge base which will enable it to project future growth rates of various industry segments.

Like strategic planning systems, corporate growth planning systems develop a set of corporate objectives. These objectives however, tend to be more ambitious than those used for strategic planning systems. For example, a typical strategic planning objective would be to increase market share by 15% within five years. In contrast, a typical growth planning system objective would be to increase market share by 25% within five years. Since it is rarely feasible to grow so rapidly using internal growth techniques, these more ambitious corporate objectives focus the company's efforts more toward acquisitions and less toward internal growth strategies.

Once a company develops a set of corporate growth objectives, it analyzes the industry segments it presently operates in and projects their future growth rates. When one or more of these industry segments is expected to have an above-average growth rate, the company will seek acquisiton opportunities in that industry segment. Next, the company identifies other industry segments which it would consider diversifying into. Then, it analyzes these industry segments and projects their growth rates. The company then selects one or more additional target industry segments from among those industry segments which it expects to have above-average growth rates over the next five years.

ADVANTAGES OF GROWTH-TYPE ACQUISITION PLANNING SYSTEMS

1. Growth planning systems offer an objective method of deciding which of a company's existing businesses it should concentrate on expanding.

2. Growth planning systems help a company's senior executives to consider a broader range of alternative acquisition growth strategies than strategic acquisition planning systems.

3. Corporate growth planning systems help management focus on the *future* growth prospects of various industry segments rather than the past growth history of these industry segments.

4. Corporate growth planning systems provide an objective approach to planning a company's diversification.

DISADVANTAGES OF GROWTH-TYPE ACQUISITION PLANNING SYSTEMS

1. It has become increasingly difficult to project future growth rates of particular industry segments with an acceptable degree of accuracy. This is due to an acceleration in the rate of economic and technological change. Therefore, there is a risk that target industry segments selected using this type of planning system will fail to have above-average growth rates over the next five years.

2. Growth planning systems overemphasize the attractiveness of diversification-type acquisition strategies. As discussed earlier in this book, this is a high-risk acquisition strategy due to the difficulty of managing businesses in different industry segments.

3. There is much more buyer competition for acquisition candidates in industry segments which are perceived as having above-average growth prospects. Therefore, these acquisition candidates tend to sell at premium prices relative to their current earnings and the value of their assets.

4. Growth planning systems tend to overlook the importance of maintaining the competitive viability of a company's existing businesses which are not in industry segments which are expected to have above-average growth prospects.

ENGINEERING-TYPE ACQUISITION PLANNING SYSTEMS

Prior to the 1960s most acquisitions involved companies acquiring businesses in their same industry segment. During the 1960s the number of mergers and acquisitions increased sharply, and many acquirers ventured outside their own industry segments. By the late 1960s, it became apparent that many of the acquisitions made a few years earlier were performing poorly. Analysts studied examples of these unsuccessful acquisitions to identify reasons for their failures. Subsequently they turned their attention to studying examples of acquisitions which had been successful to identify reasons why those acquisitions had worked well. They found that when the acquisitions had been unsuccessful, there was often a poor "fit" between the acquiring company and the business which it had purchased. They also found that when there was a good "fit" between the acquiring company and the business it had acquired, the acquisitions were much more likely to have been successful. Based upon these findings acquisition planning systems were developed which were based upon predicting how well an acquiring company and different types of selling businesses would fit together.

An acquirer and a type of business which it might purchase are considered to fit well together when:

1. Their operating strengths and weaknesses offset each other.
2. There is a similarity between the knowledge and management style of their senior executives.
3. The combination of the acquirer's and the selling company's business would produce marketing synergies and/or economy-of-scale–type cost savings.

Once acquisition planning systems were developed using variables which help to predict how well two businesses would "fit" together, it became apparent that additional variables could be added to incorporate the business growth objectives and the preferences of an acquirer's senior management. Two of the pioneers in the development and publicizing of these expanded "comprehensive" engineering-type acquisition systems were the General Electric Company and an individual, Stanley Foster Reed. Mr. Reed was the first publisher of the *Mergers & Acquisitions Journal* and lectured widely at executive seminars throughout the 1970s.

The term "engineering"-type acquisition planning system is being usd to refer to this type of acquisition planning system because they are similar in concept and methodology to the way in which other engineering systems operate, that is, to use studies of previous successes and failures to develop mathematical models which predict future success and failure. Many of the first acquisition planning systems of this type were in fact developed by executives and consultants who came from engineering backgrounds. Modern, more comprehensive versions of those earlier engineering-type planning systems are now widely used by the management consulting divisions of accounting firms and engineering firms.

The first step in developing an engineering-type acquisition planning system is to develop a list of the types of businesses which a company might consider acquiring. Then the company develops a list of variables which would make a particular type of business either more attractive or less attractive if it were owned by the acquiring company. These variables reflect the strengths, weaknesses, operating characteristics, business objectives, and preferences of the prospective acquirer. Since some variables are more important than others, a weighting system is employed which assigns higher numerical values to those variables which are more important to that acquirer and lower numerical values to those variables which are less important to that acquirer. Finally, the different types of businesses which the company is considering acquiring are given numerical ratings which reflect their relative attractiveness and are ranked based upon those ratings.

ADVANTAGES OF ENGINEERING-TYPE ACQUISITION PLANNING SYSTEMS

1. The risk of making a bad acquisition is significantly reduced.
2. The mathematical rating system can be used to evaluate additional types of acquisition candidates quickly who may be suggested in the future.
3. Personal acquisition preferences of senior executives are less likely to be overemphasized than is the case with the other two types of acquisition planning systems.
4. Medium-sized and smaller companies, and divisions of larger companies find this type of acquisition planning system especially useful.

DISADVANTAGES OF ENGINEERING-TYPE ACQUISITION PLANNING SYSTEMS

1. Chief executives find that the planning system reduces their ability to influence the selection of the types of businesses which their company should acquire.
2. This planning system does only a fair job of evaluating alternative diversification-type acquisition opportunities.
3. A larger investment of senior executive time and effort is needed than for the other two types of acquisition planning system.
4. Most companies require the assistance of an experienced consultant to develop their engineering-type planning system. The use of an experienced outside consultant is helpful, but is not as critical for companies using the other two types of acquisition planning systems.

HOW TO CHOOSE AN ACQUISITION PLANNING SYSTEM

There are many versions of each of the three types of acquisition planning systems. Once you have selected the type of acquisition planning system which will meet your company's needs and preferences, it is not especially important which particular version of that type of planning system you (or your consultant) choose to use.

There are three factors which you should consider when selecting the type of acquisition planning system which will work best for your company. These are:

1. The size and complexity of your company. For this purpose decide which of the following three categories best describes your company:

   a. Smaller companies which presently operate in one industry segment and one or two local markets
   b. Medium-sized companies which presently operate in one industry and one or two regional markets
   c. Larger companies which presently have businesses in more than one industry and several regional markets

2. Whether you wish to minimize your risk of making a poor acquisition or maximize the potential benefit of making an acquisition.

The following chart indicates the suitability of each type of acquisition planning system based upon these three variables:

x = somewhat suitable

xx = suitable

xxx = very suitable

	TYPE OF ACQUISITION PLANNING SYSTEM		
	STRATEGIC	GROWTH	ENGINEERING
Company size and complexity			
Smaller	xx	x	xxx
Medium	xx	x	xx
Large	xx	xxx	x
Risk/reward potential			
Low risk/lower reward	xx	x	xxx
Moderate risk/moderate reward	xx	x	xx
Higher risk/higher reward	xx	xxx	x
Management style			
Analytical	xx	xxx	x
Combination	xx	xx	xx
Entrepreneurial	xx	x	xxx

3. Whether your management decision making is analytical or entrepreneurial. Analytical decision making is defined as careful and well thought out, but slower. Entrepreneurial decision making is defined as opportunistic. Companies which are analytical need to use a system which makes them more aware of diversification opportunities. Companies which are entrepreneurial need to use a system which imposes greater discipline.

EXAMINING AN ACQUISITION PLANNING SYSTEM

The final sections of this chapter will describe the Basic Matrix Model acquisition planning system. Examining this particular engineering-type acquisition planning system will help you to understand key acquisition planning ideas, procedures, and strategies. Though it is designed as a teaching tool, variations of the Basic Matrix Model have been used successfully by many companies to select the types of businesses which they should seek to acquire. It has proven to be especially useful for companies which either are launching their first acquisition program or whose previous attempts at making acquisitions have had limited success.

FOUR STAGES OF THE BASIC MATRIX MODEL

The four stages of this acquisition planning system are:

1. Develop a comprehensive list of the types of businesses which your company should consider acquiring. This list is called your "acquisition opportunity menu."

2. Survey the acquisition choice preferences of your senior executives to determine which of the types of businesses listed on your acquisition opportunity menu are of only limited interest. Then eliminate those "unpopular" types of businesses from further consideration.

3. Review the five key factors which would make owning a particular type of business attractive or unattractive. Then decide how much importance to give each of these five rating factors. You may also add one or two additional rating factors which are important to your company but which were not covered by the five standard rating factors.

4. Using these rating factor values compare the relative attractiveness of the types of businesses remaining on your acquisition opportunity menu following step 2. The analytical tool which is used to make these comparisons is called a Matrix Rating Model.

HOW TO SET UP YOUR ACQUISITION OPPORTUNITY MENU

Your acquisition opportunity consists of the types of businesses which your company should consider acquiring. The idea is to develop a comprehensive listing of these types of business so that you do not overlook any which might turn out to be particularly suitable for your company. To do this you start by using seven acquisition growth strategies as the category headings for your acqusition opportunity menu. Then you list the types of businesses which you could acquire to implement each of these acquisition growth strategies. The seven acquisition growth strategies are:

1. Market intensification

2. Market extension

3. Product extension

4. Customer extension

5. Backward-type vertical integration

6. Forward-type vertical integration

7. Pure diversification

HOW TO DEVELOP YOUR ACQUISITION OPPORTUNITY MENU LISTINGS

Use the following guidelines to prepare the list of businesses to include under your seven acquisition opportunity menu categories.

1. *Market intensification.* Increasing your market share means acquiring a competitor. Since you already know who your competitors are, you start by listing these companies in order of their size (largest to smallest). Then delete from your listing those companies which are too large or too small to be realistic acquisition prospects for your company. Finally, select two or three of these competitors to use as examples on your acquisition opportunity menu.

2. *Market extension.* Expanding into a new geographic market means acquiring a company in your same line of business which operates in different geographic areas. List those geographic areas where you would be interested in operating. You should consider including geographic markets which:

a. Are adjacent to your present market.

b. Have above-average growth rates.

c. Fit the personal preferences of your senior executive(s).

3. *Customer extension.* Adding new types of customers means acquiring a business which offers the same types of products or services as your company, but sells to a different type of customer. For example, if your company manufactures shampoos sold to mass merchandisers, a shampoo manufacturer which supplied beauty salons would fit this customer extension type of growth strategy. For this growth strategy option, list the additional types of customers which you might be able to sell to, using a product line similar to the one you already offer.

4. *Product extension.* Broadening your product line means acquiring a company which produces goods or services which you could sell to your existing customer base using your existing marketing and distribution network. For example, if your company manufactured wooden office furniture, a manufacturer of steel filing cabinets would fit this product extension–type growth strategy. For this growth strategy, list the products or services which would fit well with yor existing product line.

5. *Backward integration*

a. List the principal products and services which your company purchases from third parties (e.g., other companies). For example, a chain of travel agencies might purchase the following products and services:

Packaged tours

Media advertising

Temporary clerical personnel

Travel agents (recruiting)

Travel agents (training)

Promotional gifts (e.g., calendars, novelties)

Working capital financing

b. Then list the types of businesses from which you purchase these goods and services. For our travel agency example, this list might include:

Tour sponsors (packagers and wholesalers)

Advertising agencies serving the travel industry

Temporary employment agencies

Employment agencies serving the travel industry

Vocational schools serving the travel industry

Promotional gift suppliers

Commercial banks

c. Review your list of supplier type businesses and eliminate those which it would be impractical for your company to consider acquiring and owning. For example, it might be impractical for a travel agency to acquire a commercial bank. Then list the remaining types of supplier-type businesses on your acquisition opportunity menu.

6. *Forward integration*

a. List the principal types of businesses to which your company sells. For example, a manufacturer of looseleaf binders might sell to the following types of customers:

Office supply wholesalers

Office supply store chains

Mass merchandisers (e.g., K-Mart)

Toy store chains

Schools and school systems

Promotional gift manufacturers

b. Review your list of customer-type businesses and eliminate those which it would be impractical for your company to consider acquiring. For example, it would probably be impractical for a manufacturer of looseleaf binders to acquire and operate a chain of secretarial schools. Then list the remaining types of customer-type businesses on your acquisition opportunity menu.

7. *Diversification.* Entering an unrelated business refers to acquiring a company in an industry different from the one in which you are already. List those types of businesses which your company would consider acquiring, but which were not listed under the other six categories of your acquisition opporutnity menu.

SIMPLIFY YOUR LISTINGS FOR TYPES OF BUSINESSES IN YOUR PRESENT INDUSTRY SEGMENT

Many of the types of businesses which you will include on your company's acquisition opportunity menu are in the same industry segment as your company's present business. It is somewhat cumbersome and time consuming to include this industry segment each time you list one of those types of businesses. A useful shortcut is to leave out the name of the industry segment when a type of business is in the same industry segment as your present business. For example, if your company's present business is plumbing supply distribution, and a type of business on your acquisition opportunity menu is plumbing supply distributors located in Arizona, you can list this type of business as "Arizona." When you list a type of business on your acquisition opportunity menu without designating the industry segment, it will automatically refer to the same industry segment your company presently operates in.

TWO EXAMPLES OF ACQUISITION OPPORTUNITY MENUS

Pluto Comics, Inc., publishes comic books which it sells to periodical distributors. The company's management sat down one morning and developed the following acquisition opportunity menu.

MARKET INTENSIFICATION	GEOGRAPHIC EXTENSION	PRODUCT EXTENSION	CUSTOMER EXTENSION
Comic World, Inc.	Canada	Coloring books	Direct mail (subscriptions)
Pink Pony Press	England	Children's nature magazine	

BACKWARD INTEGRATION	FORWARD INTEGRATION	DIVERSIFICATION
Comic book printing company	Periodicals distributor	Television producer (cartoon shows)
Pulp paper importer		Textbook publisher
Typesetting contractor		Pizza restaurant chain

Hair Products Supply Company manufactures liquid hair care products sold to beauty salon supply houses (distributors) located in the Southeastern states (Georgia, Alabama, and Florida). Here is an example of the acquisition opportunity menu which their management developed.

MARKET INTENSIFICATION (ACQUIRE A COMPETITOR)

COMPANY	ANNUAL REVENUES
Quality Hair Care, Inc.	$16 million
Adams Beauty Supply Co.	7 million

GEOGRAPHIC EXTENSION (ENTER ADJACENT MARKETS)

MARKET
- The Carolinas
- Tennessee
- Mississippi

GEOGRAPHIC EXTENSION (ENTER HIGH-GROWTH MARKETS)

MARKET
- California
- New England
- New York, New Jersey, Connecticut

CUSTOMER EXTENSION (LIQUID HAIR CARE PRODUCTS MANUFACTURERS WHICH SELL TO DIFFERENT TYPES OF CUSTOMERS)

TYPE OF CUSTOMER
- Department stores
- Drug stores
- Mass merchandisers
- Mail order

PRODUCT EXTENSION (OTHER PRODUCTS SOLD THROUGH BEAUTY SALON SUPPLY HOUSES)

PRODUCT
- Brushes (imported)
- Combs (imported)
- Scissors, curlers, etc.
- Hair dryers
- Facial creams and lotions
- Hand creams and lotions

BACKWARD INTEGRATION (SUPPLIERS)

- Specialty chemicals (FDA approved)
- Plastic bottles and tubes
- Aerosol containers
- Label printing
- Trucking companies (southeast region)

FORWARD INTEGRATION (CUSTOMERS)

- Beauty salon supply houses (distributors)
- Direct-mail catalog merchandisers (health and beauty aids)
- Beauty salon chains
- Health and beauty aid exporters

DIVERSIFICATION

Radio stations (Southeast United States)
Savings and loan associations (Georgia)
Nursing home chains (Southeast United States)

WHY YOU SHOULD USE YOUR SENIOR EXECUTIVE'S PREFERENCES TO SCREEN YOUR ACQUISITION OPPORTUNITY MENU LISTINGS

Companies rarely acquire a type of business which their senior executives would be uncomfortable owning. It is therefore unproductive to spend time analyzing the advantages and disadvantages of owning a type of business which your senior executives do not wish to own and operate at this time. Some of the types of businesses listed on your acquisition opportunity menu will fall within this category, which we will refer to as "unpopular" acquisition opportunities.

HOW TO USE A SENIOR EXECUTIVE PREFERENCE SURVEY TO SCREEN OUT "UNPOPULAR" TYPES OF BUSINESS

Your objective is to delete from your acquisition opportunity menu those types of businesses which your senior executives consider "unsuitable" based upon their personal preferences. A technique which can be used is a "senior executive preference survey." Each member of your acquisition planning committee is provided with your acquisition opportunity menu. Then each executive reviews the types of businesses listed on your acquisition opportunity menu and selects the types of business which he or she feels that your company should *not* consider acquiring at this time. After you compile the results of this survey, you delete from your acquisition opportunity menu those types of business with either:

1. Your chief executive and at least one other acquisition committee member indicated that your company should not consider acquiring at this time.

2. A majority of your committee members indicated that your company should not consider acquiring at this time.

HOW TO COMPARE THE ATTRACTIVENESS OF YOUR REMAINING ACQUISITION OPPORTUNITY MENU LISTINGS

To compare the attractiveness of the remaining types of businesses your company develops and employs an acquisition choice rating system called a matrix rating model. this rating system operates in the following manner:

1. Your company determines which of the acquisition objectives which it would like to achieve are the most important. These objectives are called your rating factors. For the Basic Matrix Model acquisition planning system you start with five "standard" acquisition objectives (rating factors) which are important for most prospective acquirers. Then you can add one or two additional acquisition objectives (rating factors) which are particularly important to your company. These additional acquisition objectives are called supplemental rating factors.

2. The standard and supplemental acquisition objectives (rating factors) are assigned higher or lower point values (weighting values) based upon their relative importance to your company. These point values are:

   30 points = very important
   20 points = important
   10 points = somewhat (moderately) important

3. Each type of business which you are considering is analyzed to determine how well (to what extent) it would help your company achieve each of its acquisition objectives (rating factors).

4. A type of business which would achieve a particular acquisition objective is awarded the entire point value assigned to that rating factor (e.g., low risk of postacquisition management difficulty). A type of business which partly meets a particular acquisition objective is awarded a portion of the points assigned to that rating factor. For the Basic Matrix Model acquisition planning system 50% of the rating points are assigned when a type of business partly meets a particular acquisition objective. When a type of business would not help your company achieve a particular acquisition objective (rating factor) it is awarded none of the points ("0" points) assigned to that rating factor.

5. The total number of rating points assigned to each type of business is computed by adding up the number of points assigned for each of your acquisition objectives (rating factors). The most attractive types of businesses which your company could acquire will have the highest point totals. The least attractive types of businesses which your company could acquire will have the lowest point totals.

6. Your company selects the types of businesses which it will seek to acquire from among those with the highest point totals.

HOW TO SET UP YOUR ACQUISITION CHOICE (MATRIX) RATING MODEL

1. The first column of an acquisition choice (matrix) rating model lists the alternative types of businesses your company is considering acquiring. These types of businesses are taken from your acquisition opportunity menu, after you have used your executives' preferences to screen these listings.

2. The following columns of your acquisition choice matrix are each used for five standard acquisition objectives (rating factors). These rating factors are each listed above one of these five columns. The five standard rating factors are:

   a. Low risk of postacquisition management difficulty
   b. Growth potential
   c. Customer base diversification
   d. Marketing synergy
   e. Economy-of-scale cost savings

   Two additional columns can be added to your matrix to provide room to list up to two supplemental acquisition objectives (rating factors) which your management wishes to use to evaluate types of businesses which you might acquire.

3. The last column (farthest to the right) of your business choice rating matrix is used to list the total number attractiveness rating points assigned to each type of business listed in the first column of your matrix.

   The basic framework of your acquisition–business choice rating system matrix looks like this:

				RATING FACTORS				
	A.	B.	C.	D.	E.	F.	G.	
TYPE OF BUSINESS	LOW POST AC-QUISITION MANAGEMENT DIFFICULTY	GROWTH POTENTIAL	CUSTOMER BASE DIVERSI-FICATION	MARKETING SYNERGY	COST SAVINGS			TOTAL ATTRAC-TIVENESS RATING POINTS
	(PTS)	(PTS)	(PTS)	(PTS)	(PTS)	(PTS)	(PTS)	
1____	____	____	____	____	____	____	____	____pts
2____	____	____	____	____	____	____	____	____pts
3____	____	____	____	____	____	____	____	____pts
4____	____	____	____	____	____	____	____	____pts
5____	____	____	____	____	____	____	____	____pts
6____	____	____	____	____	____	____	____	____pts
7____	____	____	____	____	____	____	____	____pts
8____	____	____	____	____	____	____	____	____pts
9____	____	____	____	____	____	____	____	____pts
10____	____	____	____	____	____	____	____	____pts

SUPPLEMENTAL ACQUISITION OBJECTIVES (RATING FACTORS)

Your acquisition choice rating system matrix provides two extra columns. These can be used to add one or two supplemental acquisition objectives (rating factors) to your acquisition choice matrix. Your supplemental acquisition objectives (rating factors) are special needs or preferences which are important to your company's management.

The following are examples of supplemental acquisition objectives (rating factors) which a company might add to its acquisition–business choice rating system matrix:

1. Nonunion work force
2. Low vulnerability to import competition
3. Preferred technology level (i.e., low tech or high tech)
4. Proprietary products or services
5. Limited government regulation
6. Nonseasonal revenues
7. Noncyclical industry
8. Low capital investment requirements (i.e., an industry segment which is not capital intensive)
9. High barriers to entry by nondomestic competitors
10. Minimum market size (e.g., $100 million)

HOW TO USE YOUR ACQUISITION RATING FACTORS

1. Each rating factor is assigned a point value which represents its relative importance to your company. The following chart indicates the importance level and the corresponding point value which is assigned to a particular rating factor:

LEVEL OF IMPORTANCE	POINT VALUE
Very important	30 pts
Important	20 pts
Somewhat important	10 pts

Guidelines and procedures are provided in the following sections of this chapter which will help your management to select the appropriate importance level and corresponding point value of each of your acquisition objectives (rating factors).

2. Each type of business which you are considering is analyzed to determine whether it would enable your company to achieve or partly achieve, or would not help your company achieve each of your key acquisition objectives (rating factors). A type of business which would enable your company to achieve a particular acquisition objective is awarded 100% of the point value assigned to that objective (rating factor). A type of business which would partly achieve a particular acquisiton objective is awarded 50% of the point value assigned to that objective (rating factor). A type of business which would not help your company achieve a particular acquisition objective is awarded 0% of the point value assigned to that objective (rating factor). The following chart summarized this relationship:

A TYPE OF BUSINESS WHICH	IS AWARDED _____% OF THE RATING POINTS ASSIGNED TO THAT OBJECTIVE:
Achieves a particular objective	100%
Partly achieves a particular objective	50%
Does not help achieve a particular objective	0%

Guidelines and procedures are provided in the following sections of this chapter which will help your management determine to what extent a particular type of business which you are considering acquiring would help your company achieve a particular key acquisition objective (rating factor).

WHY "LOW RISK" OF POSTACQUISITION MANAGEMENT DIFFICULTY IS ONE OF THE "STANDARD" ACQUISITION OBJECTIVES (RATING FACTORS)

Postacquisition management problems are one of the three principal reasons why acquisitions turn out to be unsuccessful. An acquisition is considered to be unsuccessful if the acquired business is liquidated or is sold for a lower price within five years after it was acquired.

TWO OTHER FACTORS WHICH FREQUENTLY PRODUCE UNSUCCESSFUL ACQUISITIONS

1. Economic conditions in the acquired company's industry segment become depressed within two years after the company was acquired.

2. The acquirer pays a premium price for assets which decline in value or for attractive revenue and earnings prospects which fail to be realized.

WHY "LOW RISK OF DEPRESSED INDUSTRY ECONOMIC CONDITIONS" IS NOT USED AS A STANDARD ACQUISTION OBJECTIVE (RATING FACTOR)

A company reduces its risk of acquiring a business in an industry which then becomes depressed by giving preference to industries and industry segments which have above-average growth prospects. This objective is included in the second standard acquisition rating factor which is "growth potential."

WHY "LOW RISK OF PAYING TOO MUCH FOR A BUSINESS" IS NOT USED AS A STANDARD ACQUISITION OBJECTIVE (RATING FACTOR)

This objective is included in three of the other standard acquisition rating factors. The following discussion explains why this is true:

A company reduces its risk of paying too much for a business in the following ways:

1. *Avoiding industries which its management is unfamiliar with.* Managements are less likely to recognize impending downturns in market demand, or increasing competition, in industries which their company does not presently operate in. This factor is considered when a company uses "low risk of postacquistion management problems" as a standard acquisition objective (rating factor).

2. *Identifying industry growth trends which could reduce the future value of a type of business which you are considering acquiring.* This factor is considered when your company uses the "growth potential" standard acquisition objective (rating factor).

3. *Obtaining extra profitability benefits which are not usually included in the selling price of a business.* These extra profitability benefits are derived from "marketing synergies" and "economy-of-scale cost savings." By achieving those extra profitability benefits a prospective acquirer obtains a "profitability safety margin (cushion)" which may offset the adverse effect of unanticipated declines in market demand or increased competition. Both of these two potential sources of "extra profitability benefits" ("marketing synergies" and "economy-of-scale cost savings") are included in the five standard acquisition objectives (rating factors).

WHY GROWTH POTENTIAL IS ONE OF THE STANDARD ACQUISITION OBJECTIVES (RATING FACTORS)

Companies in industries which do not grow as fast as the overall economy tend to be poor investments even though they may be well managed. The reasons are:

1. A below-average industry growth rate often produces increased price competition. Increased price competition then reduces the profit margins of companies in that industry.
2. It is difficult and expensive for a company in a low-growth industry to grow larger. This is because most of the company's growth must come from capturing market share now held by its competitors.

Berkshire Hathaway, Inc., is a large company which has prospered by acquiring businesses only in industries which have good growth prospects. In his 1985 report to shareholders, Warren Buffet, the chairman of Berkshire Hathaway, Inc., made the following observations which explain the rationale for using the growth potential rating factor:

"Major additional investment in a terrible industry usually is about as rewarding as struggling in quicksand."

"A good management record (measured in terms of economic returns) is far more a function of what boat you get in then it is how effectively you row it."

"When a management with a reputation for brilliance tackles a business with a reputation for poor fundamental economics, it is the reputation of the business that remains intact."

"Should you find yourself in a chronically leaking boat, energy devoted to changing vessels is likely to be more productive than energy devoted to patching leaks."

DEFINING THE TERM "CUSTOMER BASE DIVERSIFICATION"

For acquisiton planning purposes your "customer base" consists of the types and locations of the customers you are now selling to. In lay terms this is the present market your company serves. The reason why "market base" is not used instead of "customer base" is that a "market" is a legal term which refers only to a geographic area, rather than also including different types of customers within a geographic area.

The following example illustrates the concept of a "customer base":

ABC Plumbing Supply sells plumbing supplies to plumbing contractors located in the metropolitan Philadelphia area. The company also sells plumbing supplies to independent hardware stores located in the metropolitan Philadelphia area, southern New Jersey, and northern Delaware. ABC Plumbing Supply's present customer base consists of:

1. Plumbing contractors—metropolitan Philadelphia area

2. Independent hardware stores—metropolitan Philadelphia area

3. Independent hardware stores—southern New Jersey

4. Independent hardware stores—northern Delaware

A company diversifies its customer base by selling to additional types of customers in its present geographic markets and by selling to similar types of customers (e.g., plumbing contractors) in different geographic markets, and by selling to different types of customers in different geographic markets. For example, ABC Plumbing supply would diversify its customer base if it acquired companies which primarily:

1. Sold plumbing supplies to plumbing contractors located in the Baltimore area

2. Sold plumbing supplies to single-family home developers located in southern New Jersey

3. Sold electrical supplies to electrical contractors located in the Philadelphia area

4. Sold computers to small businesses located in the metropolitan Dallas, Texas, area

WHY "CUSTOMER BASE DIVERSIFICATION" IS ONE OF THE STANDARD ACQUISITION OBJECTIVES (RATING FACTORS)

The principal threat to the survival of a company is a prolonged period of sharply lower sales revenues. There are many reasons why a company's sales revenues may decline. For example, high manufacturing costs, low product quality, inadequate distribution facilities, or poor customer service could be the reasons why a company's sales volume declined. However, the most likely reason why a company experiences a prolonged period of sharply lower sales revenues is that its present customer base begins purchasing fewer of the types of products or services which the company supplies. For example, a drilling contractor which operates in the Permian Basin encounters a lengthy period of sharply lower sales revenues because of oil- and gas-producing companies which develop new wells in the Permian Basin region have reduced their annual exploration budgets by 50%.

Potential customers in different industry segments and geographic markets tend to reduce their purchases of a particular type of product or service at different times. Because of this factor, customer diversification will often reduce the length of the period when a company's revenues are severely depressed, thereby increasing its chances of long-term survival. The following example illustrates this concept:

A & G Drugstores has two locations, located in a Midwestern town where the principal employers are companies which manufacture parts sold to large automobile companies (e.g., General Motors). One of A & G's drugstores is located in a working-class residential area, while the other is located in a middle-class suburb. Depressed sales of automobiles lead to reduced sales of automotive parts. The automotive parts manufacturers in this Midwestern town begin laying off employees. Initially these layoffs are concentrated among the manufacturer's hourly workers. After several months of continued low sales revenues the auto parts manufacturers extend their layoffs to their salaried employees. When automobile sales recover the auto parts manufacturers first begin calling back their hourly employees. After several months of higher sales, they then begin filling vacant salaried positions.

For the purposes of this illustration assume that the lower levels of employment for hourly and salaried employees both last for six months. However, the lower employment levels of hourly employees begin and end three months before the lower employment levels of salaried workers. Here is a chart that indicates this employment pattern.

						MONTHS						
	1	2	3	4	5	6	7	8	9	10	11	12
Low employment levels of hourly employees	—	—	X	X	X	X	X	X	—	—	—	—
Low employment levels of salaried employees	—	—	—	—	—	X	X	X	X	X	X	—

These employment-level patterns have the following impact on A & G Drugstores:

1. A & G's drugstore located in a working-class residential area has sharply lower sales in months 3, 4, 5, 6, 7, 8, and 9.

2. A & G's drugstore located in a suburban middle-class area has sharply lower sales in months 6, 7, 8, 9. 10, and 11.

3. A & G's combined revenues for its two drugstores are severely depressed for three months (6, 7, and 8) when both stores are experiencing sharply lower sales. A & G's combined revenues for its two drugstores are moderately depressed for six months (3, 4, 5, 9, 10 and 11), when one store has severely depressed sales revenues and one store continues to operate at normal sales levels, and are at normal levels for three months (1, 2 and 12).

In contrast, assume that A & G had only two drugstores located in either the working-class residential area or the middle-class suburbs. A & G's sales revenues would have been severely depressed for six months and at normal levels for six months.

As shown by the A & G Drugstore example, customer base diversification often involves a trade-off. A company which sells to several different groups of customers is less likely to have lengthy periods of high revenues because not all the segments of its customer base will usually be prospering at the same time. The company is, however, less likely to have lengthy periods of severely depressed revenues because not all the segments of its customer base will usually be depressed at the same time. Since this trade-off increases the likelihood that a company will survive, it is a trade-off which is very attractive for most companies.

THE "MARKETING SYNERGY" ACQUISITION OBJECTIVE

Marketing synergy refers to the ability of one type of business to utilize the marketing resources of another type of business in order to sell more of the products and services which it produces. Marketing resources include:

1. Distribution channels (e.g., wholesalers)

2. Distribution facilities

3. Sales representatives

4. Marketing networks

5. Marketing expertise

The following example illustrates this concept:

1. A & L Cosmetics produces hair care products which it sells to beauty salons through a national network of beauty supply wholesalers.
2. Harris Brothers is a private-label manufacturer of skin creams.
3. A & L Cosmetics acquires Harris Brothers, or Harris Brothers acquires A & L Cosmetics (marketing synergy potential is not affected by whether a company is the acquirer or the acquiree).

Here are two marketing synergies which might be produced by this combination:

1. Harris Brothers uses A & L Cosmetics' national wholesaler network to market skin creams to beauty salons.
2. A & L Cosmetics produces private-label hair care products for some of Harris Brothers' customers.

WHY MARKETING SYNERGY IS A STANDARD ACQUISITION OBJECTIVE (RATING FACTOR)

Adding new distribution channels and marketing networks can significantly increase the sales and profitability of a company's present business. Therefore most companies would like to pursue this growth strategy. Acquisitions which produce marketing synergies reduce the time, expense, and risk of adding new distribution channels and marketing networks. Some of the advantages of using acquisitions are:

1. The additional distribution channels and marketing networks are already established. This reduces the risk that a company will be unable to create this marketing structure and organization in a timely fashion.
2. Until new distribution channels and marketing networks become well established, the costs of setting up, building, and maintaining these operations will usually be much higher than the gross profits generated by the increased sales volumes they produce. By owning a business which is already generating a profitable volume of sales through these distribution channels and marketing networks, a company avoids or reduces these operating losses.
3. The acquired business usually has assets and earnings which are worth a significant portion of its purchase price. Therefore, an acquirer can often obtain the benefits of marketing synergy as a valuable but inexpensive bonus.

THE "ECONOMY-OF-SCALE COST SAVINGS" ACQUISITIONS OBJECTIVE

Combining two related types of businesses may produce significant cost savings in one or more of the following areas:

- Marketing
- Manufacturing
- Distribution
- Administration
- Engineering and technical support
- Customer support (e.g., product installation, repair, and maintenance)
- New product development

These cost savings are generally derived in one of the following ways:

1. Quantity discounts from suppliers of products and services. Examples of these products and services include:

   a. Raw materials
   b. Data processing
   c. Financing
   d. Employee benefits
   e. Casualty and liability insurance
   f. Accounting services
   g. Legal services
   h. Advertising
   i. Trucking and delivery
   j. Utilities (energy and communications)

2. Elimination of duplicate assets and increased utilization of retained assets. Examples of these types of assets include:

   a. Factories
   b. Warehouses
   c. Office space

    d. Showrooms

    e. Laboratories

    f. Vehicles (trucks, corporate aircraft, etc.)

    g. Machinery

    h. Computer systems

3. Consolidation of management, operations, and staff functions. Examples of these functions include:

    a. Product development

    b. Engineering

    c. Repair and service

    d. Accounting

    e. Advertising management

    f. Personnel administration

    g. Facilities management

    h. Corporate planning

    i. Purchasing

WHY "ECONOMY-OF-SCALE COST SAVINGS" IS A STANDARD ACQUISITION OBJECTIVE (RATING FACTOR)

A company's future prosperity often depends upon whether it can:

1. Expand the market share of its present business.
2. Maintain or improve the profit margins of its present business.

Economy-of-scale cost savings are the essential ingredient which helps a company achieve these twin goals. Two of the ways in which they do this are:

1. They strengthen a company's competitive position.
2. They offset the higher administrative and management expenses required to operate a larger business.

TWO ELEMENTS OF "POSTACQUISITION MANAGEMENT DIFFICULTY"

There are two elements of "postacquisition management difficulty" which a prospective acquirer needs to consider. These are:

1. All acquisitions produce postacquisition management problems. Some of the types of businesses your company is considering acquiring are likely to produce a greater number of postacquisition management problems than are other types of businesses which you are considering acquiring.

2. Depending upon your company's management style, structure, and prior acquisition experience, you are generally more likely or less likely to be able to handle management problems at a newly acquired business without reducing your management's ability to maintain the competitive position and profitability of your present business.

HOW THE BASIC MATRIX MODEL DEALS WITH THESE TWO ELEMENTS OF "POSTACQUISITION MANAGEMENT DIFFICULTY"

Both elements of "postacquisition management difficulty" are considered when you use your "low risk of postacquisition management difficulty" acquisition objective (rating factor). This is accomplished in the following manner:

1. The importance of seeking "low risk of postacquisition management difficulty" depends upon your company's ability to handle postacquisition management problems at a newly acquired business without seriously reducing your management's ability to maintain the competitive position and profitability of your present business. This "importance level" is reflected in the number of attractiveness rating points you assign to your "low risk of postacquisition management difficulty."

    a. When your company's present management style, structure, and acquisition experience are likely to make it difficult for your company to handle postacquisition management problems, "low risk of postacquisition management difficulty" is a very important acquisition objective for your company. Therefore, you would assign the maximum number of attractiveness rating points (30 points) to this rating factor.

b. When your company's present management style, structure, and acquisition experience are likely to make it "somewhat" difficult for your company to handle postacquisition management problems, it is still "important" for your company to seek "low risk of postacquisition management difficulty." Therefore, you would assign the "average number of attractiveness rating points (20 points) to this rating factor.

c. When your company's present management style, structure, and prior acquisition experience indicate that your company is relatively well equipped to handle postacquisition management problems, it is less important ("limited importance") for your company to acquire a type of business which is likely to produce fewer postacquisition management problems. Therefore, you assign the minimum number of attractiveness rating points (10 points) to your "lower risk of postacquisition management difficulty" rating factor.

2. The number of postacquisition management problems which acquiring a particular type of business is likely to generate for your company, after you owned it, is used to determine this proportion (percentage) of the attractiveness rating points awarded to that type of business:

a. When a particular type of business is likely to produce many postacquisition management problems for your company, that type of business is awarded none (0%) of the attractiveness rating points you assigned to your "low risk of postacquisition management difficulty" rating factor.

b. When a particular type of business is likely to produce a moderate (average) number of postacquisition management problems for your company, that type of business is awarded 50% of the attractiveness rating points you assigned to your "low risk of postacquisition management difficulty" rating factor.

c. When a particular type of business is likely to produce a relatively small (below-average) number of postacquisition management problems for your company, that type of business is awarded all (100%) of the attractiveness rating points you assigned to your "low risk of postacquisition management difficulty" rating factor.

HOW TO ANALYZE YOUR COMPANY'S ABILITY TO HANDLE POSTACQUISITION MANAGEMENT PROBLEMS

A company can predict its ability to handle postacquisition management problems by examining its present management style and its present management structure. To perform this self-analysis, answer the following seven questions.

	ANSWER	
QUESTION	YES	NO

Has your company made an acquisition within the past three years?

Does your company operate two or more different types of businesses?

Are your company's facilities located in several different locations?

Is your management decision making decentralized?

Does your company have three levels of management (senior management, middle-level management, and supervisors)?

Has your company developed a written long-term (three to five year) growth plan?

Would your company continue to operate effectively if your chief executive died tomorrow?

To analyze and use results of this self-examination questionnaire use the following guidelines:

1. A "yes" answer to six or seven questions indicates that your company is likely to be well prepared to handle postacquisition management problems. Therefore, "low risk of postacquisition management difficulty" is of "limited importance" to your company. Acquisition objectives (rating factors) which are of only "limited importance" to a company are assigned the minimum number of attractiveness rating points (10 points). Therefore, you would enter "(10 points)" on the second line of your matrix in the second column, which is labeled "low risk of postacquisition management difficulty."

2. A "yes" answer to three, four, or five of the seven questions indicates that your company is likely to be somewhat prepared to handle postacquisition management problems. Therefore, "low risk of postacquisition management difficulty" is "important" to your company. Acquisition objectives which are "important" to a company are assigned 20 attractiveness rating points. Therefore, you would enter "(20 points)" on the second line of your matrix in the second column which is labeled "low risk of postacquisition management difficulty."

3. A "yes" answer to none, one, or two of the seven questions indicates that your company is likely to be poorly prepared to handle postacquisition problems at a newly acquired business. Therefore, "low risk of postacquisition management difficulty" is a "very important" acquisition objective for your company. Acquisition objectives which are "very important" to a company are assigned the maximum number of attractiveness rating points. Therefore, you would enter "(30 points)" on the second line of your matrix in the second column which is labeled "low risk of postacquisition management difficulty."

HOW YOU AWARD ATTRACTIVENESS RATING POINTS FOR YOUR "LOW RISK OF POSTACQUISITION MANAGEMENT DIFFICULTY" RATING FACTOR

1. Your company examines each of the types of businesses it is considering acquiring. These are listed in the first column of your acquisition planning matrix. Using the following guidelines, you predict whether each type of business is likely to produce few, some, or many postacquisition management problems for your company.

   a. Acquiring a type of business which is in the same industry segment as your present business is likely to produce few postacquisition management problems if it is located within two hours' travel time from your headquarters.

   b. Acquiring a type of business which is in an industry different from the one in which you now operate is likely to produce many postacquisition management problems.

   c. Acquiring a type of business which is in a different segment of your present industry is likely to produce many postacquisition problems if it is in a geographic location different from the one in which you now operate.

   d. Acquiring other types of businesses are likely to produce some postacquisition management problems.

2. Each type of business you are considering acquiring is awarded a proportion (percentage) of the attractiveness rating points you assigned to your "low risk of postacquisition difficulty objective" based upon whether it is likely to produce few, some, or many postacquisition management problems. The following chart indicated the proportions (percentages) to use:

PREDICTED NUMBER OF POSTACQUISITION MANAGEMENT PROBLEMS	PROPORTION (PERCENTAGE) OF ATTRACTIVENESS RATING POINTS TO AWARD
Few	(none) 0%
Some	(some) 50%
Many	(all) 100%

For example, assume that ABC Plumbing Supply (Philadelphia) has assigned 20 attractiveness rating points to its "low risk of postacquisition difficulty" objective (rating factor). ABC Plumbing Supply is considering acquiring the following types of businesses:

- A plumbing supply distributor located in Atlantic City
- A plumbing supply manufacturer located in Philadelphia
- A television station located in Philadelphia

Using the guidelines provided in the first part of this section, ABC Plumbing Supply predicts that these types of businesses are likely to produce few, some, or many postacquisition management problems. The results of this analysis are shown below:

TYPE OF BUSINESS	PREDICTED NUMBER OF POSTACQUISITION MANAGEMENT PROBLEMS
Plumbing supply distributor (Atlantic City)	Few
Plumbing supply manufacturing (Philadelphia)	Some
Television station (Philadelphia)	Many

Using the chart provided in this section, ABC Plumbing Supply then converts the predicted number of postacquisition problems into proportions (percentages) to use in awarding attractiveness rating points:

TYPE OF BUSINESS	PROPORTION (PERCENTAGE) OF ATTRACTIVENESS RATING POINTS TO AWARD
Plumbing supply distributor (Atlantic City)	All (100%)
Plumbing supply manufacturer (Philadelphia)	Some (50%)
Television station (Philadelphia)	None (0%)

ABC Plumbing Supply then computes the number of attractiveness rating points to award to each type of business by multiplying the number of attractiveness rating points assigned to its "low risk of postacquisition management difficulty objective" times these proportions (percentages). These computations are as follows:

Plumbing supply distributor (Atlantic City)	$100\% \times 20 \text{ pts} = 20 \text{ pts}$
Plumbing supply manufacturer (Philadelphia)	$50\% \times 20 \text{ pts} = 10 \text{ pts}$
Television station (Philadelphia)	$0\% \times 20 \text{ pts} = 10 \text{ pts}$

After computing the number of points to award to each type of business, these point scores are entered on ABC Plumbing Supply's acquisition planning matrix:

	RATING FACTORS							
TYPE OF BUSINESS	A. LOW POST-ACQUISITION MANAGEMENT DIFFICULTY (20 PTS)	B. GROWTH POTENTIAL (PTS)	C. CUSTOMER BASE DIVERSIFI-CATION (PTS)	D. MARKETING SYNERGY (PTS)	E. COST SAVINGS (PTS)	F. (PTS)	G. (PTS)	TOTAL ATTRAC-TIVENESS RATING POINTS
Plumbing dis-tributor (Atlan-tic City)	20							____pts
Plumbing manu-facturer (Phila-delphia)	10							____pts
TV sta-tion (Phila-delphia)	0							____pts

THE RISK OF PURSUING THE "GROWTH POTENTIAL" ACQUISITION OBJECTIVE

The "growth potential" acquisition objective refers to your company's desire to maintain or improve its future growth rate. Earlier in this chapter, the reasons for including "growth potential" as one of your key acquisition objectives (rating factors) were described.

Acquiring a type of business which has a high growth potential seems like an objective which should automatically be considered highly desirable. However, there are two key disadvantages involved in acquiring a type of business which is expected to have an above-average growth rate. Prior to discussing the procedure you will use to determine the importance of the "growth potential" acquisition objective for your company, it is useful to examine some of the problems implicit in acquiring a type of business which is expected to have an above-average future growth rate.

A type of business which is expected to have an above-average growth rate is generally one which is in an industry segment or geographic market which:

1. Has been growing rapidly for the past few years, and

2. Appears likely to benefit from present economic trends (e.g., rising or declining interest rates), or

3. Appears likely to benefit from demographic trends such as the increase in the number of elderly persons, or

4. Appears likely to benefit from recent changes in technology.

Types of businesses which are expected to have above-average growth rates are generally very popular with security analysts, lenders (e.g., commercial banks), and prospective acquirers. This is reflected in premium stock market valuations for public companies operating these types of businesses, generous credit arrangements from lenders, and high levels of competition among prospective acquirers. As a result these types of businesses generally command premium selling prices relative to their current earnings, cash flow, revenues, assets, and book value. In many cases acquiring one of these types of businesses requires an acquirer to pay a price which is also high relative to the business's projected earnings for the next two or three years. Therefore, a prospective acquirer which acquires a type of business which has an above-average growth rate is more likely to pay too much for the business unless it continues to grow at a rapid rate for the next five years. This is a serious risk since for the past 15 years, economic trends, business cycles, and technology have tended to change rapidly, with little forewarning. You will recall that paying too much for a business was one of the three principal reasons why acquisitions turn out to be unsuccessful.

The second disadvantage of acquiring a type of business which is expected to grow rapidly involves the risk of postacquisition management problems. Almost every type of business which is projected to have high growth potential is in an industry which has been growing rapidly for the past few years. One of the key advantages of operating in an industry which is rapidly growing is that for the first few years of this growth, a business does not have to be very well managed to grow and prosper. As a general rule companies operating types of businesses in industries which have been rapidly growing tend to be less well managed than companies operating other types of businesses. (Naturally, the executives of companies operating businesses in high-growth industries think that they are outstanding managers since their companies are performing well, and the media is praising their "talent and skill.") For the acquirer this means that acquiring a type of business in a rapidly growing industry often brings with it a management team which is unable to handle the problems which arise when there is increased competition or a slow down in historic growth rates. This, in turn, exposes the prospective acquirer to a potentially high number of postacquisition management problems.

HOW TO DETERMINE THE IMPORTANCE OF YOUR "GROWTH POTENTIAL" ACQUISITION OBJECTIVE

Growth potential refers to the growth prospects of a particular industry segment (e.g., furniture retailing) in a particular geographic market (e.g., Florida). The importance of the "growth potential" acquisition objective for a company depends upon the growth prospects of the company's present business:

1. When a company's present business has poor growth prospects, due to its industry segment and geographic location, it is unlikely to prosper and is significantly less likely to survive over the long term. For such a company acquiring a type of business which has attractive growth potential is often the only practical way of trying to improve the company's potential profitability and growth rate. Therefore, for such a company the "growth potential" acquisition objectives is "very important."

2. When a company's present business has above-average growth prospects, due to its industry segment and geographic location, it is not dependent upon using an acquisition to provide opportunities for future growth. As pointed out earlier in this chapter, however, owning a business which has poor growth prospects is generally a poor investment of company financial resources and management. There is also the risk that the growth potential of a company's present business may decline in future years due to unanticipated changes in economic trends, business cycles, or technology. Therefore, though a company's present business appears to have above-average growth prospects, it should still assign some "limited importance" to the "growth potential" acquisition objective.

3. When a company's present business has average growth prospects, due to its industry segment and geographic location, it would prefer to acquire a type of business which would maintain or improve its growth prospects. Therefore, for such a company, the "growth potential acquisition objective" is somewhat important.

After you rate the growth prospects of your company's present business as above average, average, or below average, you use the following chart to assign the appropriate number of attractiveness rating points to this rating factor:

GROWTH PROSPECTS OF YOUR PRESENT BUSINESS	IMPORTANCE LEVEL	NUMBER OF ATTRACTIVENESS RATING POINTS TO ASSIGN
Below average	Very important	30 pts
Average	Somewhat important	20 pts
Above average	Limited importance	10 pts

HOW TO RATE THE GROWTH PROSPECTS OF YOUR PRESENT BUSINESS

The growth prospects of a business refer to whether it is expected to have a growth rate which is higher, lower, or the same as the projected growth rate for the overall economy. For example, a business which is expected to grow at a higher growth rate than the overall economy has above-average growth prospects while a business which is expected to grow at a slower rate than the overall economy has below-average growth prospects. By analyzing industry and market trends, your company can project the expected growth rate of its present business and compare this with the projected growth rate for the overall economy. This is the most accurate way to estimate the growth prospects of your company's present business. A somewhat less accurate, but generally satisfactory, approach is to use average stock market price/earnings ratios comparisons to estimate growth prospects.

The average price/earnings ratios of public companies in an industry segment which has above-average growth prospects will almost always be higher than the average price/earnings ratios for public companies in all industries. In contrast, when the public companies in a particular industry segment have a lower price/earnings ratio than the average price earnings into for all public companies in all industries, this indicates that their industry segment has below-average growth prospects. Therefore, comparing the average price earnings ratios for companies in your present industry segment with the average price/earnings ratios of companies in all industries provides a convenient way to estimate the growth prospects of your present business.

There are two publications which compute the average price/earnings ratios for public companies in all industries and public companies in specific industries. These are:

- *The Value Line Investment Survey*
- *The Investor's Daily* (a newspaper)

Both of these are found in the business section of most public libraries.

When your present business is in one of the industry segments for which an average price/earnings ratio is provided, use the following procedure:

1. Compare the average price/earnings ratio for your industry segment with the average price/earnings ratio for all industries.

2. When the average price/earnings ratio for companies in your industry segment is at least 15% higher than the average price/earnings ratio for public companies in all industries, you estimate that your present business has above-average growth prospects.

3. When the average price/earnings ratio for companies in your industry segment is at least 15% lower than the average price/earnings ratio for public companies in all industries, you estimate that your present business has below-average growth prospects.

4. When the average price/earnings ratio for companies in your industry segment is neither 15% higher nor 15% lower than the average price/earnings ratio for public companies in all industries, you estimate that the growth prospects for your present business are "average."

5. Prior to using these estimates consider whether the location of your present business is expected to reduce or increase significantly your company's future growth rate. When the location of your present business is likely to have a significant effect upon its expected growth rate, you should consider adjusting the growth prospects estimate which you made based solely upon your industry price/earnings ratio comparison.

Sometimes you will find that neither *Value Line* nor the *Investors Daily* have computed an average price/earnings ratio for companies in the same industry segment as your present business. When this is the case, you will need to compute an average price/earnings ratio for companies in that industry segment. To do this, you select the public companies in the same industry segment as your present business which are listed, with their price/earnings ratios, in the stock market tables of your daily newspaper. These will be profitable companies listed on the New York and American stock exchanges. Then you compute the average price-earnings ratio for these selected public companies in your industry segment by adding up the price/earnings ratios shown and dividing by the number of companies you selected. For example, assume that you selected eight companies in your industry segment:

COMPANY	PRICE/EARNINGS RATIO
A&G	10 to 1
ABC	9 to 1
QP	13 to 1
LMN	12 to 1
OW	11 to 1
JC	12 to 1
M&G	14 to 1
WI	10 to 1
Total	91

91 divided by 8 = 11:1 average price earnings ratio.

HOW TO AWARD ATTRACTIVENESS RATING POINTS FOR YOUR "GROWTH POTENTIAL" RATING FACTOR

A particular type of business which your company is considering acquiring would be likely to improve, maintain, or reduce your company's growth potential:

1. Your company improves its growth potential by acquiring a type of business which appears likely to grow at a faster rate than your present business.
2. Your company maintains its growth potential by acquiring a type of business which appears likely to grow at a similar rate as your present business.
3. Your company reduces its growth potential by acquiring a type of business which is likely to grow at a slower rate than your present business.

Since your company would prefer to improve its growth potential you award the highest proportion (percentage) of the rating points you assign to your "growth potential rating factor" to those types of businesses which you expect to grow at a faster rate than your present business. Acquiring a type of business which would maintain your expected growth rate is somewhat attractive and is, therefore, awarded a lower proportion of the rating points you assigned to your "growth potential" rating factor. Your company would prefer to avoid acquiring a type of business which would reduce its growth potential. Therefore, a type of business which is expected to grow at a slower rate than your present business is awarded the lowest proportion (percentage) of the rating points you assign to your "growth potential" rating factor. The following chart indicates the proportion of the rating points you assign to a type of business depending upon how it would be likely to help your company achieve its "growth potential" objective:

EXPECTED GROWTH RATE IS	LIKELY EFFECT ON YOUR COMPANY'S GROWTH POTENTIAL	PROPORTION (%) OF POINTS TO BE AWARDED
Higher than your present business	Improve	All (100%)
Similar to that of your present business	Maintain	Some (50%)
Lower than your present business	Lower (reduce)	None (0%)

In order to use this chart your company will need to estimate whether the expected growth rate of a type of business which you are considering acquiring will be higher, lower, or similar to the growth rate of your company's present business.

PROCEDURE FOR ESTIMATING
COMPARATIVE GROWTH RATES

1. Start by listing the types of businesses your company is considering acquiring on the following chart:

TYPE OF BUSINESS	RELATIVE GROWTH RATE		
	LOWER	SIMILAR	HIGHER
1. _____	_____	_____	_____
2. _____	_____	_____	_____
3. _____	_____	_____	_____
4. _____	_____	_____	_____
5. _____	_____	_____	_____
6. _____	_____	_____	_____
7. _____	_____	_____	_____
8. _____	_____	_____	_____
9. _____	_____	_____	_____
10. _____	_____	_____	_____

2. Based upon your management's knowledge of industry and market trends, you will be able to estimate whether some of these types of businesses you are considering acquiring have better, similar, or worse growth prospects than your company's present business. Place a checkmark in the appropriate column for those types of businesses.

3. To estimate the relative growth rate of the remaining types of businesses which your company is considering acquiring, you estimate the projected growth rate of your company's present business and the projected growth rates of each of these remaining types of businesses. Then you compare these projected growth rates and place a check mark in the appropriate column.

HOW TO MAKE GROWTH RATE
PROJECTIONS

Use the following procedure to make growth rate projections for different types of businesses:

1. Determine the average annual growth rate for each industry segment over the past two years. Some of the sources which may provide this information include:

   a. *The Value Line Survey*
   b. *The U.S. Industrial Outlook*
   c. Published market studies
   d. Annual review issues of trade publications
   e. Industry trade associations

2. Use this average annual growth rate for the past two years as your preliminary projected growth rate for the next two years.

3. Examine recent changes in each industry segment which would be likely to improve or reduce these historic growth rates. Examples of such changes might include:

   a. Technological change
   b. Import competition
   c. Improving or declining economic conditions in the industries which companies in these industry segments sell to

Some of the information sources which may provide this information on recent changes affecting an industry segment's growth rate were listed as sources of historic growth rate data. Others include:

   a. Annual and quarterly reports of public companies in each industry segment
   b. Articles in business periodicals and newspapers

4. Based upon your examination of recent changes in each industry segment adjust the preliminary projected growth rates you developed based upon the historic (average two-year) growth rates for each industry segment.

HOW TO DETERMINE THE IMPORTANCE OF THE "CUSTOMER BASE DIVERSIFICATION" OBJECTIVE FOR YOUR COMPANY

The importance of the customer base diversification objective for your company depends upon the degree to which your company already has a diversified customer base:

1. When your company is already selling its products or services to a diversified customer base, it is preferable, but not essential, to add groups of customers in different industries or geographic markets. Therefore, this objective would have "limited importance" and is assigned the minimum number of rating points (10 points.)

2. When your company sells its goods and services to a narrow (undiversified) potential customer base, it is "very important" to add groups of customers in different industries or geographic markets. Therefore, this objective is assigned the maximum number of rating points (30 points).

3. When your company's customer base is somewhat diversified, it would be valuable to add groups of customers in different industries or geographic markets. Therefore, this objective would be "important" for your company and is assigned 20 rating points.

HOW TO ESTIMATE YOUR PRESENT LEVEL OF CUSTOMER DIVERSIFICATION

To estimate your company's present level of customer diversification, answer the following two questions:

	YES	NO
Does your company derive over 50% of its revenues from customers in a single industry?		
Does your company derive over 50% of its revenues from customers located in a single geographic market:		

1. When the answer to both questions is "no," your customer base is already diversified.

2. When the answer to both questions is "yes," your present customer base is very narrow (undiversified).

3. When you answered one question "yes" and the other "no" your present customer base is somewhat diversified.

HOW DIFFERENT TYPES OF BUSINESSES HELP YOUR COMPANY ACHIEVE ITS "CUSTOMER BASE DIVERSIFICATION" OBJECTIVE

1. Your company achieves a high level of customer diversification when it acquires a type of business which meets both the following criteria:

   a. It derives most of its revenues from sales to customers in industries different from those to which your present business sells.

   b. It derives most of its revenues from sales to customers in geographic markets different from those to which your present business sells.

2. Your company achieves a significant level of customers diversification when it acquires a type of business which derives most of its revenues from sales to customers which are in industries and geographic markets different from those of the customers to which you now sell.

3. Your company achieves a moderate level of customer diversification when it acquires a type of business which derives a majority of its revenues from sales to customers which are in industries of geographic markets different from those of the customers to which you now sell.

4. Your company achieves a low level of customer diversification when it acquires a type of business which derives less than half of its revenues from sales to customers that are in industries or geographic markets different from those of the customers to which you now sell.

HOW TO ASSIGN CUSTOMER BASE DIVERSIFICATION RATING POINTS TO THE TYPES OF BUSINESSES YOUR COMPANY IS CONSIDERING ACQUIRING

1. Types of businesses which sell their products or services to customers who are generally in the same market areas and industries as the customers you now sell to are awarded none (0%) of the rating points which you assigned to your "customer base diversification" rating factor.

2. Types of businesses which sell their products or services primarily to customers which are in industries and market areas different from those to whom you now sell are awarded all (100%) of the rating points which you assigned to your "customer base diversification" rating factor.

3. Types of businesses which sell their products or services in the same market area in which you sell, but primarily to customers in industries different from those to whom you now sell, are awarded 50% of the rating points which you assigned to your "customer base diversification" rating factor.

4. Types of businesses which sell their products or services to customers in the same industries which you now sell to, but primarily to customers in different geographic markets, are awarded 50% of the rating points which you assigned to your "customer base diversification" rating factor.

5. Other types of businesses are awarded 20% of the rating points which you assigned to your "customer base diversification" rating factor. Generally, these will be types of businesses which derive 25% to 50% of their sales from customers which are either in different industries or different geographic markets than the customers which you now sell to.

The following example illustrates this approach:

Furniture Parts Corp. manufactures metal fasteners sold primarily to furniture companies located in North Carolina. The company is considering acquiring:

1. A competing manufacturer of metal furniture fasteners which also sells primarily to customers located in North Carolina

2. A manufacturer of plastic furniture parts which sells primarily to customers located in North Carolina

3. A manufacturer of metal furniture fasteners which sells primarily to customers located in California

4. A manufacturer of precision metal fasteners sold primarily to the aerospace industry

5. An adhesives manufacturer which derives approximately half of its revenues from sales to North Carolina furniture manufacturers and approximately half its sales to building supply manufacturers located nationwide

Furniture Parts Corp. assigned 30 rating points to its "customer base diversification" rating factor. Using the guidelines presented in this section, the company awarded the following numbers of "customer base diversification" rating points to the five types of businesses it is considering acquiring:

Metal furniture fasteners, North Carolina	0% × 30 pts = 0	pts
Plastic furniture parts, North Carolina	0% × 30 pts = 0	pts
Metal furniture fasteners, California	50% × 30 pts = 15	pts
Precision metal fasteners	100% × 30 pts = 30	pts
Adhesives manufacturer	20% × 30 pts = 6	pts

HOW TO DETERMINE THE IMPORTANCE OF YOUR MARKETING SYNERGY OBJECTIVE (RATING FACTOR)

The primary role of marketing synergy is to increase the sales growth potential of your company's present business. The importance of your company seeking marketing synergy depends upon the priority which your company places on expanding its current business versus using its expansion capital to develop or acquire a business in a different industry segment.

You use the following procedure to assign an importance level and attractiveness rating points to your marketing synergy rating factor.

1. When your company seeks to grow primarily by expanding within its present industry segment (e.g., furniture manufacturing), place a "high importance level" and assign 30 rating points to your "marketing synergy objective."

2. When your company seeks to grow primarily by entering and developing a business outside its present industry segment, it is still "somewhat important" that your company seek to expand its current business. Otherwise the assets devoted to your present business will lose their value. Therefore, you assign 10 rating points to your "marketing synergy" objective.

3. When your company seeks to grow by expanding its current business and also by diversifying into a different industry segment, or when your company has not decided which of these growth strategies to pursue, your marketing synergy objective is considered to be of "average importance" and is assigned 20 rating points.

The following examples illustrate this concept:

Harmon Brothers is an oil well drilling contractor located in Tulsa. The oil well drilling business is very depressed. Harmon Brothers believes that the oil well drilling business will eventually revive, but the company intends now to concentrate on diversifying into an industry which is less cyclical. Therefore, Harmon Brothers has assigned a low priority to expanding its present business and has assigned 10 interim rating points to its "marketing synergy" acquisition objective.

Waterbury Wire Company manufacturers nonferrous metal wire, rods, strips, and eyelets. Waterbury wire is always looking for opportunities to expand within this industry segment. However, because this industry segment offers limited growth potential, and is subject to import competition, Waterbury Wire is also looking for an opportunity to diversify into another industry. Waterbury Wire Company, therefore, considers expanding within its present industry segment to be of "average importance." The company assigns 20 interim points to its "marketing synergy" acquisition objective.

HOW TO AWARD "MARKETING SYNERGY" RATING POINTS TO THE TYPES OF BUSINESSES YOUR COMPANY IS CONSIDERING ACQUIRING

Analyze your company's present business to identify potential opportunities for marketing synergy. Your objective is to answer the following two questions:

1. What other products or services might your company be able to sell through its present distribution channels and marketing network?
2. What additional distribution channels and marketing networks might be used to sell the products and services which your company now produces?

After your company has identified its potential sources of marketing synergy, examine each of the types of businesses you are considering acquiring. Then use the following guidelines to award marketing synergy rating points to each type of business:

1. A type of business which would provide additional distribution channels and marketing networks for your company's products and services is awarded 70% of the interim points you assigned to your marketing synergy objective (rating factor).
2. A type of business that produces additional products and services which your company could sell through its present distribution channels and marketing network is also awarded 70% of the interim points you assigned to your marketing synergy objective (rating factor).
3. A type of business which meets both of the preceding criteria is awarded 100% of the interim points you assigned to your marketing synergy objective (rating factor).
4. A type of business which would not produce potential marketing synergies if you owned it is awarded none (0%)— of the interim points which you assigned to your marketing synergy objective (rating factor).

The following example illustrates the approach used to award "marketing synergy" rating points to the types of businesses you are considering acquiring:

Horizon Press publishes high school textbooks which it markets to Catholic parochial schools in the Northeast through its own sales forces. The company's management seeks to expand its textbook publishing business while also diversifying another type of business. Horizon Press, therefore, assigned 20 interim points to its marketing synergy rating factor.

Horizon Press identified the following markets which might provide additional sales for its textbook product line if the company could develop or acquire suitable distribution channels and marketing networks:

- Catholic parochial high schools in other regions
- Other "Christian" parochial schools
- Public high schools
- Junior colleges
- Large retail book stores
- English language schools abroad
- Adult education programs

Horizon Press then identified other products which its existing distribution channels and marketing network might be able to market to Catholic parochial high schools in the northeast. They included:

- Other types of published instruction materials such as science lab workbooks and study guides
- Annotated fiction classics frequently used for high school English classes
- Instructional movies and video cassettes oriented to the high school market
- Standard IQ testing materials (e.g., examinations)
- Language laboratory supplies (e.g., tapes)

Horizon Press then examined the types of businesses it was considering acquiring. They included:

- Textbook publishers which sell primarily to public high schools and junior colleges
- Competing publishers of high school textbooks sold primarily to Catholic schools in the Northeast
- FM radio stations
- Newspaper publishers
- Textbook exporters

Horizon Press then awarded its "marketing synergy" rating points using the guidelines presented in the preceding section of this chapter:

- Public high school textbook publishers
$$100\% \times 20 \text{ pts} = 20 \text{ rating points}$$

- Competitors
$$0\% \times 20 \text{ pts} = 0 \text{ rating points}$$

- FM radio stations
$$0\% \times 20 \text{ pts} = 0 \text{ rating points}$$

- Newspaper publishers
$$0\% \times 20 \text{ pts} = 0 \text{ rating points}$$

- Textbook exporters
$$70\% \times 20 \text{ pts} = 14 \text{ rating points}$$

You will notice that acquiring a direct competitor does not produce potential marketing synergies. Acquiring a competitor often, however, produces significant marketing cost savings for the combined businesses. This potential benefit is included in your acquisition choice planning system when you analyze your final basic acquisition objective which is "economy of scale cost savings."

HOW TO DETERMINE THE IMPORTANCE OF YOUR "ECONOMY-OF-SCALE COST SAVINGS" OBJECTIVE

Economy-of-scale cost savings help a company to expand within its present industry. To a lesser extent these cost savings help a company which expands into a different industry but continues to operate in the same or nearby geographic markets. The greatest cost savings tend to occur when a company expands within its current industry and continues to operate in its present or nearby geographic markets. Therefore, economy-of-scale cost savings are the most important for a company which prefers to concentrate its growth efforts within its current industry and its present, or nearby, geographic markets. In order to determine the importance of your "economy-of-scale cost savings" objective, you use the following procedure:

1. Decide whether you would prefer to expand within your present industry or diversify into other industries.

   a. When your company would prefer to expand within its present industry, assign 20 rating points to your "economy-of-scale cost savings" objective.
   b. When your company would prefer to grow by diversifying into other industries, assign no ("0") rating points to your "economy-of-scale cost savings" objective.

    c. When your company does not have a strong preference for either expanding within its present industry or diversifying into a different industry, assign 10 rating points to your "economy-of-scale cost savings" objective.

2. Decide whether you would prefer to have your businesses operate in the same geographic markets which you are presently in, and nearby geographic markets, or whether you would prefer to operate businesses in more distant geographic markets. Some of the attractions of more distant geographic markets might include higher projected growth rates, less competition, and lower operating costs.

    a. When your company would prefer to operate businesses in the same geographic markets in which you operate already, or nearby markets, add 10 points to your "economy-of-scale cost savings" objective (rating factor).

    b. When your company would prefer to operate businesses in other, more distant, geographic markets, do not add any points to your "economy-of-scale cost savings" objective (rating factor).

The following example illustrates the use of these guidelines:

AAA Furniture Corp. operates a chain of retail furniture stores located in New Jersey. AAA's management team has had many years of experience in various segments of the furniture industry (retailing, manufacturing wholesaling, importing, etc.). The company has decided to expand within the furniture industry in order to take advantage of its industry knowledge. Therefore, the company starts by assigning 20 rating points to its "economy-of-scale cost savings" objective (rating factor).

AAA Furniture Corp. has done well in its New Jersey market area. The company would however prefer to expand into a different geographic market, outside the Northeast, which is less competitive and has lower operating costs. Therefore, AAA assigns no additional rating points to its "economy-of-scale cost savings" objective (rating factor).

HOW TO AWARD "ECONOMY-OF-SCALE COST SAVINGS" POINTS TO THE TYPES OF BUSINESSES YOUR COMPANY IS CONSIDERING ACQUIRING

Rating points are awarded based upon the likelihood that combining two businesses would produce opportunities for future cost savings. The two businesses are your company's present business and a type of business which you are considering acquiring.

1. When combining your present business with a type of business which you are considering acquiring is likely to produce opportunities for significant cost savings, award that type of business all (100%) of the rating points which your company assigned to its "economy-of-scale cost savings" objective (rating factor).

2. When combining your present business with a type of business which you are considering acquiring is unlikely to produce opportunities for cost savings, award none (0%) of the rating points which your company assigned to its "economy-of-scale cost savings" objective (rating factor).

3. When combining your present business with a type of business which you are considering acquiring is likely to produce some opportunities for cost savings, award 50% of the rating points which your company assigned to its "economy-of-scale cost savings" objective (rating factor).

In order to determine which of these three categories (criteria) to use for a particular type of business, use the following guidelines:

1. Combining two businesses which produce similar products or services, which they sell in the same, or nearby, geographic markets, is likely to produce significant economy-of-scale cost savings.

2. Combining two businesses which produce different types of products or services which they sell to the same types of customers in the same geographic markets is likely to produce "some" economy-of-scale cost savings.

3. Combining two businesses which operate in different segments of the same industry is likely to produce some economy-of-scale cost savings when the two businesses operate in the same geographic markets.

4. Combinations of businesses which do not fit these three categories are unlikely to produce significant economy-of-scale cost savings.

HOW TO DETERMINE THE IMPORTANCE LEVEL OF SUPPLEMENTAL OBJECTIVES (RATING FACTORS)

1. Assign the rating points to your five basic rating factors and award attractiveness rating points to the types of business you are considering acquiring.

2. Then take a fresh look at the one or two supplemental acquisition objectives your company is considering adding to your business choice matrix. Often you will find that these supplemental objectives have already been given adequate

consideration when you assigned importance levels and awarded attractiveness rating points for your five basic rating factors.

3. When your management feels that it is still important to include one or two supplemental acquisition objectives use the following guidelines:

a. when you are adding only one supplemental acquisition objective, it is assigned 20 rating points.

b. When you are adding two supplemental acquisition objectives, they are each assigned 10 rating points.

HOW TO AWARD ATTRACTIVENESS RATING POINTS FOR YOUR SUPPLEMENTAL ACQUISITION OBJECTIVES

1. A type of business which would achieve a particular supplemental objective is awarded 100% of the points assigned to the rating factor.

2. A type of business which would partly achieve a particular supplemental rating factor is awarded 50% of the points assigned to that rating factor.

3. A type of business which would not help your company achieve a particular supplemental rating factor is awarded 0% (none) of the points assigned to that rating factor.

HOW TO COMPLETE YOUR ACQUISITION CHOICE MATRIX SYSTEM

For each type of business, add together the total number of attractiveness rating points awarded to that type of business. To do this you add across each row of your matrix and enter the totals in the last column.

HOW TO USE THE RESULTS OF YOUR ACQUISITION CHOICE MATRIX SYSTEM

1. Identify the three or four types of businesses which had the highest number of total attractiveness rating points.

2. From among these three or four types of businesses, select two types of businesses which your chief executive and a majority of your acquisition committee feel that your company should seek to acquire at this time.

3. Use these two types of businesses for your company's acquisition screening criteria.

AN ACQUISITION CHOICE MATRIX EXAMPLE

ABC Plumbing Supply distributes plumbing supplies to plumbing contractors located in the metropolitan Philadelphia area. Initially, ABC Plumbing Supply was considering acquiring:

1. Other plumbing supply distributors located in Philadelphia (competitors)

2. Plumbing supply distributors serving adjacent or nearby urban markets (e.g., Trenton, NJ)

3. Plumbing supply distributors serving more distant, but faster-growing markets (e.g., Monmouth County, NJ).

4. Distributors of heating, ventilation, and air conditioning equipment (HVAC) serving the Philadelphia area

5. Manufacturers of plumbing hardware located in the Northeast

6. Retail hardware store chains located in Pennsylvania, New Jersey, and Delaware

7. Marinas located within 100 miles of Philadelphia (ABC's president owns two boats)

8. Nursing homes (Pennsylvania, New Jersey, and Delaware)

9. Single-family home builders operating within 70 miles of Philadelphia

ABC Plumbing Supply assigned 30 rating points to its "low risk of postacquisition management difficulty" rating factor and 20 rating points to its "growth potential" rating factor. Then it awarded point values to each type of business based upon whether it would be likely to achieve, partly achieve, or not achieve each of these two objectives. At this stage the company's business choice matrix looked like this:

TYPE OF BUSINESS	RATING FACTORS					
	LOW POST ACQUISITION MANAGEMENT DIFFICULTY (30 PTS)	GROWTH POTENTIAL (20 PTS)	CUSTOMER BASE DIVERSIFI-CATION (PTS)	MARKETING SYNERGY (PTS)	COST SAVINGS (PTS)	TOTAL POINTS
1. Competitors	30 pts	10 pts				
2. Nearby urban markets	30 pts	0 pts				
3. Growth markets (same region)	15 pts	20 pts				
4. HVAC	15 pts	10 pts				
5. Hardware manufacturers	0 pts	0 pts				
6. Retail hardware stores	0 pts	10 pts				
7. Marinas	0 pts	20 pts				
8. Nursing homes	0 pts	20 pts				
9. Home builders	0 pts	10 pts				

ABC Plumbing Supply then computed the interim attractiveness rating for those nine types of businesses by adding together the points assigned for its "low risk of postacquisition management difficulty" and "growth potential" objectives.

	INTERIM POINT SCORE
1. Competitors	40 pts
2. Nearby urban markets	30 pts
3. Growth markets (same region)	35 pts
4. HVAC	25 pts
5. Hardware manufacturers	0 pts
6. Retail hardware stores	10 pts
7. Marinas	20 pts
8. Nursing homes	20 pts
9. Home builders	10 pts

Three of these—hardware manufacturer, retail hardware stores, and home builders—received significantly lower interim scores than the other types of businesses ABC was considering acquiring. ABC recognized that though these three types of businesses might be awarded higher scores for some of the remaining three basic rating factors, their total scores for all five factors would not be high enough to give them a high ranking. Therefore, ABC dropped these three types of businesses from further consideration.

ABC Plumbing Supply then assigned point values to the remaining three basic rating factors and awarded points to each of the six types of businesses it was still considering acquiring. The company's completed acquisition choice matrix looked like this:

	RATING FACTORS					
TYPE OF BUSINESS	LOW POST-ACQUISITION MANAGEMENT DIFFICULTY (30 PTS)	GROWTH POTENTIAL (20 PTS)	CUSTOMER BASE DIVERSIFI-CATION (30 PTS)	MARKETING SYNERGY (20 PTS)	COST SAVINGS (20 PTS)	TOTAL ATTRACTIVENESS RATING POINTS
1. Competitors	30 pts	10 pts	0 pts	0 pts	20 pts	60 pts
2. Nearby urban markets	30	0 pts	10 pts	15 pts	20 pts	75 pts
3. Growth markets (same region)	15 pts	20 pts	15 pts	15 pts	10 pts	75 pts
4. HVAC	15 pts	10 pts	10 pts	15 pts	10 pts	60 pts
5. Marinas	0 pts	20 pts	30 pts	0 pts	0 pts	50 pts
6. Nursing homes	0 pts	20 pts	30 pts	0 pts	0 pts	50 pts

ABC Plumbing Supply's acquisition choice matrix indicates that the most attractive choices are to acquire plumbing supply distributors located either in nearby urban market areas, or in rapidly growing market areas located in the same geographic region as its present business. Acquiring a competitor and acquiring a distributor of heating, ventilation and air conditioning equipment (HVAC) also received relatively high attractiveness ratings. Therefore ABC Plumbing Supply should select two of these four types of businesses to use for its initial sets of acquisition screening criteria.

C·H·A·P·T·E·R S·I·X

HOW TO IMPROVE YOUR COMPANY'S ABILITY TO FINANCE ITS ACQUISITIONS

Acquisition financing is the pool of investment capital which a company can use to acquire another business. This includes the cash assets and unused borrowing capacity of both the acquiring company and the acquisition candidate.

WHY IS IT IMPORTANT TO INCREASE YOUR OWN COMPANY'S CASH ASSETS AND UNUSED BORROWING CAPACITY BEFORE LAUNCHING AN ACQUISITION PROGRAM

For most acquisitions the buyer must contribute 20% to 40% of the purchase price using its own cash and unused borrowing capacity. Therefore, the size company which your company can afford to acquire will usually depend upon how much money you can contribute towards the purchase price.

WHY IT IS IMPORTANT TO INCREASE THE SIZE COMPANY YOU CAN AFFORD TO ACQUIRE

1. The minimum costs associated with making an acquisition total around $120,000. These costs include legal fees, accounting fees, commissions, and

time your own executives spend searching for, evaluating, and negotiating with acquisition candidates. These costs tend to increase only gradually as the size of company you acquire increases. Thus, it might cost a company $150,000 in expenses to acquire an acquisition candidate with sales of $5 million, compared with $130,000 for a company with sales of $2.5 million.

2. It is usually easier and less expensive to finance acquisitions of larger companies. The reason is that each lender has a minimum transaction size. There are probably ten times as many lenders who will consider an acquisition loan request for $1,000,000 than there are lenders who will consider making an acquisition loan for $200,000.

3. Though most acquirers intend to retain the former owners to manage their newly acquired business, this rarely works out satisfactorily. In over 50% of the acquisitions, the purchaser is forced to bring in new senior managers within 12 months after the acquisition is made. It is easier for a new owner of a company to recruit professional management talent to run a larger business than a smaller business. A larger business is also more likely to be able to afford the salaries of these professional managers.

4. Any company which you acquire will be a combination of problems, weaknesses, and opportunities. The weakness which tends to be the most difficult and time consuming to overcome is inadequate sales volume. Therefore, it is generally less risky to acquire a larger company than a smaller company when the two companies are otherwise similar.

WHEN TO TAKE STEPS TO IMPROVE YOUR COMPANY'S ABILITY TO FINANCE ITS ACQUISITIONS

As soon as possible. You never know when a company which you would like to own will suddenly become available for purchase. Even if your company never makes an acquisition, it will benefit from improving its ability to finance investments of this type. This is because your company will also become better able to finance its internal growth. For example, when your company needs financing to purchase equipment, it will be able to borrow more money, for a longer period, at a lower interest rate.

WHY COMPANIES ARE SOLD FOR BARGAIN PRICES

An acquisition bargain is an acquisition candidate which is being sold for a lower price than similar acquisition candidates in its industry.

Bargain-priced acquisition opportunities usually occur because the selling company's owners must sell their business quickly.

Examples of situations which create the need to quickly sell a profitable business include:

- Unexpected death or serious illness of the chief executive or the principal stockholder.

- Parent company financial problems.

- The owners need cash right away to meet personal financial obligations.

WHY YOU WILL NEED MORE INTERNAL FINANCING CAPACITY TO TAKE ADVANTAGE OF THESE BARGAIN OPPORTUNITIES

The sellers will usually accept the first reasonable offer they receive from a purchaser offering all "cash." Therefore, a prospective purchaser will generally not have enough time to arrange to borrow the full amount which it could eventually obtain using the selling company's assets and earnings stream.

The following example illustrates this situation.

Alpha Electronics is a wholly owned subsidiary of Omega Oil & Gas, Inc. Alpha is a manufacturer of electronic test equipment sold to the military. Omega Oil & Gas, Inc., is in default on its bank loan and must raise cash within 45 days. It is, therefore, offering to sell its subsidiary, Alpha Electronics, for $1 million cash. The financial statements of Alpha Electronics show the following information:

Sales	$7,000,000
Net income	$300,000
Cash flow	$400,000
Accounts receivable	$1,200,000
Inventories	1,000,000
Plant and equipment	800,000
Total assets	$3,000,000
Accounts payable	$700,000
Bank loans	600,000
Long-term debt (mortgages)	700,000
Total liabilities	$2,000,000
Net worth	$1,000,000

Estimated appraised value of plant and equipment is $1,500,000.

A purchaser of Alpha Electronics could probably finance the entire purchase price if it had three to four months to do so. This could be done in the following manner:

1. Accounts receivable loan from a finance company:

70% × $1,200,000 = $840,000

2. Inventory loan from a finance company:

45% × $1,000,000 = $450,000

3. Sale and lease back to plant and equipment:

70% × $1,500,000 (appraised value) = $1,000,000

4. Total new loans:

$ 840,000
450,000
1,050,000
$2,340,000

5. Repayment of existing Alpha bank loans and mortgages ($1,300,000) leaves $1,040,000 cash available to pay a purchase price of $1,000,000.

Assume that your company is a typical privately owned electronics instrument manufacturer which has not taken steps to improve its acquisition financing capability. Your company has $50,000 in surplus cash and has not used $150,000 of its available bank credit line, secured by your accounts receivable. Your bank offers to lend you 65% of Alpha Electronics accounts receivable and would also lend your company $200,000 based upon the financial statements and personal guarantees of your company's principal shareholders. The amount of cash which your company could quickly generate would be:

Cash	$ 50,000
Accounts receivable credit line	150,000
New accounts receivable loan	780,000
Unsecured loan (personal guarantees)	200,000
Total	$1,180,000

Since you would have to repay Alpha's bank loans of $600,000, this would leave you with $580,000 to use toward the $1 million cash purchase price. Thus you would be unable to acquire this company because there would not be enough time to arrange the financing you would need.

Now assume that your company is one of the few privately owned electronics instrument manufacturers which has taken steps to improve its internal acquisition financing capacity. Your company has $100,000 in surplus cash, $200,000 in available credit from your suppliers, and $400,000 in unused accounts receivable and inventory credit lines from a finance company. Your finance company offers to lend against the selling company's current assets on the following basis:

- 70% of accounts receivable
- 40% of inventories

Your company's acquisition financing resources consist of the following:

1. Surplus cash	$100,000
2. Supplier credit	200,000
3. Finance company credit line	400,000
4. New accounts receivable loan	840,000
5. New inventory loan	400,000
Total	$1,940,000

After repaying Alpha's bank loan of $600,000 you have $1,000,000 cash for the purchase price and $340,000 cash for acquisition expenses and working capital. Temporarily your company would have assumed $1,840,000 in short-term debt and added $2,540,000 in short-term assets consisting of:

Cash	$ 340,000
Accounts receivable	$1,200,000
Inventories	$1,000,000

After you owned Alpha Electronics you would have time to arrange $1,000,000 in new long-term financing secured by Alpha's plant and equipment assets. The proceeds of this long-term financing would then be used to reduce your short-term debt back to a more manageable level and would restore some of your unused borrowing capacity.

HOW YOU IMPROVE YOUR COMPANY'S ABILITY TO FINANCE ITS ACQUISITIONS

1. Become more familiar with the types of business loan which your company could use to finance its growth.

2. Make your company more attractive to business lenders (e.g., commercial banks, finance companies, equipment lessors).

3. Use cash management techniques to increase the amount of cash which your company has available for acquisitions.

4. Increase your company's available borrowing capacity.

TYPES OF BUSINESS LOANS

Why you should become more familiar with the principal types of business loans

1. A company can either increase its borrowing capacity or reduce the interest rates it pays by using different types of loans. The first step toward utilizing this financial management flexibility is to become familiar with the different types of business loans which are available.

2. Each type of business loan represents a different lending concept. Loan officers frequently use the name of a type of loan (e.g., term loan, credit lines, mortgages) as a verbal shorthand to refer to the underlying lending concept. Understanding the different types of business loans will help you to understand and communicate more effectively with these loan officers.

The principal types of business loans

1. Supplier credit
2. Revolving credit lines
3. Term loans
4. Equipment leases
5. Commercial mortgages
6. Venture capital loans

These are described in the following sections of this chapter.

SUPPLIER CREDIT

Most companies which sell goods or services to other businesses permit these customers to defer paying for those goods and services for a period following their delivery. The reasons why suppliers generally provide credit to their business customers are:

1. It is expensive to collect and process a large number of small payments. Monthly billing reduces these administrative expenses.

2. It is considerably less expensive to package and ship a single larger order than it is to package and ship the same quantity of goods in the form of several smaller orders. The availability of supplier credit encourages business customers to make larger, but less frequent, purchases.

3. Business customers rely on their own sales to pay for the goods which they purchase. Credit provided by suppliers reduces their cash flow timing problems. They are, therefore, more likely to choose suppliers who will provide them with credit.

4. Lenders prefer to make loans secured by accounts receivables rather than inventories. A supplier can therefore borrow more money if it ships goods to purchasers rather than if it holds these goods in inventory. Accounts receivable borrowing provides the credit which suppliers then pass on to their customers.

5. Suppliers can generally increase their prices by enough to cover their interest costs for the financing that they pass on to their customers.

EXAMPLES OF CREDIT LINES PROVIDED BY SUPPLIERS TO THEIR BUSINESS CUSTOMERS

Monthly billing

Goods and services delivered during the month are not invoiced until the end of that month. The business customer can generally delay paying the bill for 30 days without being penalized. In order to encourage faster payment, the supplier may offer a discount for invoices paid within a set period (e.g., 10 days).

Extended trade credit

In order to encourage larger orders (which are more economical for the suppliers to produce, pack and ship), or to protect an order flow from a good customer, suppliers may permit a business customer to delay paying monthly invoices for up to 90 days. This tends to be a more formal arrangement than monthly billing. The supplier will generally set a maximum amount of unpaid invoices which can be outstanding before additional orders are shipped.

Seasonal credit

Suppliers to seasonal businesses often permit these customers to defer payment until their selling season is underway, or is completed. Examples of seasonal businesses include consumer goods retailing and agriculture.

Progress payments

Equipment and certain types of project-oriented services (e.g., consulting assignments, construction contracts) are paid for in installments with the final installment due 30 to 90 days after the equipment is delivered or the project is completed. When there is intense competition among suppliers, business customers may be able to pay the final installment in monthly payments over 3 to 6 months.

HOW SUPPLIERS ARE COMPENSATED FOR PROVIDING CREDIT TO THEIR BUSINESS CUSTOMERS

1. They mark up their goods or services to cover their own financing costs.
2. They capture a larger portion of a business customer's order flow for a longer period. This increases the supplier's sales volume.

REVOLVING CREDIT LINES

Revolving credit lines are preapproved short-term borrowing arrangements secured by your company's accounts receivables and inventories. Originally revolving credit lines were meant to bridge a company's seasonal cash flow gap. The banks which provided these revolving credit lines required that the principal outstanding balance of the credit lines be paid down to $0 once every 12 months. This annual "cleanup" requirement enabled the banks to classify revolving credit lines as loans having a maturity of less than 1 year. You will still find that many banks will propose an annual "clean up" requirement if you are a new customer.

Accounts receivable financing is very attractive to short-term lenders such as banks and finance companies because loan repayment is not dependent upon the borrower's profitability. The source of loan repayment is the collection of accounts receivables from the borrower's customers.

Finance companies and some banks offer attractive revolving credit facilities. Banks, however, are more selective than financing companies in choosing the smaller companies to whom they will offer these attractive revolving credit facilities. The elements of an attractive revolving credit facility are:

1. Elimination of the annual cleanup requirement. For a growing company this makes a revolving credit line equivalent to a long-term, interest-only loan, so long as the credit line is renewed each year.

2. Lending a higher portion of the accounts receivable. For example, a bank which normally permits smaller companies to borrow 65% of their outstanding receivables might permit a preferred business customer to borrow 75% of their outstanding accounts receivable.

3. Including a portion of the company's inventories (e.g., 40%) in the collateral eligible to be borrowed against. Lenders refer to this eligible collateral as the borrowing company's "loan base."

TERM LOANS

Term loans are repaid in installments (principal plus accrued interest) over a period of three to five years. They are collateralized by all the borrower's assets to the extent their value exceeds any existing secured debt. For example, if a company owns a factory which is worth $2 million and is secured by a $500,000 mortgage, the term lender will in effect have a second mortgage on the property.

The source of repayment for a term loan is the borrower's future earnings and cash flow. Since a company's future earnings and cash flow are somewhat unpredictable, lenders feel that term loans have a higher loan loss risk than working capital loans (revolving credit lines). Lenders attempt to reduce their loan loss risk by being selective in choosing companies to whom they will offer term loan facilities. Banks primarily base this decision on the borrower's financial strength and profitability. Finance companies place greater emphasis on the liquidation value of the borrower's assets which are available to collateralize the term loan.

EQUIPMENT LEASE FINANCING

Equipment leases are somewhat similar to term loans. Both types of financing are collateralized by fixed assets, such as machinery, and are repaid in installments over a period of years. Both term loans and equipment leases are repaid out of the borrower's future cash flow. The principal differences between term loans and traditional equipment leases are:

1. The borrower owns the equipment which collateralizes a term loan. The lender owns the equipment which the borrower leases, but the borrower has exclusive use of the equipment for the term of the lease. The value of the equipment at the end of the lease term is called its "residual value."

2. A term loan borrower receives the tax benefit (e.g., accelerated depreciation) which arise from ownership of the equipment which collateralizes the term loan. Usually, the lender receives the tax benefits generated from ownership of leased equipment.

3. In exchange for retaining the residual value and tax benefits generated by equipment ownership, equipment lessors will usually lend up to 100% of the cost or fair market value of the equipment. In contrast, term loan lenders typically lend a maximum of 75% of the cost of new equipment and 50% of the fair market value of used equipment.

4. The payments on an equipment lease usually stay constant throughout the term of the lease. The payments on a term loan are highest the first year and then decline each year as the principal balance is reduced.

5. Finance companies and banks are the principal source of term loans. Finance companies and equipment leasing companies are the principal source of equipment lease financing.

HOW LENDERS DEAL WITH THE DISTINCTIONS AMONG REVOLVING CREDIT LINES, TERM LOANS, AND EQUIPMENT LEASES

The distinctions between these three types of financing have become blurred as commercial banks, finance companies, and equipment leasing companies have sought to capture a larger portion of the financing business of their better customers. Lenders will frequently offer a financing package which appears to be a single loan but is actually a combined package consisting of a revolving credit line and/or a term loan and/or an equipment lease. This is confusing to many borrowers. The following guidelines will help you to analyze these loan proposals:

1. The portion of a credit line which is to be repaid in regular installments is actually a term loan. A bank or finance company which offers this type of facility will either place a lien on your fixed assets or will put requirements (called covenants) in the loan agreement which prevent you from obtaining new outside financing collateralized by your fixed assets. These are called "negative covenants."

2. The portion of a loan facility which does not require principal repayments is actually a revolving credit line. A bank or finance company which offers this type of loan facility will require that you not obtain other financing secured by your accounts receivables and inventories.

3. A revolving credit line or term loan which provides financing to purchase new equipment, which is then added to the collateral securing the loan, is viewed by the lender as being similar to equipment lease financing.

4. An equipment lease package which is collateralized by lien or negative covenant on a company's current assets (accounts receivable and/or inventories) actually includes a term loan component.

COMMERCIAL MORTGAGE FINANCING

Commercial mortgages are intermediate-term (5- to 10-year) loans secured by commercial real estate properties. Examples of commercial properties include factories, warehouse, office buildings, and shopping centers. Commercial mortgages are usually repaid in equal monthly installments. Many new mortgages are for 5 or 10 years, but the loan payments are the same as for a 25-year mortgage. At the maturity of a 10-year mortgage there will be a principal payment due which is approximately 70% of the original amount. This mortgage structure is referred to as a 10-year balloon mortgage with a 25-year amortization schedule.

Mortgage financing is similar to the equipment lease financing provided by finance companies. In both cases the present and projected future value of the underlying collateral is given greater weight than the financial strength and profitability of the borrower.

Though it is of secondary importance, equipment lessors and mortgage lenders do review the borrower's financial statements. In both cases the lenders seek to assure themselves that the borrower is unlikely to default in their loan payments for at least the next 36 months. In those instances where the equipment or the commercial real estate cannot be quickly sold for its fair market value in the event of a default, the lender will place greater emphasis on the borrower's financial strength and less emphasis on the present fair market value of the collateral.

There has been a general long-term increase in the values of most commercial real estate properties, and also in interest rate levels. This has benefited owners of commercial real estate properties but has penalized commercial mortgage lenders who granted fixed rate, long-term (e.g., 25-year) mortgages. The shift to intermediate-term (5- to 10-year) mortgages is one way in which mortgage lenders have responded to this environment.

It has also become increasingly common for mortgage lenders to seek to share in the appreciation of the underlying properties and/or to have interest rates change annually and/or to retain tax benefits generated by the commercial real estate properties. In the latter case, the mortgage financing is structured as a sale and lease back of the commercial real estate. For the borrower, the incentive for accepting these modifications to the traditional long-term fixed rate mortgage are a larger loan amount and a lower initial interest rate.

Some commercial mortgage lenders will consider providing commercial mortgages which finance both the underlying real estate and the owner/users machinery and equipment. A lender's willingness to provide a commercial mortgage of this type is based on the company's profitability and financial strength. First mortgage bonds issued by utilities are an example of this type of mortgage financing.

VENTURE CAPITAL LOANS

Venture capital loans are a hybrid form of financing. The loans usually take the form of subordinated debt or preferred stock. In exchange for accepting an unsecured position, and a below-market interest rate, the lender obtains some type of profit-sharing participation. There are dozens of different structures used for venture capital loans. The most popular are:

1. Subordinated convertible bonds.
2. Subordinated bonds with warrants to purchase common stock.
3. Convertible preferred stock.
4. Tax shelter partnerships which own depreciable assets (equipment or commercial real estate) which is leased to the company for a long period. The partnership shares in the profit and/or residual value of the assets but receives a below-market lease payment.

The supply of venture capital is less than 10% of the demand for venture capital financing. Even though some types of venture capital sources (e.g., SBICs) are oriented to smaller companies, most smaller companies have difficulty obtaining venture capital financing.

HOW THE TYPE OF LOAN AFFECTS THE ACQUIRER'S INTEREST EXPENSE AND CASH FLOW

1. Revolving credit lines have the lowest interest rate and require no principal payment as long as the collateral base (e.g., accounts receivable) remains at the same level or increases. There is a potential problem, however, because

revolving credit lines must be renewed annually. Thus, when a company's profitability and financial strength temporarily decline, it has the added risk that its revolving credit lines may be canceled.

2. Term loans carry a higher interest rate than do revolving credit lines. They require periodic payments of principal and accrued interest. The longer the repayment period, the lower the amount of each periodic principal payment. This increases the interest payment, but not nearly as much as each principal payment is reduced. The loan payments for a term loan (principal plus accrued interest) decline each year but are highest the first year.

3. Equipment lease payments stay constant throughout the term of the lease. The implicit interest rates may be higher or lower than for a term loan depending on the value of tax benefits which are retained by the lender. A key advantage of equipment lease financing is that the lease payments for the earlier years tend to be lower than the loan repayments required for a comparable term loan. This is when an acquirer is likely to need to minimize its payments because it needs its cash to pay expenses associated with the acquisition.

4. Commercial mortgages are likely to carry a higher interest rate than are the other types of financing. The principal advantage is that the monthly loan payments are much lower than for term loans and equipment leases.

5. Venture capital loans are term loans which have a lower interest rate and a lower required principal repayment rate than would be customary for term loans which did not involve an equity kicker for the lender.

MAKING YOUR COMPANY MORE ATTRACTIVE TO BUSINESS LENDERS

Factors which make a company more attractive to business lenders

The factors which make a company more attractive to business lenders fall into two categories. These are:

1. The availability of reliable written material which help a lender to analyze the prospective borrower's ability to repay a new loan and the lender's potential loss if the borrower was unable to repay the loan. In this chapter, you will learn how to develop written presentations which make a company more attractive to prospective lenders.

2. The strengths and weaknesses indicated by the financial data contained in these written presentations. In this chapter, you will become aware of practices

which make a company's financial data appear less attractive to lenders and some techniques for correcting these distortions.

Written materials which help a lender to analyze your company's borrowing capacity.

1. Written materials which indicate how much future cash flow the company can generate from operations. Examples of these written materials include your company's income and cash flow statements for past years and your business plan and financial projections for the current and future years.

2. Written materials which indicate how much cash flow your company will be able to generate by converting assets (e.g., accounts receivable) into cash. Examples of these written material include the items mentioned in (1) and your company's balance sheet and asset schedules (e.g., accounts receivable agings).

3. Written materials which indicate how much cash your company would generate if it was forced to cease operations and liquidate its assets. Examples of these written materials include your balance sheet, asset schedules, liability schedules, existing loan agreements, and appraisals of your fixed assets.

4. Written materials which help a lender to understand your company and its business. They include a business description, customer and supplier lists, market studies, an organization chart, and resumes of your key executives.

Factors which increase (in the lender's mind) the reliability of these written materials

1. *Completeness.* Lenders are more likely to believe the financial projections of a company whose management appears to be knowledgeable and professional. The availability of business plans, market studies, and asset appraisals are considered by lenders to indicate that a company has professional, knowledgeable management.

2. *Full disclosure.* Lenders (particularly banks) assume that anything not mentioned in your written materials (e.g., contingent liabilities, foreign competition, union contracts) is a problem area which reduces the reliability of your financial projections. Unless you mention and analyze the impact of such items, the lender's analysts may discount your earnings projections by unrealistically large amounts.

3. *Standard presentation formats.* Lenders are suspicious of financial data which are not presented using the same formats used by public companies and by large professional firms (e.g., real estate appraisers, marketing consultants,

accountants). You should use standard formats for presenting your company's financial data to lenders even though the formats your management uses for their own analysis and decision making may be more meaningful.

4. *Conservative assumptions.* Lenders are suspicious of financial projections which assume a rapid increase in sales or profit margins. They will generally accept a projected annual increase in sales and expenses of 6% to 8%.

	CURRENT YEAR	ADJUSTMENT	NEXT YEAR
Revenues	$5,000,000	+8%	$5,400,000
Expenses	4,700,000	+8%	5,076,000
Pretax income	$ 300,000		$ 324,000

5. *Preparation by outside professionals.* Lenders are suspicious of unaudited financial statements. They prefer that these statements be prepared by a national firm or an established regional firm. The preparation of your company's financial statements is discussed in greater detail in subsequent sections of this chapter.

WHY A PROSPECTIVE ACQUIRER SHOULD MAKE ITSELF MORE ATTRACTIVE TO LENDERS PRIOR TO LAUNCHING AN ACQUISITION PROGRAM

1. Lenders who provide financing secured by the assets and earning stream of the acquisition candidate base their decisions on the combined attractiveness and financial strength of *both* the acquiring company and the selling company. Therefore, you can increase your acquisition financing capacity by making your own company more attractive to lenders.

2. The same factors which make a company more attractive to lenders also make it attractive to the owners of profitable selling companies. Selling companies are wary of negotiating with prospective acquirers which show poor earnings or weak financial statements.

3. The volatility of the economic conditions in various industries has increased. Over the next five years, many companies will need to make unexpected capital investments in order to remain competitive. It is wise to begin now making your company attractive to lenders. Even if you fail to make an acquisition at this time, your company is likely to need better access to lenders sometime over the next few years.

WHY A PROSPECTIVE ACQUIRER SHOULD INCREASE ITS BORROWING CAPACITY PRIOR TO ITS LAUNCHING AN ACQUISITION PROGRAM

1. The amount of financing which can be obtained using the assets and earnings stream of the selling company is rarely sufficient to pay the entire purchase price of the acquisition.

2. The greater the proportion of the purchase price which the acquirer can pay without borrowing against the assets of the selling company, the more likely it is that the seller will agree to finance a portion of the purchase price.

3. A prospective acquirer will find that there is not sufficient time to line up enough outside financing in those rare instances when the selling company can be acquired for a bargain price. This is because the below-market price generally reflects the desire of the company's owners to dispose of the company quickly in an all-cash sale. Examples of when this situation occurs include:

   a. The sale of a company held by an estate
   b. The sale of a subsidiary or division by a large public company

THE BUSINESS LENDER'S OBJECTIVES

1. To maximize the difference between the interest rate which the lender pays for funds and the interest rate which the lender charges the company. Since lenders are highly leveraged, a small increase (e.g., one-fourth of 1% per year) in the interest rate charged to a borrower will significantly increase the profitability of that loan transaction. The spread between a bank's cost of funds and the interest rate which it charges smaller companies is typically 2% to 4%. The spread for finance companies is typically 3% to 6%, but they have higher administrative costs and loan losses.

2. To minimize loan losses. Lenders are very vulnerable to loan losses because their gross profit margin on losses is only 2% to 6% per year. A bank, for example, cannot afford to have more than 1 loan, out of every 40 loans it makes, fail to repay in full.

3. To maximize the average amount of loans outstanding which generate satisfactory interest rate profit margins but are unlikely to produce loan losses.

4. To reduce the proportion of its gross interest rate profit margin which is needed to pay the costs associated with establishing and maintaining a relationship with a business borrower. A lender can accomplish this by making

larger loans for longer terms. In doing so, however, the lender may increase its risk of loan losses and/or accept a lower gross interest rate profit margin.

WHAT THIS MEANS FOR YOUR COMPANY

1. Lenders (e.g., banks) who charge the lowest interest rates must offset their lower profit margin by making loans which are less likely to produce any loan losses. They are, therefore, less likely to loan as much to a smaller company and are more likely to insist on a relatively rapid loan repayment schedule.

2. Lenders (e.g., finance companies) who do a lot of asset-based lending are usually better able to liquidate collateral when a loan goes bad. This reduces their loan losses for bad loans and makes them more willing to lend larger amounts to smaller companies for longer periods.

3. Lenders who don't understand your company's business cannot accurately estimate their loan loss risk. Their typical reaction is to overestimate this risk in order to be "on the safe side." This results in their offering you a smaller loan for a shorter period.

4. You can generally obtain longer loans for longer periods if you seek out lenders who meet the following criteria:

   a. They typically charge somewhat higher interest rates than do more conservative lenders such as small local banks.

   b. They specialize in asset-based lending.

   c. They are experienced lending to companies in your industry.

5. The lending marketplace is very changeable. Lenders become more or less aggressive depending on their own availability of loanable funds, their recent loan loss experience, and the competitive environment. Keeping track of which lenders are aggressively seeking new business and which lenders are temporarily out of the market provides a good livelihood for investment bankers and finance brokers. Unfortunately, most smaller companies cannot expect to obtain the services of the better investment bankers and finance brokers because these experts cannot earn enough compensation to justify their working on loan transactions of less than $5 million. The smaller company should, therefore, periodically conduct its own survey of business financing sources.

6. A lender will give you larger loans, with a longer repayment schedule, if the lender feels that there is little risk that they will incur a loss due to your inability to make loan payments. Your job is, therefore, to show a lender that your company:

   a. Has demonstrated its ability in prior years to generate good profits and cash flow.

b. Can demonstrate that it will generate sufficient earnings and cash flow in future years to repay the loan and provide an adequate safety margin.

c. Thoroughly understands its own business and the industry trends.

d. Has the management strength, competitive position, and financial strength necessary to continue operating successfully over the next few years.

e. Can offer sufficient collateral to protect the lender in the unlikely event that your company is unable to generate sufficient cash flow to repay its loan.

THE REASONS WHY THE FINANCIAL STATEMENTS OF MOST PROFITABLE PRIVATE COMPANIES ARE AN OBSTACLE TO OBTAINING SATISFACTORY FINANCING FROM FINANCIAL INSTITUTIONS

1. Many privately owned companies do not have audited financial statements. Lenders automatically discount the earnings shown in unaudited statements because they feel that they are less reliable than audited statements.

2. Many private companies prepare their financial statements on a tax basis rather than a "book basis." This substantially understates a profitable company's net worth.

3. The financial statements of many private companies reflect their owner's aggressive use of tax avoidance techniques. These techniques save taxes but reduce the reported earnings and net worth shown on a company's financial statements.

PRINCIPAL DIFFERENCES BETWEEN FINANCIAL STATEMENTS PREPARED ON A TAX BASIS AND FINANCIAL STATEMENTS PREPARED ON A BOOK BASIS

1. Fixed assets (plant, equipment, vehicles, tools, etc.) are depreciated more rapidly for tax purposes than for book purposes.

2. Some types of costs such as research and development expenditures are expensed for tax purposes but are amortized over several years for book purposes.

3. For tax purposes a company typically seeks to set up the maximum loss reserve for bad debts permitted by the IRS. For book purposes, a company typically seeks to set up a smaller loss revenue.

WHEN TO USE EACH TYPE OF FINANCIAL STATEMENTS

1. Your tax-basis financial statements accompany your annual corporate tax returns.
2. Your book-basis financial statements are used when you seek financing.

WHEN A PRIVATE COMPANY SHOULD HAVE AUDITED FINANCIAL STATEMENTS

Audited financial statements significantly improve a profitable company's ability to obtain debt financing. Companies which have audited financial statements can generally borrow larger amounts, for longer terms, at lower interest rates, than similar companies which do not have audited financial statements. The annual costs of audited financial statements for a smaller company is approximately $10,000 to $30,000 higher than its accounting expense for unaudited statements. Therefore, your decision whether or not to have audited financial statements will depend on how important debt financing availability is to your present business, and whether your company is likely to need more debt financing in the future.

WHOM TO USE TO PREPARE YOUR AUDITED FINANCIAL STATEMENTS

Lenders prefer to deal with companies whose audited financial statements are prepared by an accounting firm which they know and trust. Generally, these are the national and regional accounting firms. A small company switching to audited statements should therefore employ one of these accounting firms which are acceptable to most lenders.

A LENDER'S OBJECTIVES WHEN THEY REVIEW YOUR COMPANY'S FINANCIAL STATEMENTS

1. To determine whether your company competes effectively within its industry in terms of profitability

2. To determine whether your company's competitiveness has been improving or deteriorating in recent years

3. To determine how much money your company will have available for loan repayment

4. To determine your company's chances of surviving a temporary decline in sales volume and profitability

5. To determine how much they would be likely to lose if your company failed to repay its loans and they were forced to liquidate your company's assets which they hold as collateral

HOW A LENDER ANALYZES YOUR COMPANY'S FINANCIAL STATEMENT

1. The lender compares your profit, cash flow, and revenue generation with that of similarly sized companies in your industry. The following are examples of ratios which are used to make these comparisons:

   a. Return on equity (pretax profit divided by net worth)
   b. Return on assets (pretax profit divided by total assets)
   c. Cash flow on equity (cash flow divided by net worth)
   d. Cash flow on assets (cash flow divided by total assets)
   e. Sales on equity (sales divided by net worth)
   f. Sales on assets (sales divided by total assets)

2. The lender analyzes the year-to-year changes in your sales, profitability, and cash flow generation.

3. The lender compares your leverage with that of other similarly sized companies in your industry, and with their own internal credit guidelines. The following are examples of the ratios used to make these comparisons.

   a. Debt to equity (total liabilities divided by net worth)
   b. Current assets to current liabilities (current assets divided by current liabilities)

4. The lender analyzes year-to-year changes in your leverage ratios.

TRENDS AND RATIOS WHICH A LENDER LIKES TO SEE WHEN THEY ANALYZE YOUR FINANCIAL STATEMENTS

1. A general upward trend in sales, pretax profits, and cash flow.

2. Reasonably stable profit margins.

3. Profitability, cash flow, and revenue generation ratios which are not too different from those of other similarly sized companies in your industry. When your ratios are significantly lower than the industry average, a lender becomes concerned that your company may not be competing effectively. When your ratios are significantly higher than the industry average, a lender becomes concerned that over the long term they cannot be maintained at these high levels.

4. Current assets at least 50% higher than the current liabilities.

5. A debt-to-equity ratio which is similar to the industry average and which has not increased significantly in recent years.

WHAT TO DO BEFORE YOU USE YOUR FINANCIAL STATEMENTS TO SEEK ACQUISITION FINANCING

1. Obtain comparative financial statement information for similarly sized companies in your industry. The preferred source of this information is an annual publication called *Robert Morris Statement Studies.*

2. Analyze your financial statements in the same manner that the lender will. There are many good handbooks on financial statement analysis that can guide you. These are available at many large bookstores and most business libraries. One such book is *Financial Tools for the Non-Financial Executive,* written by Bryan E. Milling and published by Chilton Press, Radnor, PA (1983).

3. When time permits, take steps to improve your balance sheet and/or income statement ratios, if they do not meet industry standards.

4. When your income statement ratios (e.g., gross profit margins) are significantly higher or lower than the industry averages, provide a written explanation. When these differences are due to your use of tax avoidance strategies which understate your company's income, you should prepare pro forma income statements. These pro forma statements will show your pretax profits and cash flow prior to any direct or indirect compensation paid to owner executives, and to affiliated entities (corporations, partnerships, trusts, retirement plans, etc.).

STRATEGIES WHICH PRIVATELY OWNED COMPANIES CAN USE TO IMPROVE THEIR BALANCE SHEET RATIOS

1. Replace short-term loans with longer-term loans. This will improve your liquidity ratio, reduce your monthly debt service, and increase your cash flow. The disadvantage of this strategy is that your annual interest expense will be higher, which will reduce your pretax income.

2. Sell and then lease back undervalued fixed assets. This will increase your current assets and net worth. The disadvantage of this strategy is that the lease payments are likely to be higher than the annual depreciation charges and mortgage interest payments you are now deducting as annual expenses.

3. Swap income-producing assets held by the corporation's shareholders for additional common stock or preferred stock in the corporation. This strategy increased the company's net worth and cash flow. The disadvantage is that it may create tax liabilities for the former asset owners. This strategy works best when the assets were originally purchased to provide tax shelter benefits for the individual owners, but these tax benefits have not been used up.

4. Sell additional stock in the company. This strategy increases short-term assets and net worth. The disadvantage is that it dilutes the ownership of the company's current shareholders. Selling new stock to company employees through an employee stock option plan or trust generates special tax benefits which are valuable for some companies.

HOW PROFITABLE COMPANIES CAN IMPROVE THE CASH FLOW AND EARNINGS WHICH THEY SHOW ON THEIR BOOK BASIS INCOME STATEMENTS

1. Reduce your company's use of tax avoidance techniques which reduce the corporation's reported cash flow and after-tax income. Over the long term this will also increase the company's net worth by increasing retained earnings.

2. Steady growth in sales and earnings is more attractive to a lender than are sharp changes in a company's year-to-year sales and earnings. In order to take advantage of this lender attitude, you need to determine at the beginning of the year the level of sales and earnings which you want to report at the year end. Generally a company can legitimately show about 15% of its revenues and/or expenses in the current year or can shift them to the following year. A company should use this flexibility to even out its year-to-year reported sales and earnings.

EXAMPLES OF TAX AVOIDANCE TECHNIQUES USED BY PRIVATE COMPANIES

1. The company reduces its taxable income by maximizing the direct compensation (e.g., generous salaries) and the indirect compensation it pays to owners and their close relatives (e.g., wives, parents, and children). Indirect compensation typically includes company cars, club memberships, and generously funded pension plans.
2. The company artificially reduces its current earnings by expensing investments in fixed assets, setting up unnecessarily high reserves for bad debts, and writing off usable inventory (based on fictitious obsolescence).
3. The owners of the company reduce their personal taxable income by investing their overly generous personal compensation (e.g., salaries) in various tax advantaged investments.

THE EFFECT OF THESE TAX AVOIDANCE STRATEGIES ON A COMPANY'S FINANCIAL STATEMENTS

1. The company's business appears to be considerably less profitable than it really is.
2. The net worth of the company shown on its balance sheet is significantly understated.

HOW A COMPANY CAN OFFSET THE HIGHER TAX LIABILITIES IT WILL INCUR WHEN IT REDUCES ITS USE OF TAX AVOIDANCE TECHNIQUES WHICH PENALIZE ITS REPORTED EARNINGS

1. The company uses the cash it formally distributed as overly generous owner management compensation to purchase tax advantaged investments for its own account. The company can hold such investments without adversely impacting its reported earnings for borrowing purposes because accelerated depreciation does not appear on its book basis financial statements. Corporations have an important advantage as tax shelter investors. They are exempt from many of the IRS regulations which are designed to restrict an individual's ability to obtain maximum benefits from lower-risk tax-oriented investments such as leveraged finance–type leases.

2. The company chooses to own or lease the depreciable assets used in its business based upon the impact this choice will have on both its tax liabilities and its reported book earnings. For example, a company should generally;

    a. Own rather than lease depreciable assets when the expense deductions for tax purposes are greater than the expense deductions for book purposes. In effect you have created your own tax shelter.

    b. Sell and lease back your existing depreciable assets when the expense deductions for tax purposes are less than the expense deductions for book purposes. Special care must be taken when using this technique to first determine the tax consequences.

    c. Rent or lease depreciable assets to your customers instead of giving them title to the assets. This can create a tax shelter for your company's earnings. However, for book purposes it will defer a portion of your profit from the sale and will temporarily increase your leverage ratios.

WHERE TO FIND SUITABLE TAX-ADVANTAGED INVESTMENT OPPORTUNITIES

1. Many equipment leasing companies specialize in creating investment programs tailored to the needs of privately owned corporations.

2. Corporate tax lawyers and tax accountants are usually aware of these opportunities.

You should not seek tax-advantaged investment opportunities from your stockbroker. Most stockbrokers think that they have a good tax shelter product. However, it is usually designed for private investors rather than corporations and is heavily loaded with unnecessary fees and expenses.

YOU CAN SOMETIMES USE ACQUISITIONS TO SHELTER YOUR COMPANY'S TAXABLE INCOME

There are two types of acquisitions which profitable companies use to shelter their income. These are:

1. Acquiring a company which has a tax loss carryforward and/or unused investment tax credits. There are many complicated rules and regulations which the federal government has developed to discourage use of this technique, but it still works. You will need the assistance of a good tax attorney to help you avoid potential problems if you seek to use this type of acquisition to shelter income.

2. Acquiring a company which is in a business which generates surplus tax shelter benefits. Examples of such businesses include:

a. Equipment leasing
b. Real estate development
c. Magazine and newsletter publishing
d. Oil/gas drilling and production

HOW TO ANALYZE OPPORTUNITIES TO IMPROVE YOUR COMPANY'S REPORTED EARNINGS

You will need to be able to make relatively accurate financial projections, and you will need the assistance of an accountant who understands sophisticated corporate finance and tax planning. Fortunately, there are a number of excellent computer programs which make it relatively easy to compare alternative tax shelters, asset purchase, and leasing strategies. These computer programs have made the use of sophisticated financial planning techniques much more accessible to smaller companies and their financial advisors.

INTERNAL RESOURCES WHICH COMPANIES CAN USE TO HELP FINANCE THEIR ACQUISITIONS

1. Current assets not needed to support current operations.
2. Unused credit lines from suppliers.
3. Unused revolving credit loan facilities from banks and finance companies.

HOW A COMPANY CAN INCREASE ITS POOL OF CURRENT ASSETS WHICH IS AVAILABLE FOR INVESTMENT

The various techniques which a company can use to accomplish this objective are called "cash management." They are designed to obtain faster use of revenues while delaying the payment of expenses. The following are examples of cash management techniques:

1. Customers make their payments directly into your bank account. This enables your company to gain use of the funds a day sooner.
2. Employees are paid biweekly rather than weekly.
3. Payment of bills from suppliers is delayed, but not for so long as to either cause the loss of cash discounts or impair the company's credit rating.

HOW A COMPANY CAN INCREASE ITS CREDIT LINES FROM SUPPLIERS

1. Request new credit arrangements or increased credit facilities from all your present suppliers. Provide them with your audited financial statements prepared on a book basis and your financial projections.
2. Occasionally use each of your new credit facilities even though you don't need them. This is necessary to keep the facilities available.

PRINCIPAL SOURCES OF REVOLVING CREDIT LINES

Revolving credit lines are provided by working capital lenders. The two types of lenders which provide revolving credit lines (working capital financing) to smaller companies are commercial banks and finance companies.

WHY YOU WANT TO BE ABLE TO BORROW AGAINST YOUR INVENTORIES

1. It enables you to borrow a larger amount than if you can only borrow against receivables.
2. It can provide you with opportunities to get cash discounts from your suppliers which are often higher than the interest cost of your loan.
3. It reduces your need to use the credit lines provided by your suppliers. These credit lines are valuable when you need cash for an investment because they permit you to borrow 100% of the cost of new inventory. By comparison a bank or finance company will generally only lend 40% to 60% against inventories.

HOW LENDERS VIEW WORKING CAPITAL FINANCING

Lenders love to provide working capital financing (revolving credit lines) to companies because they consider it to be a particularly safe type of lending. They prefer, however, to lend only against account receivables.

WHAT THIS MEANS FOR YOUR COMPANY

1. Working capital lenders will automatically grant a profitable company a revolving credit line secured by its accounts receivables which are not delinquent (over 60 days old).

2. In order to attract new business or retain their present customers, working capital lenders will consider increasing the proportion of a company's receivables against which they will lend. They will rarely, however, volunteer to make this change. A company must usually ask for the change in their accounts receivable lending formula and threaten to take its business elsewhere if not satisfied.

3. Lenders are generally receptive to increasing the maximum dollar amount of a company's revolving credit line if the company has repaid its previous borrowings in a timely fashion. Once again, however, the company must ask for the increase and threaten to take its business elsewhere if not satisfied.

4. The willingness of a lender to offer a company a larger, more liberal revolving credit line facility depends on the following factors:

   a. How attractive the company appears to be in terms of creditworthiness. Earlier in this chapter there is a discussion of how a company can make itself more attractive to lenders.

   b. The interest rate charged by the lender. Generally lenders (e.g., finance companies) which charge higher interest rates for revolving credit loans tend to use more generous formulas to determine borrowing capacity of a smaller company.

   c. The lending institution's current lending philosophy. Lending institutions which are aggressively seeking to increase their loan volume are generally more willing to offer a larger, more liberal revolving credit line facility in order to capture new accounts.

5. Every two years a company should shop around to see whether its present lender is providing it with the largest, most liberal revolving credit facility for which the company qualifies. Frequently, a company's present lender will only

give the company a more generous revolving credit line facility when faced with the prospect that the company might take its business elsewhere.

THE ADVANTAGE OF OBTAINING WORKING CAPITAL FROM A COMMERCIAL FINANCE COMPANY RATHER THAN A BANK

1. A finance company does not have a compensating balance requirement. Many banks require a 10% compensating balance. Thus you may only get 90% of the money you borrow from a bank versus 100% from the finance company.
2. A finance company will lend you a higher proportion of your receivables and inventory.

THE DISADVANTAGE OF BORROWING FROM A FINANCE COMPANY

Finance companies charge higher interest rates. Typically they charge 4% to 6% over prime. This compares with an interest rate of 1% to 2% over prime on revolving bank credit lines.

THE REASONS WHY AN ACQUISITION-MINDED COMPANY SHOULD CONSIDER OBTAINING FINANCE COMPANY FINANCING IN PREFERENCE TO BANK FINANCING

1. The finance company will usually lend you a larger dollar amount against your receivables and inventory. This increases your pool of investment capital.
2. Finance companies are more comfortable than banks, lending against the receivables and inventory of a company you want to acquire.

HOW TO SELECT A FINANCE COMPANY

You should look for a commercial finance company which is actively providing financing to companies in your industry and is actively providing financing for acquisitions.

WHEN TO PREPARE A WRITTEN ACQUISITION FINANCING PRESENTATION

You should begin preparing the presentation as soon as you feel that there is a better than 50-50 chance that you will buy the acquisition candidate. Generally, this is the point at which your company and the owners of the selling company execute a letter of intent. The letter of intent outlines the terms and conditions of the sale which the two parties have agreed to, but it is not a legally binding contract.

THE PURPOSE OF A WRITTEN ACQUISITION FINANCING PRESENTATION

1. To give the prospective lender the information needed to analyze the amount and type of financing they will offer

2. To make your acquisition financing request more attractive to prospective lenders

ELEMENTS OF AN EFFECTIVE WRITTEN ACQUISITION FINANCING PRESENTATION

An effective acquisition presentation consists of two sections. These are:

1. A narrative presentation which includes the following:

   a. A brief description of the terms of the proposed acquisition.
   b. An outline of how you propose to finance the purchase price of the acquisition candidate.
   c. A comprehensive description of your company.
   d. A business plan for your company covering the next two years.
   e. Your rationale of acquiring the acquisition candidate.
   f. A description of the acquisition candidate.

2. A financial presentation which includes:

   a. Financial statements for your company.
   b. Actual and pro forma financial statements for the selling company.
   c. Projected financial statements for the combined companies.

HOW CAN YOU MAKE THE SELLING COMPANY'S FINANCIAL STATEMENTS MORE ATTRACTIVE TO A PROSPECTIVE LENDER

Earlier in this chapter there was a discussion of how to make your own company's financial statements more attractive to a lender. Unless the selling company has taken similar steps to make its financial statement more attractive to prospective acquirers, you are likely to find that the selling company's financial statements understate its income and net worth. When this is the case you will need to develop new pro forma financial statements for the selling company. The following are some of the techniques which are used to develop these pro forma financial statements.

1. The selling company's income statement

   a. Switch from a tax-basis to a book-basis income statement.
   b. Show income prior to expenses for direct and indirect compensation paid to the company's owner/executives.

2. The selling company's balance sheet

   a. Eliminate excess reserves for bad debts.
   b. Show tangible assets (inventories, supplies, plant and equipment, etc.) at their fair market value.

You will need to include a written explanation justifying the differences between the selling company's actual financial statements and the pro forma statements you prepare. When there are substantial differences between the assets shown on the selling company's balance sheet and their fair market value, you should have appraisals prepared by a creditable third party to substantiate the fair market value of these assets.

HOW TO PREPARE YOUR PROJECTED FINANCIAL STATEMENTS FOR THE COMBINED COMPANIES

1. Prepare a new balance sheet for the selling company by allocating the purchase price among the different types of tangible assets owned by the selling company. Then make the changes in your own balance sheet to reflect payment of the purchase price, and combine the balance sheets of the two companies. Your liability accounts for the combined companies will need to include the acquisition financing which you hope to borrow.

2. Prepare projected income statements for the next two years for the combined companies. When these income statements include anticipated cost savings arising from the combination of the two businesses a narrative explanation should be included. You should also provide a narrative explanation justifying projected year-to-year increases in revenues and expenses. Lenders are more likely to accept the accuracy of your revenue and expense projections if you increase both by the same percentage (e.g., 6% per year) and try to be conservative in your growth estimates.

C·H·A·P·T·E·R S·E·V·E·N

ACQUISITION FINANCING SOURCES AND TECHNIQUES

SOURCES OF ACQUISITION FINANCING

Principal sources

1. Banks.
2. Finance companies.
3. Equipment leasing companies (equipment lessors).
4. The portion of the purchase price which the owners of the selling company agree to defer receipt of. This unique source of acquisition financing is discussed separately in the final section of the next chapter.

Secondary sources

1. Insurance companies
2. Thrift institutions
3. Small business investment corporations (SBICs)
4. Private venture capital firms

TYPES OF FINANCING OFFERED BY THESE SOURCES OF ACQUISITION FINANCING

FINANCING SOURCE	REVOLVING CREDIT (WORKING CAPITAL)	TERM LOANS	EQUIPMENT LESSORS	COMMERCIAL MORTGAGES	VENTURE CAPITAL
Banks	X	X			
Finance companies	X	X	X	X	
Equipment lessors			X		
Insurance companies				X	
Thrifts	X	X		X	
SBICs					X
Venture capital firms					X

HOW BANKS VIEW WORKING CAPITAL AND TERM LOAN LENDING

1. Banks usually incur a substantial loan loss if they must take back and liquidate the borrower's collateral. These losses are highest when the collateral consists of plant, equipment, and inventories and are lowest when the collateral consists of cash, marketable securities, and accounts receivable. They therefore prefer to make working capital loans rather than term loans.

2. The purpose of collateral for a bank is to reduce its losses if a loan cannot be repaid. Since a bank assumes that it will incur substantial losses if it is forced to liquidate collateral, its primary objective is to make business loans which will be repaid in full, and on time.

3. Banks rely primarily on a company's financial statements to determine:

    a. Whether to provide financing

    b. Whether to only offer a revolving credit line

    c. Whether to also offer the company a term loan

In reviewing a company's financial statements a bank looks for:

    a. Consistent profitability over a period of years

    b. A moderate amount of debt relative to the company's net worth

HOW BANKS EVALUATE THE BORROWING COMPANY

A bank analyzes a business borrower from three different points of view. These are:

1. *Repayment capacity.* The bank will project your cash flow for the term of the loan and then assume that a portion of this amount will be available for loan repayment. The cash flow projections will be based upon your cash flow for prior years and the cash flow shown on your financial projections.

2. *Liquidity.* This is really two computations. The bank looks at the amount by which your short-term assets exceed your short-term liabilities and the ratio of your short-term assets divided by your short-term liabilities.

3. *Net worth.* This is the amount by which your assets exceed your liabilities. Based on a company's net worth a bank will compute the maximum amount of liabilities which they feel you can handle. This is usually expressed as a leverage ratio which is computed by dividing liabilities by net worth. Different ratios are used as a standard for different industries.

HOW BANKS DECIDE WHAT TYPE OF ACQUISITION FINANCING TO OFFER YOUR COMPANY

1. The bank first decides whether your company is eligible to borrow a revolving credit line secured by accounts receivable.

2. Then the bank decides whether they would also grant your company a revolving credit line secured by your inventories.

3. Then the bank decides whether your company qualifies for a term loan facility.

4. Finally, the bank offers to provide the same types of financing secured by the assets and earnings of the acquisition candidate that they will be willing to lend to your company.

HOW BANKS ANALYZE THE AMOUNT OF ACQUISITION FINANCING THEY WILL OFFER

1. First, the bank decides which type of financing they would offer. This process was described in the preceding section. The type of financing determines

which assets will be included in determining the collateral value of the
acquisition candidate. Revolving credit lines are collateralized by current
assets. Term loans are collateralized by fixed assets.

2. Banks use a set of special criteria to determine the maximum amount which a
company can borrow using the earnings flow, net worth, and assets of an
acquisition candidate. A bank will lend the lesser of:

a. 80% of the acquisition purchase price. Banks never like to lend 100% of
anything. They want to see that the acquirer is putting up at least 20% of the
price using its own resources. Thus if you purchase a company for $1
million which has sufficient earnings to support a $1 million loan, the bank
will still only lend a maximum of $800,000.

b. Two times $(2\times)$ the net worth which would appear on the balance sheet of
your company following the acquisition. This is called the leverage
limitation.

c. The loan value of the selling company's assets less any debt already secured
by those assets. Assuming that the bank is willing to offer both a revolving
credit line and term loan facilities, the loan value of the selling company's
assets are computed using the following formulas:

Accounts receivable	60 to 70%
Inventories	30 to 40%
Plant and equipment	40 to 60%
Other tangible assets	0 to 40%

d. The loan amount which the combined companies should be able to repay
using 70% of the projected cash flow available for loan repayment. They will
generally accept cash flow projections which assume a 6% to 8% per year
increase in revenues and expenses.

3. Banks liberalize their acquisition lending criteria under the following
circumstances:

a. Interest rates and business loan demand are declining.
b. The borrower is considered a "good" customer which the bank does not
want to lose.
c. The borrowing company is very profitable and/or the acquisition candidate
is very profitable.

4. Banks tend to be more cash flow than asset oriented. They will offer larger
acquisition loans to very profitable service companies than the loan value of

their collateral would support. They will offer marginally profitable companies smaller acquisition loans than their collateral would support. Generally, you can expect that a bank will lend three to five times the pretax income of the selling company if both the acquirer and the selling company have good financial statements.

5. Banks will consider the loan value of the assets owned by the company's principals who are guaranteeing the acquisition loan. They are the only type of lender which will lend more money for an acquisition based upon personal guarantees.

WHY OBTAIN ACQUISITION FINANCING FROM A BANK

1. Banks usually grant quick approval for acquisition loan requests from companies with strong financial statements. Finance companies do not respond as quickly because they must conduct a field audit of the acquisition candidate's assets.

2. Banks charge a lower interest rate than other types of lenders.

3. Banks give some consideration to the assets of the company's principals who guarantee the acquisition loan.

4. Some banks are prepared to provide acquisition financing (e.g., an accounts receivable credit line) in partnership with the other types of lenders (e.g., equipment lessors).

5. There are a lot of banks. Some bank in your geographic area is almost always actively seeking to add new business loan accounts.

PRINCIPAL DISADVANTAGES OF OBTAINING ACQUISITION FINANCING FROM A BANK

1. Banks usually offer a smaller loan amount to manufacturing companies than a finance company will offer.

2. Banks usually assign their young, inexperienced loan officers to be the account officers for smaller companies.

3. Bank term loans tend to have a shorter maturity than term loans provided by finance companies. This makes the required loan payments higher even though the interest rate is lower.

HOW BUSINESS FINANCE COMPANIES OPERATE

Business finance companies (e.g., asset-based lenders) borrow from the commercial banks at the prime rate (or sell commercial paper) and then lend to the acquirer at a higher interest rate. They are able to borrow larger amounts for longer terms than your company can borrow directly because the finance company's own net worth and cash flow provides the bank with an additional source of repayment.

Business finance companies are organized to take back and liquidate your assets. They are generally able to liquidate this collateral and lose only 25% of their loan as compared with a 50% loan loss for collateral taken back and sold by a bank.

Business finance companies charge high interest rates (4% to 6% over prime). This enables them to set up a 2% loss reserve (versus one-half of 1% loss reserve for a bank lender).

HOW FINANCE COMPANIES DIFFER FROM BANKS IN THEIR ROLE AS ACQUISITION LENDERS

1. Finance companies will lend to smaller companies which are less profitable or are more highly leveraged than a bank is prepared to lend to.

2. Finance companies will lend a higher proportion of the acquisition candidate's assets than a bank will generally lend. The following chart shows this comparison.

	MAXIMUM LOAN AMOUNT	
LOAN COLLATERAL	BANK LENDER	FINANCE COMPANY
Accounts receivable	60 to 70%	70 to 80%
Inventories	30 to 40%	40 to 50%
Machinery[1]	50%	80%
Other plant and equipment[2]	50%	70%

[1]Quick liquidation value.
[2]Fair market value.

3. Banks and finance companies both grant revolving credit lines secured by accounts receivables. Finance companies are, however, more likely to permit you to borrow against the acquisition candidate's inventories.

4. Banks and finance companies both offer term loans. Finance companies are, however, less restrictive in selecting the companies which are eligible to obtain term loans.

5. Banks generally make three-year term loans to smaller companies. Finance companies also make three-year term loans, but they are more willing than banks to offer a five-year term loan for an acquisition.

6. Finance companies tend to be more familiar with acquisitions than the loan departments of banks.

7. Finance company account officers tend to be older, more experienced, brighter, and better paid than the bank account officers assigned to work with smaller companies.

8. Finance companies charge higher interest rates than banks.

9. Finance companies are primarily asset rather than cash flow lenders. They tend to offer higher loan amounts than banks for acquisitions of manufacturing companies. They tend to offer less attractive financing packages than banks for acquisitions of profitable service companies.

THE DIFFERENT TYPES OF FINANCE COMPANIES

1. *Large national finance companies such as G.E. Credit.* These lenders finance themselves by selling their own commercial paper. These finance companies sometimes pass on a portion of their lower cost of funds to borrowers. These finance companies typically charge interest rates 3% to 4% over prime.

2. *Local and regional independent finance companies.* These lenders finance themselves by borrowing from banks, at the prime interest rate. They typically charge interest rates 4% to 6% over prime. In order to compete, these lenders tend to offer slightly higher loan amounts with somewhat longer repayment terms than the large national finance companies.

3. *Finance company operations of commercial banks.* These finance companies require stronger borrower financial statements than the other two types of finance companies, but charge lower interest rates (2% to 3% over prime). They specialize in lending to companies which are not quite strong enough to qualify for bank term loans.

HOW EQUIPMENT LEASING COMPANIES ANALYZE LOAN RISK

There are two types of equipment leasing companies. One type of equipment leasing company makes loans to large strong companies which qualify for traditional term loans, but prefer to use an equipment lease format. These equipment leasing companies are balance sheet rather than asset-based lenders. They are usually a subsidiary of a large bank. They are of little use to smaller companies. You can usually identify them because they share office space with their parent bank.

Our discussion will focus on the second type of equipment leasing company. These are asset-based lenders which have a lending philosophy similar to that of finance companies. In many cases they are a subsidiary or affiliate of a finance company. Asset-oriented equipment lessors lease equipment to smaller companies because they want to own the equipment when the lease term is completed or they feel that the liquidation value of the equipment significantly reduces their loan risk. Though they want the equipment user to be able to make the required lease payments, they don't care how profitable the borrower will be. Their analysis is therefore based on the following factors:

1. The market for the equipment being leased. They prefer to finance general-purpose machinery and equipment which they can dispose of easily at the end of the lease term, or if there is a default in the lease payments.

2. The depreciation characteristics of the equipment. They prefer to finance equipment which has a long useful life.

3. The likelihood that the company leasing the equipment will remain in business for the life of the lease. They are not particularly concerned that a company is highly leveraged so long as it has demonstrated its ability to survive during periods of poor economic conditions. They do, however, expect a company to show a positive annual cash flow regardless of how profitable or unprofitable it has been.

4. The amount of equipment to be leased. Leasing companies prefer to work on transactions which the amount of equipment to be leased has a fair market value of at least $250,000.

THE ROLE OF EQUIPMENT LEASING COMPANIES IN FINANCING ACQUISITIONS

Equipment leasing companies are the most generous source for financing the acquirer's and selling company's machinery and equipment. In comparison with the banks and finance companies, leasing companies usually:

1. Lend for a longer term (e.g., five years versus three years). This reduces the amount of monthly payments.

2. Lend a larger proportion of the fair market value of used machinery and equipment (e.g., 75% versus 50%).

Equipment lease financing can be used in two ways to help finance an acquisition.

1. An acquirer can often increase its pool of investment capital by selling and leasing back its own machinery and equipment.
2. An acquirer can usually increase the amount of financing secured by the assets of the acquisition candidate by selling and leasing back that company's machinery and equipment.

In both cases a key consideration is the type of equipment to be sold and leased back. Most standard manufacturing equipment and transportation equipment (e.g., trucks, helicopters, tank cars, containers, ships) are eligible for equipment lease financing. Equipment which is very specialized or which depreciates rapidly (e.g., office machines, store fixtures) is usually not eligible for attractive lease financing.

THE DISADVANTAGES OF USING EQUIPMENT LEASING AS PART OF AN ACQUISITION FINANCING PACKAGE

1. There are adverse tax consequences when equipment is sold and leased back. Whether or not these will be significant depends on the structure of your acquisition. They will be a major negative factor if the acquisition is a stock purchase, but are not likely to create a problem if the acquisition was structured as an asset sale. (In an asset sale, the selling company has to absorb most of the adverse tax consequences arising from the sale of used equipment.)
2. The effective interest rate is likely to be higher than for other types of acquisition financing.
3. The borrower gives up some or all of the potential residual value of the equipment being leased.

THE ROLE COMMERCIAL MORTGAGE LENDERS PLAY IN PROVIDING ACQUISITION FINANCING

Companies can borrow a higher proportion of the fair market value of real estate assets than they can borrow against other tangible assets. Generally, the commercial real estate owned by both the acquiring company and the selling company can be refinanced to generate cash which can be used to finance a portion of the cost of an acquisition.

The amount of real estate financing which a company can borrow depends on five factors. These are:

1. The fair market value of the commercial real estate properties.
2. The location and type of properties. Lenders don't care how useful the property is to the owner/user. They look for properties for which they are a large number of prospective users in the event that they are forced to foreclose on the property.
3. The borrower's ability to make the monthly loan payments for at least the next 36 months.
4. The willingness of the borrower to give up a portion of the future appreciation in market value of the property and/or the borrower's willingness to give up the tax benefits generated by the ownership of commercial real estate. A borrower can, for example, obtain a larger loan at a lower interest rate if the real estate financing is structured as a sale and lease back.
5. Interest rate levels and the availability or scarcity of long-term credit.

In addition to being able to borrow a larger proportion of fair market value, real estate loans have the lowest required monthly repayments per dollar borrowed. This benefit is due to the small amount of principal repayment. During the first ten years of a mortgage, or sale and lease back, real estate financing is almost equivalent to a long-term interest loan only.

THE DISADVANTAGES OF USING REAL ESTATE LOANS TO HELP FINANCE AN ACQUISITION

1. The interest rate on the new debt is likely to be significantly higher than the present mortgages on the properties. Lenders who hold existing mortgages frequently have the right to prevent the owner from obtaining a second mortgage on the property. Thus it is often necessary to pay off old low-interest-rate mortgages with new higher-interest-rate mortgages in order to increase the mortgage loan amount.
2. In order to obtain a new mortgage at a reasonable interest rate, the borrower may need to give up to the lender a portion of any future increase in the value of the real estate properties.

3. The interest rates for commercial mortgages are higher than are the interest rates for other types of business financing such as revolving credit lines and term loans.

SOURCES OF COMMERCIAL MORTGAGE FINANCING

Traditionally life insurance companies and commercial banks have been a principal source of commercial mortgages for smaller companies. Commercial banks viewed such mortgage financing as an accommodation for their better business borrowers. Since 1988 thrift institutions have become less active funding commercial mortgages. Finance companies are becoming an important source of commercial mortgages. The term "credit companies" refers to the real estate lending divisions of finance companies.

Mortgage brokers play a key role in arranging commercial real estate financing. Smaller companies are advised to use this resource for the following reasons:

1. The lenders who are active providing commercial real estate financing change each month. It is impractical for a company to keep track of who is currently in the market.
2. Special expertise is required to prepare an effective real estate financing proposal for out-of-town lenders. These lenders may offer better rates and terms than local lending institutions.
3. There is wide variation between the terms and conditions and the interest rates offered by different lenders. A good mortgage broker can help you select among the alternative types of real estate loans, and then help you find the lender offering the lowest interest rate.

HOW TO FIND AN EXPERIENCED COMMERCIAL MORTGAGE BROKER

The better large mortgage brokerage firms are members of the Mortgage Bankers Association of America, 1125 15th Street, NW, Washington, DC 20005. The better smaller mortgage brokers will be members of your state's mortgage banking association. You can purchase the membership directory of these trade associations or use one at your local library, bank, or S&L.

SOURCES OF VENTURE CAPITAL

1. Small business investment corporations (SBICs)

2. Private venture capital groups

HOW SMALL BUSINESS INVESTMENT CORPORATIONS (SBICs) OPERATE

Small Business Investment Corporations (SBICs) borrow funds from the U.S. Treasury at fixed interest rates, for up to ten years. The amount which an SBIC can borrow is a multiple (e.g., $3\times$) of its own capital. An SBIC generally makes its investments in smaller companies in the form of subordinated debt or preferred stock. The subordinated debt or preferred stock is convertible into common stock, or the SBIC receives warrants which permit it to purchase common stock at a set price per share. An SBIC cannot own more than 49% of a company's stock.

THE ROLE OF SBICs IN PROVIDING ACQUISITION FINANCING

Small business investment corporations are in the business of making loans to companies in order to obtain the right to purchase equity in the company or to convert their loans into an equity interest. The SBICs make their profit by selling these equity investments and then using the proceeds to make new venture capital loans to other companies. Since their objective is to "roll over" their investment portfolio, they prefer to provide financing to private companies which are likely to go public or which are likely to be sold to a larger company, within five years. In order to be of interest to an SBIC, a company should therefore have a plan to go public or sell itself within five years.

SBICs have two objectives. These are:

1. To obtain high enough dividends, interest, and principal repayments from their investment portfolios to repay their loans from the federal government.

2. To earn a 25% to 30% annual compound return on their successful equity investments. This means they want to triple their money within five years. This explains the SBIC's preference for companies in high-growth industries. SBICs tend to be very fad oriented. They typically limit investment to industries which are popular. Areas of present interest include medical and environmental technology companies. (Several years ago they were entranced by the energy and agribusiness industries.)

The typical SBIC financing is a three- to seven-year subordinated loan at a below-market interest rate. The SBIC receives warrants to purchase common stock or has the right to convert the loan into common stock. When the company is already public the conversion price is 20% higher than the current market value of the stock. When the company is privately owned the conversion price is 20% over the current book value of the company's stock.

SBICs are receptive to making venture capital loans to a company which is using the funds to help finance an acquisition. However, they are only a potential source of financing for companies in popular, high-growth industries.

THE ROLE PRIVATE VENTURE CAPITAL GROUPS PLAY IN PROVIDING ACQUISITION FINANCING

Private venture capital groups seek to obtain a high return on their investment by purchasing equity at a bargain price. They look for opportunities to invest in undervalued, profitable, well-established companies, in unromantic industries. Their financial objective is to earn a 30% to 40% annual return on their investment over a five-year period.

Private venture capital groups typically purchase preferred stock or common stock. The company has the right to buy back its stock at the end of the five years, but if this option is not exercised, the venture capital group has the right to buy out the company's other shareholders. The price at which the company can buy back its stock is not unreasonably high if the company continues to generate good profits and has some growth. The price at which the venture capital group can buy out the management's shareholders is based on the company's earnings or net worth at the end of five years. Thus, if the company performs poorly, the venture capital group can buy out the other shareholders for a low price and install new management.

Venture capital groups closely monitor and advise the companies they invest in. This involvement gives conventional lenders a greater degree of comfort. As a result, private venture capital groups tend to be successful at arranging acquisition loans from lending institutions. This is however a frequent source of misunderstandings between the company and the venture capital group. Although the venture capital group has the capital necessary to contribute the necessary equity for the acquisition, their objective is to invest as little of their own money as possible. A company which thought it was getting a larger equity contribution from a venture capital group frequently finds when the transaction is almost completed that it is getting less equity capital and is assuming a larger debt burden than it had anticipated.

Private venture capital groups like to finance acquisitions when the purchase price is relatively low relative to the company's earnings. They generally will lend or arrange to finance up to 80% of equity required for the acquisition so long as the owner/managers contribute the other 20% in cash. They like management buyouts and purchases of larger companies by smaller companies which have excellent managements.

Private venture capital groups are usually good partners. They tend to be sophisticated entrepreneurs and contribute their financial expertise to the companies they invest in. They are, however, tough negotiators and will try to get the maximum equity interest for the lowest possible investment of their own money.

HOW TO IDENTIFY WHICH LENDERS YOU SHOULD CONTACT TO DETERMINE WHETHER THEY ARE POTENTIAL SOURCES OF ACQUISITION FINANCING FOR YOUR COMPANY

Lenders are constantly becoming more or less aggressive and are constantly changing their lending criteria. You must therefore periodically survey those lenders who have provided acquisition financing for growing companies to learn their current lending criteria. Your objective is to determine which of these lenders would consider providing financing for the type of acquisition you plan to make.

There are three sources which can help you to identify which lenders to contact. These are:

1. *Financing directories.* Two such directories are:

> *Corporate Finance Sourcebook*
> National Register Publishing Company
> 3004 Glenview Road
> Wilmette, IL 60091

> *Handbook of Business & Capital Resources*
> Interfinance Corporation
> 305 Foshay Tower
> Minneapolis, MN 55042

2. *Business publications.* Lenders who are aggressively seeking new business may advertise and/or publicize their financing activities. It is a good idea to keep a file of advertisements placed by lenders and articles that mention the lenders providing financing for an acquisition. Good places to look for such advertisements and articles are:

    a. The principal trade periodicals in your industry

    b. Business magazines such as *Inc.*

    c. Business magazines and newspapers oriented to your metropolitan area, state, or region

3. *Industry trade associations*

Lenders who are interested in providing financing to companies in your industry are often associate members of your industry trade association. You can check the association's membership directory. It is also helpful to phone the executive secretary of your trade association. He or she will be able to tell you which lenders have joined the association since the last directory was published.

HOW TO ANALYZE THE FINANCING POTENTIAL OF THE SELLING COMPANY

1. Obtain a realistic appraisal of the selling company's fixed assets (e.g., property, plant, and equipment).

2. Identify and value any surplus assets of the selling company which can be liquidated shortly after it is acquired. Begin lining up purchasers for these assets once the letter of intent is signed by the owners of the selling company. Examples of surplus assets may include supplies, inventories, equipment, and warehouses.

3. Estimate the additional mortgage financing that could be obtained using any real estate owned by the selling company.

4. Estimate the additional equipment lease financing that could be obtained using any equipment owned by the selling company.

5. Estimate the additional term loan financing that could be obtained using the cash flow, profits, and collateral of the selling company.

6. Estimate the additional revolving credit lines that could be obtained using the accounts receivables and inventories of the selling company.

7. Compare the amounts of acquisition financing you could obtain by combining different types of financing. Keep in mind that you cannot use the same assets to collateralize two different loans. For example, a commercial mortgage loan will reduce the collateral available to support a term loan.

ANOTHER SOURCE OF ACQUISITION FINANCING

Another source is the portion of the purchase price which the owners of the selling company agree to defer receipt of.

WHY OWNERS OF PROFITABLE SELLING COMPANIES PREFER TO RECEIVE THE ENTIRE PURCHASE PRICE, IN CASH, AT CLOSING

1. Once the owner/executives of a profitable company have made the psychologically difficult decision to sell their company, they become increasingly reluctant to continue to be involved financially after the sale is completed.

2. The accountants and lawyers who are advising the sellers will usually encourage them to make an "all-cash" sale.

WHY THE OWNERS OF SMALLER SELLING COMPANIES FREQUENTLY PROVIDE SOME FINANCING TO THE PURCHASER OF THEIR COMPANY

This is frequently the only way in which the owners can realize the full fair market value of their company.

WHY THE OWNERS OF A SMALLER COMPANY ARE FREQUENTLY UNABLE TO REALIZE ITS FAIR MARKET VALUE IN AN ALL CASH SALE

1. The accounting and tax avoidance techniques used by many privately owned companies understate their profitability and net worth. This often reduces the amount of financing which the purchaser can obtain to finance the acquisition. As a result, prospective purchasers become less willing to pay a premium over the selling company's book value.

2. Many young growing companies may have excellent future earnings prospects, but their present earnings and net worth do not yet reflect this future value. A prospective purchaser cannot obtain acquisition financing based upon the acquisition candidate's anticipated higher future earnings. The prospective purchaser is, therefore, less willing to pay a premium over the selling company's book value.

3. There may be a few interested buyers for a particular company. This situation frequently occurs when a company is currently unprofitable, or when it is in a depressed industry (e.g., oil/gas production).

PRINCIPAL REASONS WHY PURCHASERS SEEK SELLER FINANCING

1. To enable them to purchase a larger business than they could afford to buy otherwise.
2. To meet the seller's minimum price requirement. When this is higher than the company's fair market value, the purchaser offsets the purchase price premium with a below-market interest rate on the seller's financing.
3. To obtain a lower interest rate, or a longer repayment period, or a larger loan amount than an institutional lender would offer.
4. To motivate former owners who will continue to manage the business by making a portion of the purchase price contingent upon future earnings.

PRINCIPAL WAYS IN WHICH SELLER FINANCING ARRANGEMENTS ARE STRUCTURED

1. Earnouts
2. Installment sales
3. Consulting contracts

EARNOUTS

The purchase price of the acquisition candidate is based, in part, upon its future earnings performance.

How earnouts are structured

1. At closing, the selling company's owners receive the base price in cash. This base price is usually equal to the company's net worth.
2. Additional payments are paid to the seller if earnings from the acquired business exceed certain specified levels.
3. The acquired company continues to operate as a separate entity, managed by its former owners, until the earnout period is over. The typical earnout period is two to five years.

When earnouts are used

Earnouts tend to be used under the following circumstances:

1. The sellers and the purchaser cannot agree on a price, but both agree that the acquisition candidate may be worth more than its book value because of its future earnings potential.
2. The acquirer wants the former owners to continue managing their company for at least the next two years.

Disadvantages of an earnout for the acquiring company

1. It postpones combining operations of the two companies.
2. The additional purchase price payments will be based upon the selling company's future earnings during the two- to five-year period following the acquisition. It is very difficult to develop a formula for computing these future earnings which is comprehensive enough to avoid future disputes. Some examples of issues which must be addressed are:

   a. Will the new subsidiary be charged for a portion of parent company overhead?
   b. What accounting principles will be used to compute bad-debt reserves and depreciation?
   c. What interest rate will be used for loans between the two companies?
   d. What tax rate will be used to compute the subsidiary's after-tax income?
   e. What will be the terms and conditions of the catastrophe clause?

You need a catastrophe clause

A catastrophe clause gives the acquiring company the right to terminate the earnout and replace subsidiary's management. This termination option becomes available only if the subsidiary's earnings fall below a set level for a period of at least a year. It is important for the acquirer that any earnout agreement have such a catastrophe clause.

INSTALLMENT SALES

The owners of the selling company accept interest-bearing promissory notes for a portion of the purchase price. This makes the seller dependent upon the new owner's ability to make these note payments, but induces the purchaser to pay a higher price for the company. At one time installment sales were popular as a tax deferral technique for the owners of the selling company. However changes in the tax laws have reduced the tax benefits of an installment sale versus an all-cash sale.

HOW AN INSTALLMENT SALE SHOULD BE STRUCTURED

1. The seller's loan should be secured by shares in the selling company which are held in escrow by a trustee. The escrow agreement provides that the trustee will vote the escrowed shares as directed by the acquiring company, so long as the note payments are kept current. As the notes are repaid, the shares are released to the acquiring company.

2. The seller's loan is a subordinated debt. This is frequently a source of conflict in the acquisition negotiations. The seller's attorney wants his or her client's loan to be secured by the company's assets. This is, however, impractical because the acquirer will need to use the company's assets to collateralize its working capital credit lines.

HOW EXPERIENCED ACQUIRERS USE INSTALLMENT DEBT ARRANGEMENTS AS A NEGOTIATING TOOL

The acquirer offers a higher purchase price but offsets this by requiring the seller to take back promissory notes at a below-market interest rate for a longer period (e.g., five to seven years) that an institutional lender would offer. This higher purchase price appeals to the seller's ego and is attractive to those sellers who want to have a steady flow of cash rather than a large lump-sum payment. It also enables the prospective acquirer to shut out competing purchasers by making a higher initial price offer. Frequently, acquisitions which are initially negotiated as installment sales at a premium price wind up being cash sales at a lower price when the negotiations are completed.

THE TYPE OF CONSULTING ARRANGEMENTS USED FOR ACQUISITIONS

The consulting agreements offered to owners of selling company are somewhat different from normal consulting arrangements. Some of the terms may include:

1. A much higher annual payment than would be paid for the actual consulting hours which the former owners are expected to provide

2. An expensive automobile provided at company expense

3. Free use of an office and a secretary

4. Continuation of health insurance and other benefits such as country club memberships

5. A generous travel and entertainment allowance

6. The consulting contract is noncancelable for several years

WHY SUCH CONSULTING ARRANGEMENTS ARE ATTRACTIVE TO OWNERS OF MANY ACQUISITION CANDIDATES

1. They appeal to the individuals' egos.

2. They provide a way for the seller to pay less taxes on the portion of the purchase price which would be taxed as ordinary income at the maximum tax rate if received as a lump-sum payment.

3. They help the former owners to make the transition to semiretirement or to fill in the period until they embark on new business ventures.

WHY SUCH CONSULTING ARRANGEMENTS ARE ALSO ATTRACTIVE FOR THE ACQUIRING COMPANY

1. It reduces the cash price which must be paid at closing.

2. The former owners feel more obligated to help the new owners during the transition period which follows the closing.

3. It enables the purchaser to expense for tax purposes the portion of the purchase price which is paid out under the consulting arrangement, rather than assigning that portion of the purchase price to goodwill or to depreciable assets.

YOUR NEGOTIATING STRATEGY WHEN YOU NEED SELLER FINANCING TO MAKE THE PURCHASE

1. Offer 25% more than a cash purchaser would be likely to offer. Typically, this is 25% over book value. For psychological reasons many owners of smaller companies don't want to sell their companies for book value.

2. Set the interest rate on the seller financing at 1% over the equivalent five-year certificate of deposit (CD) rate. For example, if a five-year CD is paying 11%, offer the seller 12% if it is providing financing for five or more years. The seller winds up getting a higher return than if it invested the proceeds of a cash sale and the purchaser obtains a lower interest rate than by borrowing from outside sources. This interest cost saving will offset most of your higher purchase price.

3. Offer to provide the seller with a five-year consulting contract that provides an office, a secretary, a company car, club memberships, travel and entertainment reimbursement, and some cash. This helps to reduce the sellers' resistance to giving up their "baby."

4. Be prepared personally to guarantee the loan. You are probably already guaranteeing so many of your own company's debt obligations that a few more contingent liabilities won't make any difference.

5. The seller's lawyer and accountant will always try to kill a purchase that is not all cash. Your job is to make them aware that the price you are offering is significantly higher than the price the sellers would receive from an all-cash sale.

C·H·A·P·T·E·R E·I·G·H·T

HOW TO DEVELOP AND USE ACQUISITION CANDIDATE VALUATION TECHNIQUES

THE PURCHASE PRICE PROBLEM

Most companies that find a business they want to acquire are still trying to figure out how much they should offer to pay for it when an announcement is made that some other company has contracted to buy that business.

There are two reasons why most prospective acquirers have difficulty valuing acquisition candidates. These are:

1. They fail to recognize the limitations of business valuation techniques. These techniques will not produce a single "right" price which it is okay to pay for a particular selling business. The value which they provide are intelligent estimates based upon a series of assumptions.

2. There are many different ways to estimate the value of a business. Each of these business valuation techniques will produce a different estimated value for a particular selling business. Most prospective acquirers are unsure how and when to use these different value estimates.

THE ROLE OF BUSINESS VALUATION ESTIMATES

The various techniques which can be used to estimate the value of a particular selling business provide guidelines which help a prospective acquirer reduce its risk of either paying too much for a business, or offering too little for a business. When an acquirer pays too much for a business, it wastes scarce capital which could have been used by the company for other purposes such as plant modernization, product development, debt reduction, and making other acquisitions. When an acquirer offers too little for a business, it often loses the opportunity to negotiate to purchase that business. This is because a seller's reaction to a "low-ball offer" is generally to find a different prospective acquirer to negotiate with.

FOUR WAYS TO VIEW THE VALUE OF A SELLING BUSINESS

A business is a complex combination of people and assets which can create wealth for its owners and attractive compensation for its executives. There are four different ways in which a selling business can give value to the company or investors who purchase it. Each provides the basis for one or more of the valuation techniques described later in this chapter. The four ways of viewing the value of a selling business are:

1. The acquired business has a market value which can be realized by selling the business to some other acquirer. An example of a valuation technique which emphasizes this viewpoint is the comparative market value technique.
2. The assets of the business have a value based upon how much it would cost to replace them. The replacement value technique for valuing a business is based upon this viewpoint.
3. The assets of the business have a value based upon how much they could be sold for. The liquidation value techniques for valuing a business is based upon this viewpoint.
4. The business can produce future cash flow which can either be paid to the owner or which can be reinvested to expand or improve the business. Some of the valuation techniques which assign primary importance to project future cash flow are a return on investment, discounted cash flow, and payback period.

YOUR BUSINESS VALUATION OBJECTIVES

When your company finds a selling business which it would like to acquire you have three valuation objectives. These are:

1. To determine how much the owners of that business can expect to receive based upon current acquisition market conditions. This is called the "fair market value" of a business.

2. To estimate how much the business would be worth to your company if you owned and operated it. This will be referred to as the "acquisition investment" value of a business.

3. To estimate how much money you would recover if the business failed to perform satisfactorily after you owned it, and you therefore subsequently liquidated the business. This will be referred to as the "forced liquidation value" of a business.

WHEN YOU SHOULD ESTIMATE THE FAIR MARKET VALUE OF AN ACQUISITION CANDIDATE

You should make a preliminary fair market value estimate as soon as you determine that an acquisition candidate meets your company's acquisition screening criteria, and you have obtained the financial statements for the selling business. Then you should revise your fair market value estimate when you learn more about the sellers business.

WHY YOU SHOULD ESTIMATE THE FAIR MARKET VALUE OF AN ACQUISITION CANDIDATE

1. *To use your limited acquisition program personnel more effectively.* Few businesses are sold for less than 80% of their fair market value. It is expensive and time consuming to investigate, analyze, and negotiate to purchase a selling business. Therefore, you do not want to waste your limited time and energy pursuing a selling business unless you decide that you might be willing to pay *at least* 70% of its fair market value.

2. *To prepare your initial price offer for an acquisition candidate.* The owners of a business will rarely provide you with access to the confidential information which you need to evaluate their business until after you have made an initial price offer which the owners feel is somewhat reasonable. Your preliminary fair market value estimate provides you with a basis for determining your initial price offer. A "somewhat reasonable" initial price offer is 70% to 80% of the fair market value of a business. As explained in the following paragraph, you can gain a competitive advantage by quickly offering the owners of a business, which you would like to own, a "somewhat reasonable" preliminary price offer.

Once the owners of a selling business receive a somewhat satisfactory preliminary price offer from your company, they will usually refrain from entering into negotiations with other prospective acquirers while their negotiations with your company are continuing. Therefore by making a somewhat satisfactory preliminary price offer to the owners of a selling business, before other prospective acquirers do so, your company in effect obtains an exclusive opportunity to investigate and negotiate to acquire that seller's business, without paying anything for this option.

3. *To avoid overpaying for an acquisition candidate.* You will usually be able to find suitable acquisition candidates in your target industry segment which can be purchased for 80% to 120% of their estimated fair market value. Therefore, you should not let your enthusiasm for a particular acquisition candidate lead you to pay more than 120% of its estimated fair market value.

THE PRIMARY ROLE OF FAIR MARKET VALUE ESTIMATES

Fair market value estimates are primarily designed to help owners estimate the value of their business. Some of the reasons why the owners may wish to know how much their business is worth include:

1. To help them evaluate offers from prospective acquirers.

2. To provide them with "ammunition" to use in their price negotiations with a prospective acquirer.

3. To establish a value to be used to determine how much to pay for, or to receive for selling, an equity interest in their business. For example, a company may wish to sell an equity ownership in the business to employees, key executives, new partners, or investors.

4. To determine the taxable gain or loss when equity interests in a privately owned business are sold or transferred.

It is important to remember that the fair market value of a business is an estimate of how much the business is worth to its owners. It is not an indication of how much the business would be worth to your company. You should only consider paying the fair market value of a business if its value to your company (its acquisition investment value) is the same or is greater than its fair market value.

TECHNIQUES USED TO ESTIMATE THE FAIR MARKET VALUE OF A BUSINESS

There are five types of valuation techniques used to estimate the fair market value of a business. These are:

1. *The comparative market value of the business.* This is an estimate of how much the business would be sold for based upon the prices which were paid for other similar businesses.

2. *Public market value comparisons.* This is a substitute for the comparative market value technique. You use the public market value of similar businesses as your estimate of how much these businesses would be sold for.

3. *The replacement value of the selling business.* This is an estimate of how much it would cost to start up a similar business and grow it to the same size as the selling business.

4. *The liquidation value of the business.* This is an estimate of how much the seller could receive if it sold off its assets and operations in an orderly manner over a period of one to three years.

5. *The investment value of the future annual cash flow which the business is expected to produce for its owners.* There are two techniques which can be used to estimate this investment value. They are the return-on-investment technique and the discounted present value technique.

THE COMPARATIVE MARKET VALUE TECHNIQUE

One of the best ways to estimate the current fair market value of a business is to determine how much that business would be likely to sell for. To do this you first examine, and analyze, the prices paid to acquire other similar businesses in the same industry segment. Though these selling prices will reflect a combination of the size profitability and book values of a selling business, usually only one of these factors will be the primary variable determining the selling prices of similar businesses. Once you have identified which of these factors (size, profitability, or book value) is the principal factor determining the selling prices of these businesses, you can derive a formula which will enable you to estimate the fair market value of the business which you are considering purchasing. Here is an example of how this technique works.

First United Bank of Pennsylvania seeks to acquire a small commercial bank in New Jersey. First United is contacted by a broker representing Sussex Community Bank, a small New Jersey bank which would consider being acquired. First United Bank wishes to estimate the price which it would probably have to pay to acquire Sussex Community Bank. This expected selling price is the fair market value of Sussex Community. Since there have been several recent sales of small New Jersey banks, and the preacquisition financial statements and the selling prices of these banks are known, First United is able to use the market value comparison technique to estimate the fair market value of Sussex Community Bank.

First United starts by obtaining the selling prices and preacquisition financial data for four small New Jersey banks which were sold over the past 18 months. These banks and Sussex United are to be compared in terms of their size, profitability, and book value. There are several different indications of company size and profitability which can be used. The most common size indicator is annual sales. However, in some industries such as banking, a different indicator is used to compare company size. For the banking industry this size indicator is total assets. You can determine the company-size indicator used in a particular industry by reviewing company descriptions in industry trade publications and the reports of industry security (stock and bond) analysts.

Just as there are several different indicators of company size which can be used, there are also several different indicators of profitability which can be used to compare companies in a particular industry. In the banking industry and most service industries net income usually is a good indicator of relative profitability. For manufacturing industries pretax earnings (rather than net income) tend to be the most reliable indicator of relative company profitability because it eliminates distortions in reported net income created by variations in depreciation rates used for fixed assets. When comparing small privately owned businesses which may underreport their earnings in order to reduce their income tax liability, cash flow tends to be the most accurate measure to use when comparing company profitability in a particular industry.

The following is the size, profitability, book value, and selling price data for Sussex Community and the four comparable New Jersey bank acquisitions.

Sussex Community Bank

Assets	$300 million
Book value	$30 million
Net income	$3.6 million

Estimate for fair market value
? (to be determined)

Bank A

Assets	$400 million
Book value	$30 million
Net income	$1 million
Selling price	$40 million

Bank B
Assets	$200 million
Book value	$20 million
Net income	$2 million
Selling price	$30 million

Bank C
Assets	$700 million
Book value	$40 million
Net income	$2 million
Selling price	$60 million

Bank D
Assets	$350 million
Book value	$20 million
Net income	$2 million
Selling price	$28 million

The next step is to compute the relationship of the selling prices of the four banks relative to their size (assets), profitability (net income), and book value. The ratios which are used are:

- Selling price divided by assets
- Selling price divided by book value
- Selling price divided by net income (called the "price/earnings ratio")

These ratio computations for the four banks are:

- Bank A

    Selling price divided by assets = ?

    $40 million divided by $400 million = 10%

    Selling price divided by book value = ?

    $40 million divided by $30 million = 1.3 to 1

    Selling price divided by net income = ?

    $40 million divided by $1 million = 40 to 1

- Bank B

    Selling price divided by assets = ?

    $30 million divided by $200 million = 15%

Selling price divided by book value = ?

$30 million divided by $20 million = 1.5 to 1

Selling price divided by net income = ?

$30 million divided by $2 million = 15 to 1

- Bank C

    Selling price divided by assets = ?

    $60 million divided by $700 million = 9%

    Selling price divided by book value = ?

    $60 million divided by $40 million = 1.5 to 1

    Selling price divided by net income = ?

    $60 million divided by $2 million = 30 to 1

- Bank D

    Selling price divided by assets = ?

    $28 million divided by $350 million = 8%

    Selling price divided by book value = ?

    $28 million divided by 20 million = 1.4 to 1

    Selling price divided by net income = ?

    $28 million divided by $2 million = 14 to 1

The next step is to summarize these ratio relationships:

BANK	SELLING PRICE/ ASSETS	SELLING PRICE/ BOOK VALUE	SELLING PRICE/ NET INCOME
A	10%	1.3 to 1	40 to 1
B	15	1.5 to 1	15 to 1
C	9	1.5 to 1	30 to 1
D	8	1.4 to 1	14 to 1

After preparing a chart such as this you will usually find that a company's selling price tended to be determined primarily by either company size, or company book value or company profitability. Though company profitability (e.g., net income) is more likely to be the principal variable affecting the selling price of a company, this is not the case in some industry segments. In the preceding New Jersey bank example, the principal factor determining selling prices was book value.This was indicated because the selling price–to–book value ratios all fell within a narrower range (1.3 to 1 minimum to 1.5 to 1 maximum) than the other ratios.

Once you have identified the principal ratio determining the selling prices of companies in our target industry segment, you estimate the fair market value of your acquisition candidate by applying the same ratio. In the New Jersey bank example, the selling price–to–book value ratio ranges from 1.3 to 1 to 1.5 to 1. Therefore, the estimated selling price (fair market value) of Sussex Community Bank is computed in the following manner.

- Sussex Community Bank

    Book value × 1.3 to 1 = ?

    $30 million × 1.3 = $40 million

    Book value × 1.5 to 1 = ?

    $30 million × 1.5 to 1 = $45 million

    Estimated fair market value = $40 million to $45 million

THE PUBLIC MARKET VALUE COMPARISON TECHNIQUE

As you know from Chapter 2 of this book, one of the obstacles to developing an effective acquisition program is that the selling prices of companies are rarely disclosed. This can prevent you from being able to use the comparative market value comparison technique described in the preceding section. Fortunately, there is an acceptable (though slightly less reliable) valuation technique which you can use when you are unable to obtain the selling prices, financial performance data (e.g., revenues and profits) and book values for companies which have recently been sold, which are similar to the company which you are considering acquiring. This technique is called "public market value comparisons."

The public market value comparison uses the valuation which the stock market places on a company as a substitute for the actual selling prices of companies which have recently been sold. After you have selected public companies which are similar to the acquisition candidate which you wish to value, you compute their public market value. Then you substitute this amount for the selling price and follow the same procedures which were used for the comparative market value technique described in the preceding section.

The first step in using the public market value appraisal technique is to identify public companies which are similar to your acquisition candidate. These are public companies which are in the same segment of the same industry as your acquisition candidate. For example, if your acquisition candidate manufactured metal fasteners, you would look for public companies whose primary business was manufacturing metal fasteners. To find these public companies you should use the following directories of public companies:

Standard & Poors Corporation Records
Moody's Manuals (OTC, industrial, finance, etc.)

These directories are found in the business reference departments of most larger public libraries.

After you have identified the public companies which are in the same industry segment as your acquisition candidate, your next step is to select from those companies those which are the most similar to your acquisition candidate in terms of size (i.e., annual revenues). Then you obtain current financial statements for these selected public companies by telephoning the companies and requesting their annual reports, Form 10-K, and latest quarterly reports. (The Form 10-K is similar to the annual report but contains some additional information which the SEC requires public companies to file.) Though not necessary for your appraisal, it is also useful to request and read these materials for all the public companies whose primary business is similar to that of your acquisition candidate. The reason is that these materials often contain valuable insights into the current trends and competitive conditions in an industry segment.

In order to compute the value which the stock market is giving to a public company, you multiply the number of shares of common stock outstanding times the current selling price for share. For example, if a public company has 1,000,00 shares of common stock outstanding and its stock is selling for $3.50 per share, its public market value would be $3,500,000 (1,000,000 shares × $3.50 per share = $3,500,000). The number of shares of common stock outstanding is indicated on the company's balance sheet, which you will find in its latest quarterly report. The current selling price per share for most public companies is listed in *The Wall Street Journal* and *Barrons*. When a bid and asked price is listed rather than a selling price per share, you should take the average of these two prices.

Public market value comparisons are one of the most popular techniques for estimating the fair market value of a business. Most appraisal firms rely primarily on this technique when they estimate the value of a business. There are, however, circumstances which can make it impractical or inappropriate to use public market value comparisons to estimate the fair market value of a particular business. These circumstances include:

1. The business is smaller in size than the public companies which operate in the same industry segment in which it operates.

2. The future sales and earnings growth prospects of the selling business are significantly better or worse than the future sales and earnings growth prospects of typical public companies which operate in the same industry segment.

3. There are few public companies which are in the same line of business as the business which is to be valued.

When these circumstances apply, it is necessary to use one of four remaining techniques for estimating fair market value. These are:

1. Asset replacement value

2. Asset liquidation value

3. Return on investment

4. Discounted present value (also called "discounted cash flow")

THE ASSET REPLACEMENT VALUE TECHNIQUE

The asset replacement value of a business is an estimate of how much it would cost to start up a similar business and grow it to the point where it would have the same level of sales, profitability, and market share as the existing business which you wish to value. There are three components of replacement value. The first is an estimate of how much it would cost to replace the assets shown on the balance sheet of the business. The second component is the cost of replacing the assets of the business which are not shown on its balance sheet. Examples of these assets include the company's customer base, sales organization, supplier relationships, product development capabilities, and distribution network. The third component of replacement cost is an estimate of the lost earnings during the period while the start-up business is grown to the size of the business being valued.

The replacement value of a business is most likely to be a good indication of its fair market value when its primary value is the assets which it owns, rather than its current earnings. Examples of this type of business are natural resource producers (e.g., mining companies), real estate holding companies, and companies which own media properties such as newspapers, TV stations, and magazines.

THE ASSET LIQUIDATION VALUE TECHNIQUE

One of the options which the owners of a business have is to convert their business into cash by winding down and liquidating the business over a period of months or years.

The asset liquidation value is an estimate of how much the owners of a business would realize if they used this approach. A rationale for using this fair market valuation technique is that the owners of an acquisition candidate would not sell it for less than they would realize from an orderly, long-term liquidation. However, since the owners would usually prefer to realize this price now, rather than over a period of months or years, they may accept this as being a "fair" price for their business.

The procedure which is used to determine the seller's liquidation value of a business is as follows:

1. List all the assets of the business which could be sold or liquidated by the owners. Examples of such assets might include:

   a. Buildings
   b. Leasehold improvements
   c. Leases
   d. Land
   e. Product line
   f. Machinery and equipment
   g. Inventory (raw materials and finished goods)
   h. Accounts receivable
   i. Securities
   j. Trademarks and trade names
   k. Franchises
   l. Sales organization
   m. Laboratories
   n. Patents
   o. Customer base (market share)
   p. Mailing lists

2. Estimate the amount which each of these assets could be sold for and then add up these amounts.
3. Subtract the selling company's liabilities (debts).

For example, assume that the selling business is an unprofitable wallpaper manufacturing company which has the following assets:

- Two factory buildings
- Three acres of undeveloped land zoned for industrial use
- Manufacturing machinery and equipment

- Inventory
- Cash
- Accounts receivable
- Trademarks and trade names
- Patterns and dies

Since the seller's liquidation value estimate is based on a slow, orderly liquidation of the business, the following assets are assigned 100% of the values shown on the company's balance sheet:

- Cash
- Inventory
- Accounts receivable

The liquidation value of the other assets (e.g., machinery and equipment) is estimated by having appraisals prepared which are based upon the recent selling prices of similar assets. Unless the seller has obtained these appraisals and provided them to your company, you will need to make your own estimates of these asset values in order to come up with a preliminary fair market value for the seller's business. Later you would employ an appraiser to confirm or adjust these value estimates.

There is another faster, though less accurate, way to develop a preliminary estimate of the seller's liquidation value of a company. This is called the "adjusted book value technique." To use this technique, you first take the balance sheet section of the selling company's financial statements. The balance sheet indicates the accounting values of the selling company's assets and liabilities. For example, assume that the balance sheet for the wallpaper manufacturing company showed the following assets and liabilities:

Assets		
Cash	$ 50,000	
Inventory	250,000	
Accounts receivable	300,000	
Current assets		$600,000
Buildings	$400,000	
Less: Accumulated depreciation	(250,000)	
	$150,000	
Land	50,000	
Machinery	300,000	
Less: Accumulated depreciation	(175,000)	
	$125,000	

Total fixed assets	325,000	
Goodwill and other assets	50,000	
Total assets		$975,000

Liabilities

Accounts payable	$100,000	
Loans	100,000	
Total liabilities		200,000
Net worth (book value)		$775,000

In order to compute the adjusted book value you add to the book value shown on the company's balance sheet the amounts indicated for accumulated depreciation. The rationale for this approach is that due to inflation, the current value of buildings, machinery, equipment, and other fixed assets often totals their original cost rather than the depreciated values shown on the balance sheet. Here is the computation for our wallpaper manufacturing company example.

Book value	$775,000
Plus: Accumulated depreciation of buildings	250,000
Plus: Accumulated depreciation of machinery and equipment	175,000
Adjusted book value	$1,200,000

The adjusted book value is then used as your preliminary estimate for the seller's liquidation value.

In the preceding example you will note that it is assumed that the values shown for the nondepreciable assets on the selling company's balance sheet (e.g., accounts receivable) are the same as their liquidation value if disposed of by the present owners of the company. This may seem to represent an overvaluing of these assets since some of thee assets (e.g., inventory) are likely to have a market value which is lower than the amounts indicated on the selling company's balance sheet. You will find, however, that it is usually reasonable to use the balance sheet values indicated. The reason is that most companies will own enough assets which are not shown on their balance sheets (e.g., good inventory which has been written off to avoid income or property taxes) to offset the effect of this apparent overvaluation.

The liquidation value technique is most likely to be a good indicator of fair market value when a business is unlikely to continue to be operated as a "going concern." Usually, these are businesses which have poor earnings and growth prospects.

THE RATIONALE FOR USING FUTURE CASH FLOW–TYPE VALUATION TECHNIQUES

There are many reasons for owning a business. They include power, prestige, independence, job security, financial compensation, investment income, and the creation of wealth. All these are dependent upon the level of future cash flow generated by the business. Therefore, a useful way of valuing a business is to estimate the value of the future cash flow which the business is expected to produce for its owners.

HOW TO ESTIMATE OWNERS' ANNUAL CASH FLOW

The first step in using a future cash flow valuation technique is to determine how much annual cash flow a business is now producing for its owners. This is the amount of cash flow from operations which is available to be distributed to the owners of that business, while still maintaining the competitive strength and the earnings generating capacity of the business. This will be referred to as the "owners cash flow." The procedure which you use to estimate the owners cash flow is to start with the reported after-tax earnings of the business for either the previous fiscal year or a more recent 12-month period. Then three adjustments are made to derive the cash flow available for distribution to the owners of the business. The three adjustments are:

1. Add to the reported after-tax earnings any cash paid to the owners which could have been reported as earnings, but was not. This usually consists of excess compensation paid to owner/executives. Excess compensation is the difference between the salaries benefits provided to owner/executives and the amounts which would have been provided to nonowner executives if they were performing the same job functions. The reason for providing higher than necessary compensation to owner/executives is to reduce the amount of the company's earnings which are taxed twice. Earnings which are to be paid out as dividends are taxed first as corporate income, and then the recipients must pay state and federal personal income tax on their dividend income. In contrast earnings are paid to owner/executives as salaries and benefits they are only taxed as personal income.

2. Add to the reported after-tax earnings expenses which are deducted for tax and accounting purposes but which do not actually involve any cash payout. The two principal noncash charges which need to be added to reported earnings are depreciation expenses and amortization expenses. The combination of reported earnings and noncash charges is often referred to as cash flow. Owners cash flow consists for this amount plus the two additional types of adjustments described in this section.

3. Subtract the average annual amount of cash payments which are not deducted from revenues and earnings, but which do reduce the cash available for distribution to the business owners. These are:

a. Purchases of assets which are amortized or depreciated over a period of years rather than being deducted as expenses when the expenditures are made. Examples of assets which are amortized or depreciated include leasehold improvements, machinery, and buildings.

b. Loan principal payments on the long-term debt of the business.

The following example illustrates how these adjustments are made:

Reported earnings	$100,000	
Depreciation expense	$ 14,000	
Amortization expense	2,000	
Total noncash charges	$ 16,000	
Owner/executives salaries and benefits		$300,000
Comparable salaries and benefits for nonowner/executives		(230,000)
Excess owner compensation		$ 70,000
Purchase of fixed assets	$ 20,000	
New leasehold improvements	5,000	
Purchases of patents and licenses	5,000	
Loan principal payments	4,000	
Total cash expenditures for noncurrent assets and loan repayment	$ 34,000	

Reported earnings	+	noncash charges	+	excess compensation	−	cash expenditures	=	Owners' adjusted cash flow
$100,000		$ 16,000		$ 70,000		$ 34,000		$152,000

Once you have determined the amount of cash flow which the business is now producing for its owners, the next step is to project how much annual owners' cash flow the business will produce in future years. The following are some of the approaches which you might use to project future annual owners' cash flow for a business:

1. The simplest approach is to assume that owners' cash flow in future years will be at the same annual level as it was for the previous fiscal year or 12-month period. This approach should only be used when the owners cash flow is expected to remain relatively stable from year to year.

2. Another approach is to take the average annual owners' cash flow for the past few years and then use this amount as your estimate of the future annual cash

flow which the business will generate for its owners. This approach is appropriate to use when the owners' cash flow generated by a business tends to fluctuate from year to year but there is no long-term trend of increasing or declining annual owners' cash flow. The following is an example of this approach.

YEAR	OWNERS' CASH FLOW
Current year	$100,000
Previous year	80,000
Two years ago	100,000
Three years ago	90,000
Total	$370,000

$$\frac{\$370,000}{4 \text{ years}} = \text{projected annual owners cash flow}$$

$$\$ 92,500 = \text{projected annual owners cash flow}$$

3. Another approach which uses historic annual owners' cash flow to predict future annual owners' cash flow is to compare the current year's owners cash flow with the owners cash flow for some previous year, such as five years ago. Next you compute the average annual increase or decrease in the owners' cash flow. Then you increase or decrease each future year's projected owners' cash flow by this amount. This approach is appropriate to use when the historic trends affecting the owners' cash flow from the business are expected to continue into the future. The following example illustrates this approach:

Current year's owners' cash flow $100,000
Owners' cash flow five years ago   (60,000)
Change in owners' annual cash flow $ 40,000

$$\text{Average annual change in owners cash flow} = \frac{\$40,000}{5 \text{ years}} = \$8,000 \text{ per year}$$

YEAR	PROJECTED OWNERS' CASH FLOW
1 (current year)	$100,000
2	$100,000 + $8,000 = $108,000
3	$108,000 + $8,000 = $116,000
4	$116,000 + $8,000 = $124,000
5	$124,000 + $8,000 = $132,000

A variation of this approach is to compute average annual percentage change in the owners' cash flow for the past few years. Then you apply this point percentage to each years' projected cash flow in order to estimate the owners cash flow for the following year. The following is an example of this approach.

PERIOD	PERCENTAGE CHANGE IN OWNERS' CASH FLOW
Four years ago	5% increase
Three years ago	2% decrease
Two years ago	7% increase
Current year	6% increase
Total net change	16% increase

Average annual change in owners cash flow = $\dfrac{16\%}{4 \text{ years}}$ = 4% increase per year

Current year owners' cash flow = $500,000

Projected cash flow next year = 104% × $500,000 = $520,000

Projected cash flow for the following year (year 2) = 104% × $520,000 = $540,800

Projected cash flow for the following year (year 3) = 104% × $540,800 = $562,432

4. Rather than projecting the change in future owners' cash flow based upon how the earnings level of this business has changed in the past, you could choose to use the historic or projected earnings trend for companies which operate in the same industry segment. This approach is appropriate to use when the future earnings of a business are likely to be determined primarily by industry trends. The following is an example of this approach:

Current year's owners' cash flow = $100,000

Projected industry cash flow trend = +8% year-to-year increase

YEAR	PROJECTED OWNERS' CASH FLOW
1 (current year)	$100,000
2	$100,000 + (8%) $ 8,000 = $108,000
3	$108,000 + (8%) $ 8,640 = $116,640
4	$116,640 + (8%) $ 9,331 = $125,971
5	$125,971 + (8%) $10,078 = $136,049

4. The most sophisticated approach for projecting the future cash flow of a business is to project separately for each future year reported earnings, noncash charges, excess owner/executive compensation, and cash expenditures which are not deducted from current earnings. Then you make the necessary adjustments to the projected reported earnings using the procedures described for computing the current year's owners' cash flow. This approach is the most difficult to use since you need to analyze how several different items (e.g., depreciation) are likely to change each year. However, it provides the most realistic estimate of future owners' cash flow. This is the approach which should be used when the future annual earnings of a business are expected to be significantly different than its present level of earnings. The following is an example of this approach.

YEAR	PROJECTED EARNINGS		NONCASH CHANGES		EXCESS OWNER/ EXECUTIVE COMPENSATION		CASH EX- PENDITURES FOR FIXED ASSETS AND LOAN REPAYMENT		OWNERS CASH FLOW
1 (current year)	$ 50,000	+	$ 20,000	+	$ 25,000	−	$ 50,000	=	$ 45,000
2	50,000	+	20,000	+	25,000	−	80,000	=	15,000
3	200,000	+	30,000	+	30,000	−	50,000	=	210,000
4	200,000	+	35,000	+	35,000	−	100,000	=	170,000
5	275,000	+	45,000	+	35,000	−	70,000	=	285,000
6	300,000	+	45,000	+	35,000	−	50,000	=	330,000
7	325,000	+	50,000	+	40,000	−	150,000	=	265,000
8	350,000	+	55,000	+	45,000	−	50,000	=	400,000
9	375,000	+	60,000	+	50,000	−	50,000	=	435,000
10	400,000	+	75,000	+	55,000	−	50,000	=	480,000
Totals	$2,525,000	+	$345,000	+	$375,000	−	$700,000	=	$2,635,000

In the preceding example you will notice that the current year's owners' cash flow would not have been a good indicator of future annual owners' cash flow for this business.

TWO METHODS FOR VALUING FUTURE OWNERS' CASH FLOW

There are two popular ways of estimating fair market value based upon the projected annual owners' cash flow for a business. These are:

1. *Return of investment (rate of return).* This method is used when the annual owners' cash flow from the business is expected to remain relatively stable or is expected to grow at a steady rate.
2. *Discounted cash flow.* This method is used when the future levels of owners' cash flow are expected to be significantly different than the owners' cash flow for the current year.

THE RETURN-ON-INVESTMENT (RATE-OF-RETURN) TECHNIQUE FOR VALUING OWNERS' PROJECTED CASH FLOW

An individual, partnership, or company which is considering investing in a business which operates in a particular industry segment will usually seek to obtain a specific average annual return on their equity investment. This return on investment is a percentage called the "target rate of return." For larger businesses which are owned by public shareholders or private businesses which are large enough to be likely to be purchased by public corporations, the annual return is the annual cash flow which the business is expected to produce. This cash flow is defined as the reported after-tax earnings plus the expenses deducted for noncash charges to income, such as depreciation and amortization. For small businesses which are likely to remain privately owned, or which are likely to be sold to a privately owned company, the annual return is the owners' annual cash flow. Techniques for estimating the owners' annual cash flow were discussed earlier in this chapter.

The following are the formulas used to estimate the fair market of a business using the return-on-investment technique:

For larger (e.g., regional and national) businesses:

Fair market value = Projected annual cash flow divided by the target rate of return

For smaller (e.g., local) businesses:

Fair market value = Projected owners' annual cash flow divided by the target rate of return

The return on investment technique is generally employed to estimate the fair market value of smaller businesses which are difficult to value using the public market value comparison technique. Therefore, our discussion will focus on how the return or investment technique is used to value smaller, privately owned businesses.

The first step is using the return on investment technique is to estimate the annual owners cash flow which the business is expected to generate. This is the projected owners' cash flow for the next fiscal year, calendar year, or 12-month period. The next step is to estimate the target annual rate-of-return percentage (return on investment) which a purchaser of businesses in the same industry segment would expect to obtain. When the future annual owners cash flow from the business is expected to increase more rapidly than the industry average you adjust for this by using a lower target rate of return. If the future annual owners' cash flow from the business is expected to increase at a slower rate than the industry average, you adjust for this by using a higher target rate of return. The rationale for these adjustments to the target rate of return are:

1. The purchasers of a business would want to receive a higher current rate of return from a business which has below-average growth prospects.
2. The purchasers of a business would accept a lower current rate of return on their investment if the business has above-average growth prospects.

The following example illustrates the use of lower target rates of return for businesses which are expected to grow more rapidly.

COMPANY	NEXT YEAR'S PROJECTED OWNERS' CASH FLOW	PROJECTED ANNUAL % INCREASE IN OWNERS' CASH FLOW
A	$120,000	6%
B	100,000	9 (industry average)
C	80,000	12

PROJECTED ANNUAL CASH FLOW, GROWTH RATE	INVESTOR/PURCHASER TARGET RATE OF RETURN
6%	15%
9 (industry average)	12
12	9

COMPANY	NEXT YEAR'S PROJECTED OWNERS' CASH FLOW	DIVIDED BY	TARGET RATE OF RETURN	=	FAIR MARKET VALUE
A	$120,000		15%		$800,000
B	100,000		12		833,000
C	80,000		9		888,000

In the preceding example Company A had the highest projected owners cash flow for the next 12 months, but had the lowest fair market value due to its poor growth prospects. In contrast Company C had the lowest projected owners' cash flow for the next 12 months, but it had the highest fair market value due to its above-average growth prospects.

THE DISCOUNTED CASH FLOW METHOD OF VALUING OWNERS PROJECTED CASH FLOW

The cash flow which a business produces for its owners this year is more valuable than the cash flow which a business will produce for its owners next year. The reason is that the cash flow generated this year could have been reinvested to generate additional income for one year. The same applies in each subsequent year. The following example illustrates this concept:

Business A

YEAR	OWNERS' CASH FLOW FROM THE BUSINESS	AMOUNT INVESTED	INTEREST RATE ON CASH INVESTED	INVESTMENT CASH FLOW	COMBINED OWNERS' CASH FLOW
1	$100,000	$100,000	10%	$ 0	$100,000
2	0	0	10	10,000	10,000
3	0	0	10	10,000	10,000
Totals	$100,000	$100,000		$20,000	$120,000

Business B

YEAR	OWNERS' CASH FLOW FROM THE BUSINESS	AMOUNT INVESTED	INTEREST RATE ON CASH INVESTED	INVESTMENT CASH FLOW	COMBINED OWNERS' CASH FLOW
1	$ 0	$ 0	10%	$ 0	$ 0
2	0	0	10	0	0
3	100,000	100,000	10	0	100,000
Totals	$100,000	$100,000		$ 0	$100,000

As you can see from this simplified example both Business A and Business B generated owners' cash flow of $100,000. However, because Business A generated its cash flow in year 1, it was reinvested for two years. Therefore, the owners' combined cash flow was 20% higher ($120,000 versus $100,000) for Business A than for Business B, even though both businesses generated the same level of cash flow from operations over the three-year period.

The discounted cash flow method seeks to adjust the value of projected future owners' cash flow for a business to reflect the timing differences illustrated in the preceding example. It does this by reducing ("discounting") the value of future cash flow according to how long it will be until that cash flow is generated by the business, and is therefore available for reinvestment by the business owners to generate interest income. The estimated interest rate for the reinvested cash is called the annual discount rate. The cash flow which is expected to be generated by the business in year 1 is valued at 100%. The projected cash flow for the following year (year 2) is valued at 100% minus the interest rate which the business owners would have earned if this cash flow had been available to be reinvested in year 1. For example, if the owners could have invested the cash income in bonds yielding a 9% interest rate, the cash income for year 2 would be valued at 100% minus 9%, which is 91%. The percentage (91%) or equivalent fraction (0.91) which is used to reduce the value of the second year's cash income is referred to as the "discount factor" for that year. For the third year, the discount factor is computed by taking the discount factor for the second year and subtracting 9% times that discount factor. This computation would be

$$91\% - (91\% \times 9\%) = 0.91 - (0.91 \times 0.09) = 0.9100 - 0.0819 = 0.8281$$

There is considerable disagreement regarding the appropriate discount rate to use when computing the annual discount factors. The most commonly used approach is to use a 10% discount rate. The following schedule indicates the discount factor which would be used for each year using a 10% discount rate. These discount factors will be used in the example illustrating the use of the discounted cash flow method for estimating the fair market value of a business.

YEAR	DISCOUNT FACTOR	
1	100%	(1.0)
2	90	(0.90)
3	81	(0.81)
4	73	(0.73)
5	66	(0.66)
6	59	(0.59)
7	53	(0.53)
8	48	(0.48)
9	43	(0.43)
10	39	(0.39)

The following is an example of how the discounted cash flow method is used to estimate the present value of the projected future owners cash flow for a business:

Modern Wallpaper Company, Inc., is expected to generate cash flow of $200,000 this year. While annual cash flow has fluctuated from year to year, for the past five years it has increased by an average of $30,000 per year. It appears that this trend is likely to continue. Therefore, the projected annual cash flows for the company are:

Year 1	$200,000
Year 2	230,000
Year 3	260,000
Year 4	290,000
Year 5	320,000
Year 6	350,000
Year 7	380,000
Year 8	410,000
Year 9	440,000
Year 10	470,000

Assuming a 10% discount rate, the present value of these cash flows would be computed by multiplying each years cash flow by that year's discount factors. The following chart indicates these computations:

YEAR	OWNERS' CASH INCOME		DISCOUNT FACTOR		PRESENT VALUE
1	$ 200,000	×	1.0	=	$ 200,000
2	230,000	×	0.90	=	207,000
3	260,000	×	0.81	=	211,000
4	280,000	×	0.73	=	212,000
5	320,000	×	0.66	=	211,000
6	350,000	×	0.59	=	207,000
7	380,000	×	0.53	=	201,000
8	410,000	×	0.48	=	197,000
9	440,000	×	0.43	=	189,000
10	470,000	×	0.39	=	183,000
Totals	$3,350,000				$2,018,000

In this example the estimated value of the projected future owners cash income for the next 10 years was approximately $2 million. However, in this presentation no value was given for projected annual owners' cash flow beyond the tenth year. One way of handling this would be to project annual owners' cash flow for a longer period such as 20 years, and then compute and add the present value at these subsequent earnings. The problem with this approach is that it is difficult to predict accurately the cash flow which a business would generate for its owners so far into the future. Therefore, an alternative approach which is generally employed is to assume that the businesses will be sold or liquidated the end of the tenth year and to add this "residual" value to the owners' cash flow in the tenth year. One method used to estimate this residual value is to assume that the current book value (net worth) of the business will be equivalent to its residual value at the end of the tenth year. The rationale for using this estimate is that declines in the value of the fixed assets of the business due to depreciation and technological change will be offset by increases in the value of these assets due for inflation. Assuming that Modern Wallpaper Company has a current book value of $700,000 and this is used as our estimate of its liquidation value at the end of the tenth year, the computation would be:

$$\text{Liquidation value} \times \text{discount factor} = \text{Present value}$$
$$\$700,000 \quad \times \quad 0.39 \quad = \quad \$273,000$$

Present value of future owners cash income for years 1 to 10	$2,018,000
Plus: Present value of liquidation value	273,000
Estimated fair market value	$2,291,000

HOW TO CHOOSE WHICH FAIR MARKET VALUATION TECHNIQUES TO START WITH

Once you have obtained the financial statements of a selling business, the sellers will expect you to make a purchase price offer within two to three weeks. Unless this initial purchase price offer is at least 70% of the fair market value of the selling business it is unlikely that its owners will consider you to be a serious buyer. Unless the owners of a selling business feel that you are a serious buyer, you will have little chance of negotiating the acquisition of that business. Therefore, you want to start with a fair market valuation technique which you can use quickly and easily so that you will obtain your fair market value estimate before you need to make your initial price offer for the selling business.

The second factor which you need to consider is which of these fair market valuation technique is likely to provide a more accurate estimate of the fair market value of a particular selling business. Different valuation techniques tend to produce better fair market value techniques for different types and sizes of businesses. Therefore, you want to try to select a valuation to technique which is appropriate to the type and size of the business you wish to value.

The way in which you combine these two objectives is to start with the three fair market value techniques which require the least amount of time and effort to employ. These are:

1. Public market value comparisons
2. The adjusted book value method of estimating the liquidation value of a business
3. The return-on-investment method of estimating the value of projected owners' cash income.

Then you use the following guidelines to help you decide which of these three techniques to employ:

	SUITABLE VALUATION TECHNIQUES		
	PUBLIC MARKET VALUE COMPARISONS	ADJUSTED BOOK VALUE	RETURN ON INVESTMENT
Small, local business		x	x
Medium-sized regional business	x		x
Large national business	x		x
Profitable, growing business	x		x
Unprofitable business		x	
Depressed/unpopular industry segment		x	x
Manufacturing industry	x	x	
Wholesaling industry	x	x	
Service industry	x		x

DEFINING ACQUISITION INVESTMENT VALUE

Acquisition investment value is an estimate of how much a particular selling business would be worth to your company if you owned it. The value of a selling business to your company can come from either of two sources. These are:

1. *The additional cash flow which your company is likely to obtain by owning that business.* This additional cash flow is the difference between the cash flow you expect your own business to generate and the cash flow which your company

expects to be able to obtain if you owned both your present business and the selling business. The following example illustrates this concept.

A&L Plumbing Supply Company is a plumbing supply distributor located in Dallas. The company generates annual cash flow for its owners of approximately $400,000 per year. A&L Plumbing Supply Company is considering purchasing a smaller competitor, Quality Plumbing Supply Company. Quality Plumbing Supply Company generates annual cash flow of $100,000 for its owners. A&L Plumbing Supply has analyzed the revenues and expenses of its company if the two businesses were combined. Due to the projected cost savings from combining duplicate facilities and functions, A&L Plumbing Supply estimates that the combined businesses would generate owners cash flow of $525,000 per year. Therefore, the additional cash flow which A&L Plumbing Supply expects to obtain if it owned Quality Plumbing Supply Company would be $125,000. The computation used to derive this was $525,000 minus $400,000 equals $125,000.

2. *The value to your company of the tangible and intangible assets owned by the selling business.* This is the replacement value of those assets of the selling business which your company would like to own and retain, plus the liquidation value of those assets which your company does not need or desire to retain if you owned the selling business. The following example illustrates this concept:

Plastic Components, Inc., manufactures plastic parts sold to furniture manufacturers located in the Carolinas. The company has a modern, efficient nonunion manufacturing facility located in Raleigh, North Carolina, which is operating at 65% of capacity. Plastic Components, Inc., is considering acquiring Peter Brothers Plastics Company. Peter Brothers is both a manufacturer and distributor of plastic parts sold to furniture manufacturers. Its manufacturing facility is a less modern plant located in Richmond, Virginia, which has a more costly union work force. Plastic Components, Inc., would like to own Peter Brothers' wholesale distribution operations and facilities. It does not, however, desire to own Peter Brothers manufacturing facility since it can shift this production to its underutilized Raleigh plant. Plastic Components has analyzed the replacement and liquidation value of Peter Brothers manufacturing and its wholesale distribution operations. The results of this analysis were:

	REPLACEMENT VALUE	LIQUIDATION VALUE
Peter Brothers wholesale distribution operation	$1,000,000	$500,000
Peter Brothers manufacturing operation	1,500,000	750,000

Since Plastics Components intends to retain Peter Brothers wholesale distribution operation but sell its manufacturing operation, it would add the replacement value of the wholesale operation and the liquidation value of Peter Brothers manufacturing operation in order to estimate the acquisition investment value. This computation is:

Replacement value of their wholesale distribution operation	$1,000,000
Plus: Liquidation value of their manufacturing operation	750,000
Acquisition investment value	$1,750,000

WHEN AND HOW TO USE YOUR PRELIMINARY ACQUISITION INVESTMENT VALUE ESTIMATE

Your company should develop a preliminary acquisition investment value estimate for a selling business once you decide that it meets your company's acquisition screening criteria and you obtain the seller's financial statement. This preliminary acquisition investment value estimate will give you a "rough" estimate of how much that selling business would be worth to your company if you owned it.

The way in which you use your preliminary acquisition investment value estimate is to compare this value with the preliminary fair market value estimate you developed for that selling business. You will recall that the acquisition investment value of a business is an estimate of how much the business would be worth to your company if you owned it. On the other hand, the preliminary fair market value of that business is an estimate of how much you would probably have to pay to acquire that business. When your preliminary acquisition investment value estimate is either approximately the same, or less than the preliminary fair market value estimate for that selling business, you should continue investigating and negotiating with that acquisition candidate. When the preliminary fair market value estimate of a selling business is higher than your preliminary acquisition investment value estimate for that business, you should either cease investigating and negotiating with that acquisition candidate or devote only limited resources to continuing to investigate and negotiate with that acquisition candidate. This is because it is unlikely that the owners of the selling business would accept a low enough price to make it worthwhile for your company to purchase and own that business. The following examples illustrate this priority-setting procedure:

Johnson Floor Lamp Company seeks to acquire profitable lighting fixture manufacturers with annual revenues of $5 million to $25 million. The company has found three such acquisition opportunities and has estimated the preliminary fair market value and the initial (preliminary) acquisition value of each of these three selling businesses. The following chart indicates these values and the priority which Johnson should assign to pursuing each of these opportunities:

SELLING BUSINESS	FAIR MARKET VALUE	ACQUISITION INVESTMENT VALUE
Smith Lighting, Inc.	$3,000,000	$2,500,000

Priority recommendation. Johnson would not be willing to pay more than $2,500,000 to acquire Smith Lighting. Therefore, it is likely to be outbid by other prospective acquirers. Since its chances of purchasing this business is low, it should limit the time and energy it devotes to pursuing this acquisition opportunity.

Golden Lamps, Inc.	$4,000,000	$4,000,000

Priority recommendation. Johnson is probably one of many prospective acquirers who would be willing to pay approximately $4,000,000 to purchase this acquisition candidate. Therefore, Johnson should move quickly to initiate serious price negotiations with this seller before other competing acquirers have an opportunity to do so. However, if a bidding contest develops, Johnson would lose out if the competing acquirer is prepared to pay a premium for Golden Lamps, Inc.

Lamp Lighting Associates	$3,000,000	$4,000,000

Priority recommendation. This acquisition candidate would be more valuable to Johnson that it would be to most prospective acquirers. Johnson, therefore, has an excellent chance of purchasing this acquisition candidate because, if necessary, it can afford to pay a premium over the price which most competing acquirers would be prepared to pay. Johnson should concentrate more of its time and resources on pursuing this acquisition opportunity than on either of the other two acquisition opportunities, since it has the best chance of being able to acquire Lamp Lighting Associates for a price which does not exceed its acquisition investment value.

HOW TO USE ACQUISITION INVESTMENT VALUE ESTIMATES TO GUIDE YOUR PURCHASE PRICE NEGOTIATIONS

The acquisition investment value of a selling business estimates how much that business would be worth to your company if you owned it. Therefore, this is the maximum price which your company should consider paying to acquire that selling business. As you continue to investigate the selling business, you will be constantly improving and adjusting the cash flow projections and asset value estimates you used to prepare your preliminary acquisition investment value estimate. Since these improved cash flow and asset value estimates will change your acquisition investment value estimate, you should update your acquisition investment value estimate prior to each negotiating session with the owners of the selling business. Your negotiators should then be kept aware of any changes in the maximum price which your company would consider paying to acquire the selling business.

ACQUISITION INVESTMENT VALUE VERSUS FAIR MARKET VALUE TECHNIQUES

In order to estimate the acquisition investment value of a selling business you employ techniques which are somewhat similar to those used to estimate the fair market value of a selling business. Due to the similarities between the techniques used to estimate acquisition investment value and those used to estimate fair market value there is a tendency for acquirers to confuse these techniques and to use fair market value techniques inadvertently to estimate acquisition investment value. Therefore, prior to discussing the techniques used to estimate acquisition investment value, it is helpful to highlight the differences between how these two types of valuation techniques view owners cash flow, asset liquidation and replacement value, and return on investment.

Owners' cash flow

For estimating fair market value you use the future cash flow which a business is expected to produce for its present owners.

For estimating acquisition investment value, you use the additional future cash flow which your company expects to generate if it owned and operated the selling business. This will, therefore, include any additional cash flow which your company expects to generate from combining the selling business with your company's existing business. For example, the two businesses might realize cost savings or marketing synergies which would result in their producing more cash flow if you owned them than if they continued to operate as independent businesses.

Asset liquidation value and asset replacement value

For estimating the fair market value of a selling business based upon the assets which it owns you use *either* the liquidation value of these assets or the replacement value of these assets. Liquidation value is used to estimate fair market value when most prospective acquirers would be primarily interested in owning the tangible assets of the selling business rather than its intangible assets such as market share, management expertise, reputation and so on. Replacement value is used when most prospective acquirers would want to maintain the selling business as an operating entity to preserve the value of its intangible assets.

For estimating the acquisition investment value of a selling business based upon its assets you use a combination of the asset replacement value and the asset liquidation value techniques. For tangible and intangible assets of the selling business which your company would want to retain after you owned that business, you use their replacement value. Assets of the selling business which your company will not need to retain are valued at their liquidation value.

Return on investment (rate of return)

The return-on-investment technique was one of the ways in which to estimate the fair market value of a business based upon its annual cash flow. This technique employed the following formula:

$$\text{Fair market value} = \text{Annual owners cash flow divided by the}$$
$$\text{Target rate-of-return percentage}$$

The rate-of-return percentage used was the return on investment which a typical acquirer or investor would expect to obtain if he or she purchased an equity interest in a typical business in the same industry segment as the selling business.

For estimating the acquisition investment value of a selling business based upon its annual cash flow, you can also used a rate-of-return percentage. However, this rate-of-return percentage is the return on investment which your company would want to obtain in order to make it worthwhile of you to use your company's investment capital and surplus borrowing capacity to acquire the selling business. This may be higher, lower, or the same rate-of-return percentage used to estimate the fair market value of a business operating in the same industry segment.

METHODS USED TO ESTIMATE ACQUISITION INVESTMENT VALUE

There are four principal ways of estimating the acquisition investment value of a selling business. These are:

1. The asset value method

2. The return-on-investment method

3. The cash investment payback period method

4. The borrowed funds payback period method.

The preferred approach when estimating the acquisition investment value of a selling business is to use the asset value method *and* one of the three cash flow value methods (return on investment, investment payback period, or borrowed funds payback period). Then you can either average together these two value estimates or choose one of these two value estimates based upon whether the assets owned by the selling business or the cash flow produced by the selling business is of primary importance to your company.

THE ASSET VALUE METHOD OF ESTIMATING ACQUISITION INVESTMENT VALUE

The first step in using the asset value method is to list all the tangible and intangible assets of the selling business which either would be useful for your company to own or which could be sold. While the assets listed on the balance sheet of the selling business provide a useful starting point, it does not include most of the intangible assets which you would be purchasing. Examples of these tangible assets might include:

- Supplier relationships
- Purchasing personnel and expertise
- Senior management personnel and expertise
- Distribution networks and expertise
- Customer base
- Market share
- Product lines
- Product development expertise
- Engineering and technical personnel and expertise
- Management systems
- Information and control systems
- Repair and service networks
- Mailing lists
- Sales organizations
- Marketing personnel and expertise
- Production capacity and expertise

- Industry reputation
- Leasehold improvements which were expensed rather than capitalized
- Experienced, trained work force
- Administrative staff and systems
- Lender relationships
- Goodwill
- Low-cost financing (e.g., low-interest-rate mortgages that are assumable)

Once you have done your best to compile a comprehensive list of the tangible and intangible assets owned by the selling business, you need to assign values to these assets. For those assets which your company would want to retain after you owned the selling business, you estimate the cost of replacing these assets. A useful way to estimate the replacement value of key personnel whom you would want to retain is to take one-half of their salary compensation. The rationale for doing this is that recruiting, hiring, and training new personnel, and the lost productivity while they become good at doing their jobs, could easily cost you half their annual compensation. For these assets which your company would not desire to retain, you estimate how much you could sell these assets for within three to six months after acquiring the selling business. The final step in estimating the acquisition value of the selling business is to reduce the total value you computed for the assets of the selling business by 30%. Some of the reasons for applying this discount factor are:

1. You will lose and need to replace some of the key employees at the selling business who you had hoped to retain.

2. Some of the tangible assets which you are buying and retaining will be less suitable to your needs than the tangible assets which you would have chosen to purchase if you were starting from scratch. For example, the seller might own a distribution facility which you can utilize but which is not located in as good a location as you would select if you were setting up a new facility to serve that market area.

3. You will lose some of the supplier and customer relationships which you had hoped to retain.

4. After you own the business, you are likely to find hidden problems which reduce the values you assigned to some of the assets which you retain.

5. The liquidation values which you assigned to assets which you plan to sell after you own the selling business may be overly optimistic. For example, you may have failed to subtract the commissions and legal expenses you will incur to market and dispose of these assets.

HOW TO USE YOUR ASSET VALUE ESTIMATE OF THE ACQUISITION INVESTMENT VALUE OF THE SELLING BUSINESS

1. When your company's primary objective in purchasing a selling business is to obtain its tangible and intangible assets, this acquisition investment value is the maximum price which your company should consider paying to purchase the selling business. The reason why a company would purchase a business primarily to obtain its assets is that it intends to merge the operations of the selling business into its existing business.

2. When your company's objectives in purchasing the selling business are both to obtain valuable assets and also to obtain the future cash flow of the selling business, you should average together the acquisition investment values you obtained using both the asset value method and one of the three cash flow valuation methods (return on investment, cash investment payback, or borrowed funds payback).

3. When your company's primary objective in purchasing a selling business is to obtain its future cash income, you should still estimate its acquisition value using the asset value method. The reason is that this gives you some idea of how much the selling business would be worth to your company if the selling business, produces a lower level of annual cash flow than anticipated, after you own it.

THE RETURN-ON-INVESTMENT METHOD OF ESTIMATING ACQUISITION INVESTMENT VALUE

The return-on-investment method for estimating acquisition investment value of a business is similar to the return-on-investment value technique used to estimate the fair market value of a business. For both, the formula is:

$$\text{Estimate value of the business} = \frac{\text{Annual owners cash flow}}{\text{Return on investment}}$$

When computing the acquisition investment value of a selling business, the annual cash flow of the selling business refers to the additional cash flow which your company expects to generate after it owns the selling business. This is generally the annual cash flow which the business would be likely to generate for its present owners plus an additional cash flow which your company expects to obtain if it owned the selling business. Some of the factors which might produce this additional cash flow are:

1. Economies of scale and other efficiencies resulting from combining the personnel, operations, facilities, or purchasing power of your company's existing business and the selling business
2. Marketing synergies between your company's existing business and the selling business
3. Improved management of the selling business

In contrast you will recall that when the return-on-investment technique was used to estimate the fair market value of a business, annual owners' cash flow was defined as the annual cash flow which the *present* owners of the business would be likely to receive if they continued to own and operate the business.

When computing the acquisition investment value of a selling business, the return on investment (rate-of-return percentage) is the return on investment which your company would expect to obtain from investing its expansion capital. Expansion capital consists of the extra cash and borrowing capacity which your company could use to make either internal or external growth investments.

In contrast you will recall that when the return-on-investment technique was used to estimate the fair market value of a business, the return on investment (rate of return percentage) was the average return which purchasers and investors would expect to obtain from making equity investments in the same industry segment as the business which is to be valued.

A PROCEDURE FOR COMPUTING ADDITIONAL ANNUAL CASH FLOW

In order to compute the additional annual cash flow which your company could expect to obtain from owning a particular selling business, the following procedure can be used. First, you combine the current annual revenues of your company's existing business and the selling business. Then you add to this total any additional revenues which you expect to obtain from owning both businesses. The following example illustrates this procedure:

Health Vitamins Corp. manufactures vitamin supplements which it markets via direct mail to individual consumers. The company's annual sales are $4 million.

Natural Fruits of Florida produces organically grown citrus fruits which it markets to health food stores in the Northeast. The company's annual sales are $7 million.

Health Vitamins Corp. is considering acquiring Natural Fruits of Florida. Health Vitamins estimates that adding some of Natural Fruits product line items to its mail-order catalog would add $2 million to its annual sales. Therefore, the projected combined revenues of the two businesses would be $13 million.

The next step is to estimate the combined annual operating expenses of your company's existing business and the selling business. To do this you first add together the annual operating expenses of both businesses. Since your final objective is to determine the cash flow which the owner of the combined businesses could expect to obtain, you exclude from these expenses direct and indirect excess compensation which consists of salaries and benefits paid to owner/executives which would not have been paid to nonowner executives if they were employed to perform the same management functions. After you have combined the operating expenses of the two businesses, you need to make two adjustments to this total. These are:

1. Add any additional expenses required to generate the extra revenue you expected to receive from marketing synergies between the two businesses.

2. Subtract any cost savings you expect to obtain if your company owned and operated both businesses.

In our example the precombination annual operating expenses are as follows:

Health Vitamins Corp.	$2,500,000
Natural Fruits of Florida	5,500,000
Combined annual operating expenses	$8,000,000

The additional operating expenses required to support the projected $2 million increase in direct-mail sales of organic fruits were $1.5 million. The anticipated cost savings from combining the two businesses in this example are only $200,000 since the two operations are quite different and would therefore need to retain most of their existing facilities and personnel. The projected combined operating expenses of the two businesses are:

Combined current annual operating expenses	$8,000,000
Plus: Additional operating expenses to support projected $2 million sales increase	1,500,000
Less: Anticipated cost savings	(200,000)
Projected annual combined operating expenses	$9,300,000

Once you have estimated the combined revenues and expenses of your company's present business and the business which you are considering acquiring, you compute the combined cash flow of the two businesses by subtracting the total operating expenses from the total revenues. The following chart compares the cash income of the two businesses if they continued to operate separately and the anticipated cash income obtained by combining the two businesses under common ownership.

	PREACQUISITION	POSTACQUISITION
Combined revenues	$11,000,000	$13,000,000
Combined operating expenses	(8,000,000)	(9,300,000)
Combined cash flow	$ 3,000,000	$ 3,700,000

After you have computed the postacquisition combined cash flow of the two businesses, you subtract the cash flow generated by your company's present business. This difference is the amount of additional cash flow which your company expects to obtain by owning and operating the selling business. In our example this computation was:

Combined cash flow	$3,700,000
Current cash income (Health Vitamins)	1,500,000
Projected increase in each income	$2,200,000

You will recall that the fair market value of a selling business is based upon the cash flow it produces for its present owners. In the Natural Fruits example, this was $1,500,000 (annual revenues of $7,000,000 minus annual operating expenses of $5,500,000). However, for Health Vitamins Corp. the ownership of Natural Fruits is expected to generate $2,200,000 in additional cash income. Therefore, the acquisition value which Natural Fruits would have for Health Vitamins would be based upon $2,200,000 in annual cash flow rather than $1,500,000.

APPLYING THE RETURN-ON-INVESTMENT VALUATION FORMULA

Once you have estimated the additional annual cash flow which you could obtain by owning and operating the selling business, you divide this amount by your target rate of return-on-investment percentage to obtain the estimated acquisition investment value for the selling business. For example, if the target rate of return used by Health Vitamins Corp. were 15% per year the computation would be:

Acquisition investment value =
Additional annual cash flow
Target rate of return

Acquisition investment value =
$2,200,000
15%

Acquisition investment value = $14,666,666

WHEN TO USE THE RETURN-ON-INVESTMENT METHOD TO ESTIMATE ACQUISITION INVESTMENT VALUE

The return-on-investment method utilizes a single year's projected additional cash flow from your company owning and operating its present business and the selling business. This approach produces satisfactory acquisition investment value estimates when the additional cash flow in subsequent years is expected to either:

1. Remain relatively stable in constant (inflation adjusted) dollars
2. Increase at a steady rate from year to year

In the latter case (increasing annual additional cash flow) you would use a somewhat lower target rate of return on investment when you value the projected additional annual cash flow for the first five year you would own and operate the selling business. This is the same type of adjustment which appraisers use when estimating the value of an income producing real estate property when the cash flow generated by that property is expected to increase more rapidly than the expected inflation rate. It is also the same type of adjustment which was made when the return-on-investment technique was used to estimate the fair market value of a business.

WHEN TO USE A PAYBACK PERIOD METHOD TO ESTIMATE ACQUISITION INVESTMENT VALUE

When the projected additional annual cash flow from owning the selling business for the first year is not a good indication of the expected additional cash flow in subsequent years, one of the two payback period methods should be used, rather than the return-on-investment method. The payback period methods value a business combination based upon its expected additional cash flow for the next few years. The following is an example of when a purchaser should use one of the two payback methods to estimate the acquisition investment value of a selling business:

Health Vitamins Corp. manufacturers vitamin supplements which it markets via direct mail to individual consumers. The following chart indicates the projected annual revenues, expenses, and cash flow for Health Vitamins Corp.

YEAR	REVENUES	EXPENSES	CASH FLOW
1	$4,000,000	$2,500,000	$1,500,000
2	4,400,000	2,700,000	1,700,000
3	4,800,000	2,900,000	1,900,000
4	5,200,000	3,100,000	2,100,000
5	5,600,000	3,300,000	2,300,000
6	6,000,000	3,600,000	2,400,000
7	6,400,000	3,800,000	2,600,000
8	6,800,000	4,000,000	2,800,000
9	7,200,000	4,200,000	3,000,000
10	7,000,000	4,500,000	3,100,000

Health Vitamin is considering purchasing Generic Medicinals, Inc. Generic Medicinals is in the process of developing generic versions of several prescription drugs for which the patents expire in two years. These drugs are difficult to manufacture, but Generic has purchased the necessary technology from a foreign drug manufacturer. Generic is expected to be one of the only producers of the generic versions of these drugs for two year (years 2 and 3) and then is expected to face increased competition from other generic drug manufacturers. Generic also owns a profitable subsidiary which manufacturers fine chemicals (used in drug and vitamin manufacturing) which has been growing at a slow but steady rate.

The following chart indicates the projected revenues, expenses and cash flow for Generic Medicinals, Inc.:

YEAR	REVENUES	EXPENSES	CASH FLOW
1	$2,000,000	$1,800,000	$ 200,000
2	2,200,000	2,000,000	200,000
3	5,000,000	3,000,000	2,000,000
4	7,200,000	4,000,000	3,000,000
5	8,000,000	5,500,000	2,500,000
6	8,500,000	6,500,000	2,000,000
7	9,000,000	6,900,000	2,100,000
8	9,500,000	7,300,000	2,200,000
9	10,000,000	7,700,000	2,300,000
10	10,500,000	8,100,000	2,400,000

Health Vitamins Corp. has analyzed the marketing synergies and the operating efficiencies which they could expect to obtain from owning and operating both their present business and that of Generic Medicinals, Inc. Their analysis uncovered the following potential synergies and cost savings opportunities.

1. Health Vitamins Corp. would begin to purchase the fine chemicals it uses to make vitamins from Generic Medicinal's subsidiary. This would add $300,000 to Generic's annual sales, $250,000 to its operating expenses, and $50,000 to its annual cash flow.
2. Combining the purchasing power of Health Vitamins Corp. and Generic Medicinals would generate $160,000 in annual cost savings beginning in year 3.

The following chart indicates the additional annual cash flow which Health Vitamins Corp. expects to obtain if it owned and operated Generic Medicinals.

YEAR	PRECOMBINATION CASH FLOW OF GENERIC MEDICINALS	CASH FLOW IMPROVEMENT FROM COMBINATING THE TWO BUSINESSES	TOTAL ADDITIONAL CASH FLOW
1	$ 200,000	$ 150,000	$ 250,000
2	200,000	50,000	250,000
3	2,000,000	150,000	2,150,000
4	3,000,000	150,000	3,150,000
5	2,500,000	150,000	2,650,000
6	2,000,000	150,000	2,150,000
7	2,100,000	150,000	2,250,000
8	2,200,000	150,000	2,350,000
9	2,300,000	150,000	2,450,000
10	2,400,000	150,000	2,550,000

You will notice that there is a considerable variation in the annual additional cash flow which the acquisition of Generic Minerals by Health Vitamins would be likely to generate.

The following chart illustrates why the return on investment method (which relies on a single year's increased cash flow) would not yield a good estimate of acquisition investment value for Generic Minerals. the computations assume that Natural Vitamins' target rate of return is 15%, per year.

Year 1 additional cash flow: $\dfrac{\$250,000}{15\%}$ = acquisition investment value

$$= \$1.7 \text{ million}$$

Year 3 additional cash flow: $\dfrac{\$2,150,000}{15\%}$

= acquisition investment value = \$14.3 million

Year 4 additional cash flow: $\dfrac{\$3,150,000}{15\%}$ =

acquisition investment value = \$21 million

TWO PAYBACK PERIOD METHODS FOR ESTIMATING ACQUISITION INVESTMENT VALUE

The two payback period methods of estimating acquisition investment value are:

1. *The cash investment payback period method.* This approach assumes that the funds which would be used to purchase the selling business would come from the purchaser's own surplus cash and working capital. The prospective purchaser's objective is to recover this investment within a maximum number of years (the investment payback period) using the projected additional annual cash flow generated from its ownership of the selling business.

2. *The borrowed funds payback period method.* This approach assumes that a constant payment term loan is used to finance the purchase price of the selling business. The purchaser's objective is to repay this loan within a maximum number of years (the borrowed funds payback period) using the projected additional annual cash flow generated from its ownership of the selling business.

HOW TO USE THE CASH INVESTMENT PAYBACK PERIOD METHOD TO ESTIMATE ACQUISITION INVESTMENT VALUE

The first step in using this method is to project the additional annual cash flow which your company expects to obtain from owning the selling business. To do this, you can use the same procedure which was described in the previous section on the return-on-investment method. However, instead of doing this only for the first year you would own the selling business, you do this for each of the next ten years. The Health Vitamins/Generic Medicinals example illustrated this procedure.

The next step is to select your company's target return on investment (percentage rate of return). This is the same rate of return which you would have used for the return-on-investment method of estimating the acquisition investment value of a selling business. You will recall that this was the minimum rate of return which your company uses when it evaluates the attractiveness of long-term capital investments such as purchasing new machinery. After you have selected your target rate of return, you compute your desired acquisition investment payback period (in years) by dividing 100% by that target rate-of-return percentage. For example, if your target rate of return was 25% per year, your payback period would be 100% divided by 25%, which equals 4 years.

The final step in computing the acquisition investment value of a selling business is to total the additional annual cash flow which your ownership of that business is expected to produce over the period. Using the Natural Vitamins/ Generic Medicinals additional annual cash flow projections and a 4-year payback period the estimated acquisition value of Generic Medicinals would be:

Additional cash flow for years 1, 2, 3 and 4 = acquisition investment value

$250,000 + $250,000 + $2,150,000 + $3,150,000 = Acquisition investment value = $5,800,000

Though this method of estimating acquisiton investment value is simple and convenient to use, it has the disadvantage of giving equal value to each year's additional cash flow. You will recall from the discussion of the discounted cash flow method of estimating fair market value that additional cash flow method received in earlier years is more valuable than is additional cash flow recovered in later years due to the additional interest income which would be obtained frm reinvesting this money for a longer period. This concept is sometimes referred to as "the time value of money." When the projected additional annual cash income for some years is much higher or lower than for other years, it is more accurate to use a payback period which incorporates a discounted cash flow adjustment. A payback period method which does this is the borrowed funds payback period method.

AN ALTERNATIVE RETURN-ON-INVESTMENT METHOD

Instead of using the cash investment payback period method to estimate the acquisition investment value of a selling business, you can derive a similar value estimate by using the following variation of the return on investment method:

1. Project the additional owners' annual cash flow for each of the next four years. In the Health Vitamins/Generic Medicinals example these additional annual owners cash flow were:

YEAR	ADDITIONAL OWNERS CASH FLOW
1	$ 250,000
2	250,000
3	2,150,000
4	3,150,000
Total	$5,800,000

2. Compute the average annual additional owners cash flow:

$$\frac{\$5,800,000}{4 \text{ years}} = \$1,450,000$$

3. Apply the return-on-investment formula to compute the estimated acquisition investment value for the selling business:

Target rate of return = 22%
Average annual additional owners' cash flow = $1,450,000
Acquisition investment value = Additional annual owners' cash flow divided by your target rate of return
Acquisition investment value = $1,450,000
22%
Acquisition investment value = $6,590,909 rounded off to $6,590,000

This is a convenient approach to use when your target rate of return would yield a fractional payback period (100% divided by 22% = 4.4545 years).

WHY TO USE THE BORROWED FUNDS PAYBACK PERIOD METHOD TO ESTIMATE ACQUISITION INVESTMENT VALUE

The borrowed funds payback period method defines the acquisition investment value of a selling business as the amount of borrowed funds which would be repaid using the projected annual additional cash flow to pay loan interest and principle, during the target payback period.

There are three advantages to using the borrowed funds payback period method. These are:

1. The sooner you receive additional cash flow which can be used to repay borrowed funds the more interest you will save and the more cash flow which you will be able to use to repay loan principal. This is equivalent to using cash flow discounting to give higher value to additional cash flow received in the earlier years.

2. Generally an acquirer borrows around 75% to 85% of the purchase price of a business. Therefore, the borrowed funds payback period is more realistic than the cash investment payback period method.

3. Higher interest rates make it more expensive for your company to use borrowed funds to make capital investments, while lower interest rates make it less expensive to do so. This makes capital investments such as acquisitions more attractive when the interest rates you would pay are lower and less attractive when interest rates you would pay are higher. The interest rate which your company would pay are determined by general interest rate levels, and by how safe leaders view the loans which they would make to your company to purchase the selling business. The borrowed funds payback method adjusts the acquisition investment value of a selling business to reflect the interest rates which you expect to pay on the funds which you would borrow to purchase the selling business.

Though the borrowed funds payback period method of estimating the acquisition investment value of a selling business offers these advantages, it has one principal disadvantage. That is, that it is somewhat complicated to estimate the amount of principal which will be repaid during different payback periods. Included in this section, however, are formulas which you can use to estimate the approximate amount of loan principle repaid for the two most commonly used borrowed funds payback periods (four and five years).

HOW TO USE THE BORROWED FUNDS PAYBACK PERIOD METHOD

The procedures used to compute the acquisition investment value of a selling business using the borrowed funds payback period method are:

1. Select your target borrowed funds payback period based upon the degree to which the selling business meets your company's acquisition goals and objectives. For a selling business which your company would have a special interest in owning, use a five or six year payback period. For other businesses which would help your company achieve its acquisition goals and objectives, use a four-year payback period.

2. Estimate the interest rate which your company would need to pay if you financed the acquisition of the selling business using a bank term loan. The best way to do this is to ask your bank what interest rate they would use if you took a five-year loan to pay for some new machinery and equipment. Another approach is to use the average interest rate which B grade corporate bonds are yielding. A bond salesman at your securities brokerage firm can provide you with this information.

3. Apply the following formulas to get an approximation of the cumulative loan principal repayment during the payback period.
   a = year 1 additional cash flow
   b = year 2 additional cash flow
   c = year 3 additional cash flow
   d = year 4 additional cash flow
   e = year 5 additional cash flow
   i = the interest rate on the borrowed funds
   p = the total principal repayment during the payback period = acquisition investment value

• Four-year payback period:

$$p = \frac{a + b + c + d + 3(i)a + 2(i)b + ic}{1.0 + 4i + ci^2}$$

• Five-year payback period

$$p = \frac{a + b + c + d + e + 4(i)a + 3(i)b + 2(i)c + i(d)}{1.0 + 5i + 10i^2}$$

To illustrate the use of the borrowed funds payback period method the Health Vitamins Corp./Natural Fruits of Florida example will again be used:

YEAR	PROJECTED ADDITIONAL OWNERS CASH FLOW
1	$ 250,000
2	250,000
3	2,150,000
4	3,150,000
5	2,650,000
6	2,150,000

7	2,250,000
8	2,350,000
9	2,450,000
10	2,550,000

Interest rate on acquisition financing = 12% = i
Target payback period = 4 years

First-year owners' cash flow = a	=	$ 250,000
Second-year owners' cash flow = b	=	250,000
Third-year owners' cash flow = c	=	2,150,000
Fourth-year owners' cash flow = d	=	3,150,000
	$a + b + c + d =$	$5,800,000

$$p = \frac{a + b + c + d + 3(i)a + 2(i)b + ic}{1.0 + 4(i) + 6i^2}$$

$$p = \frac{\$5,800,000 + 3(0.12)\$250,000 + 2(0.12)\,\$250,000 + 0.10(\$2,150,000)}{1 + 4(0.12) + 6(0.12)^2}$$

$$p = \frac{\$5,800,000 + (0.36)(\$250,000) + (0.24)(\$250,000) + (0.20)(\$2,150,000)}{1 + 0.48 + 6(0.0144)}$$

$$p = \frac{\$5,800,000 + \$90,020 + \$60,000 + \$258,000}{1.48 + 0.864}$$

$$p = \frac{\$6,208,000}{1.54}$$

$$p = \$4,020,725 = \text{acquisition investment value}$$

FORCED LIQUIDATION VALUE ESTIMATES

The planning, analysis, and valuation techniques described in this book will help you reduce your risk of making a bad acquisition. Nonetheless you cannot entirely avoid the risk that a business which you purchase will fail to perform satisfactorily after you own it. Economic and competitive conditions can change rapidly, and unpredictably. Key personnel at a business which you purchase may leave, or they may prove to be incompetent or dishonest. The average failure rate among acquisitons ranges from 20% to 40%. Therefore, you should generally not acquire a business if the failures of that acquired business would cause your own company to go out of business. The forced liquidation value of a selling business helps you to analyze this risk.

HOW TO ESTIMATE THE FORCED
LIQUIDATION VALUE OF A BUSINESS

The forced liquidation value of a business is an estimate of how much you could recover from liquidating the assets of that business. To estimate this value, you make the following assumptions:

1. You acquire the business and attempt to operate it for a period of two years.
2. The business fails to generate the minimum level of revenues and profits necessary to justify its continued operation.
3. At the time you decide to give up and liquidate the business economic conditions in its industry segment are depressed.

The procedures for estimating the forced liquidation value of a business which you are considering acquiring is to first estimate the fair market value of the business using the liquidation value technique described earlier in this chapter. Then you reduce this fair market value estimate by 35% to give you an estimate of the forced liquidation value of the business. For example, if the fair market liquidation value of a business was $4,200,000, you would subtract $1,470,000 (33%) to yield a forced liquidation value estimate of $2,730,000.

HOW TO USE YOUR FORCED LIQUIDATION
VALUE ESTIMATE

Your objective is to estimate how much your company would lose if it purchased the selling business and was then subsequently forced to liquidate it. To do this you first, take the fair market value of the selling business you estimated using one of the valuation techniques described in the first sections of this chapter. This fair market value is an estimate of how much you would probably need to pay to purchase the selling business. Then you subtract from this purchase price estimate your forced liquidation value estimate for this business. This difference is an estimate of how much your company would lose if the selling business failed to perform satisfactorily after you owned it. The final step is to decide whether your company could survive a loss of this magnitude. When the answer is that your company would be unlikely to survive such a loss, you should generally avoid pursuing this acquisiton opportunity. The key exception to this rule is if your company's existing business is failing. In that case you should continue to pursue this acquisition opportunity if you feel that it would improve your company's chances of surviving.

C·H·A·P·T·E·R N·I·N·E

STAFFING AND MANAGING YOUR ACQUISITION PROGRAM

ACQUISITION PROGRAM WORK REQUIREMENTS

Carrying out your acquisition program is a major undertaking. The following is a list of some of the key work assignments which your company will need to perform in order to implement various phases of your acquisition program.

Acquisition search

1. Developing sources of acquisition candidate referrals
2. Identifying companies that meet your acquisition criteria, and then contacting them to learn whether they are for sale
3. Compiling sufficient information on an acquisition candidate to enable you to decide whether or not they meet your acquisition criteria

Acquisition candidate investigation

1. Investigating and analyzing the key aspects of an acquisition candidate company. These include the acquisition candidate's earnings history, financial

position, growth potential, product lines, personnel, operating strengths and weaknesses, and market position.

2. Determining the nonfinancial objectives of the owners of the selling company. Examples might include continuation of the company name, employment guarantees, access to additional growth capital, management autonomy, and so on.

Acquisition candidate valuation

1. Estimating the acquisition candidate's fair market value. Fair market value is the price at which a particular company is likely to be sold based upon current market conditions.

2. Projecting the acquisition candidate's future earnings and cash flow, assuming it was owned by your company.

3. Determining how much the acquisition candidate would be worth to your company. This valuation estimate may be higher or lower than the selling company's "fair market value."

4. Determining the availability (amount, terms, and conditions) of outside acquisition financing.

5. Determining how much you would be prepared to pay for the acquisition candidate assuming alternative payment terms (cash sale, installment sale, contingent payments based on future earnings, etc.).

Negotiations

1. Negotiate the purchase price, tax liabilities, payment terms, and the indirect compensation to be provided to the sellers (company cars, management contracts, noncompete payments, etc.).

2. Negotiate the degree of autonomy to be provided to the management of the acquired company.

3. Negotiate the other nonfinancial considerations of the purchase (e.g., continuation of the selling company name, membership on the board of directors of the combined company).

ACQUISITION PROGRAM WORK REQUIREMENTS CREATE PROBLEMS FOR MANY COMPANIES

The amount and the complexity of the work required to carry out an acquisition program causes many companies to give up in the middle of their acquisition programs. Prospective acquirers often find that:

1. Their acquisition program is damaging their company's existing business by absorbing too much of their senior executive's time and energy.

2. The work required to find, investigate, analyze, or negotiate to purchase suitable acquisition candidates is not being performed satisfactorily.

3. The acquisition decision-making process is creating conflicts among the company's senior executives. These conflicts are preventing key acquisition decisions from being made in a timely manner. These conflicts are also creating morale problems.

WHY IT IS DIFFICULT FOR A COMPANY TO STAFF AND MANAGE AN ACQUISITION PROGRAM

1. Acquisition programs are very labor intensive. An acquisition program requires a company to provide over 2,000 executive laborhours concentrated over a six- to nine-month period. This is equivalent to three executives devoting over half their time to the company's acquisition program.

2. The most effective way for a company to handle its acquisition program work load is to employ a full-time corporate development staff. In addition to working on their company's acquisition program, a corporate development staff also works on the development of strategic growth plans and the analysis and selection of proposed internal growth investments (e.g., building a new manufacturing plant). However, most companies only seek to make acquisitions or large internal growth investments every two or three years. Therefore, it is not cost effective for them to employ their own full-time corporate development staffs.

3. An acquisition program requires the skills of many different types of acquisition specialists such as finder/brokers, corporate finance experts, investigators, accountants, attorneys, and corporate development consultants. Most company staffs do not include many of these specialists. Therefore, the

companies must rely on outside acquisition specialists. Unless these outside specialists are effectively monitored and coordinated by the company's executives, these specialists will not perform their work in a timely, cost-effective manner.

4. Unless a company's chief executive is actively involved in its acquisition program, it is unlikely to make an acquisition. Generally, however, the chief executive's time is already fully occupied managing the company's existing business.

5. Successfully operating a newly acquired business requires the active cooperation and support of the acquirer's senior executives. Therefore, the acquirer's senior executives each need to have a stake in making the newly acquired business a success. The acquirer's senior executives develop this commitment by being involved in the company's acquisition program from beginning to end. However, these same senior executives cannot devote too many laborhours to the company's acquisition program and still be able to handle their ongoing management responsibilities effectively.

STRATEGIES WHICH HELP YOUR COMPANY

There are five strategies which can help your company overcome the difficulties associated with staffing and managing your acquisition program. They are:

1. Develop an acquisition work plan.

2. Utilize techniques which reduce the number of laborhours which your *senior* executives would have to spend carrying out acquisition work assignments. This is important because if your senior executives must devote too many hours to implementing your acquisition program, they will not have enough time to perform their duties managing your existing business.

3. Identify those of your executives who will need to devote a significant amount of time to your acquisition program. Then utilize techniques which increase the amount of time which they will have available to work on your acquisition program.

4. Create a special acquisition program management structure instead of trying to use your company's existing management structure.

5. Make proper use of outside acquisition specialists such as attorneys, accountants, and consultants.

THE PURPOSE OF YOUR ACQUISITION WORK PLAN

The purpose of your work plan is to help your company prepare to handle the management and staffing needs of your acquisition program. Unless you take the time to develop a plan for managing and staffing the hundreds of work assignments which will comprise your acquisition program, you are likely to encounter the following problems:

1. Many work assignments will have been overlooked. Then the operation of your acquisition program will be stalled while you figure out how to handle them.

2. You will not have identified some of the types of outside acquisition experts you will need to supplement your in-house personnel resources and expertise. Then you will not have the time to find and select outside experts whose experience and talents are best suited to your company's needs and management style.

3. As your acquisition program progresses, you will probably give the first work assignments to your most talented and experienced executives and support personnel. They will, therefore, wind up working on some assignments which could have been handled by your less talented or experienced employees. Then when you need to begin work on important assignments which occur later in your acquisition program (e.g., negotiations), you will be unable to utilize your most experienced and talented executives and support personnel to carry out these assignments because their available time will already have been devoted to less important work assignments which occurred in the earlier stages of your acquisition program (e.g., acquisition search).

HOW TO BEGIN TO PREPARE YOUR ACQUISITION WORK PLAN

In order to prepare your acquisition work plan, you need to identify the work assignments which you will need to manage and staff and the personnel resources which you have available to work on these assignments. To do this, you need to prepare two lists. These are:

1. A list of the acquisition work assignments required to carry out the various phases of your acquisition program. As your acquisition program progresses, you will be constantly adding to this list of work assignments. It is important,

however, to try to identify each work assignment as early as possible. This gives you more time to figure out who you should have manage and staff that work assignment. A good starting point is the list of work assignments presented earlier in this chapter. Your listing of acquisition work assignments is entered in the first column of a three-column form. This form provides space for you to insert the name of the person responsible for managing or coordinating each work assignment and the support staff who will work on each work assignment. The following is an example of a filled in section of this form:

WORK ASSIGNMENT	MANAGER/COORDINATOR	SUPPORT STAFF
C. ACQUISITION SEARCH		
1. Search program planning and coordination	Jim Williams (acquisition manager)	Paul Johnson (acquisition consultant)
2. Contact finder/brokers	Jim Williams	Paul Johnson
3. Evaluate finder/brokers	Paul Johnson	
4. Prepare standard finder/ broker compensation agreement	Bud Aspin (attorney)	
5. Negotiate finder/broker compensation arrangements	Jim Williams	Bud Aspin
6. Maintain log of finder/ broker submissions	Jim Williams	Carol Ellis (administrative assistant)
7. Undertake direct-mail solicitation	Paul Johnson	Ace Typing Service
8. Prepare and place advertisements	Jim Williams	Al Smith Advertising Agency
9. Develop employee referral compensation program	Joan Goodson (V.P., Personnel)	Jim Williams Bud Aspin
10. Prepare employee memorandum outlining growth plans and acquisition criteria	Peter Walsh (V.P., Marketing)	Joan Goodson
11. Initial screening of acquisition opportunities	Jim Williams	Paul Johnson John Riccardo (sales manager)

2. A list of your company's executives and outside specialists (e.g., your accountant) who would be available to manage, coordinate, or staff acquisition program work assignments. When you retain additional outside specialists, or decide to utilize other company executives to work on your acquisition program, they are added to this personnel resource list. Your list of company executives and outside specialists who would be available to work on your acquisition program is entered in the first column of a two-column form. This form provides space to indicate the acquisition program responsibilities assigned to each individual. The following is an example of a filled in section of this form.

NAME	TITLE	ACQUISITION PROGRAM RESPONSIBILITIES
John Henry	Chief Financial Officer	1. Acquisition committee member 2. Negotiating team alternate
Paul Douglas	Assistant Treasurer	1. Exploratory meeting representative 2. Task force member
Herbert Glasgow	Outside Accountant	1. Task force member
Paul Walsh	V.P., Marketing	1. Acquisition committee member 2. Preparer of employee memorandum 3. Preparer of company brochure
John Riccardo	Sales Manager	1. Acquisition candidate screening—staff support 2. Task force member
Jim Williams	Assistant Sales Manager	1. Acquisition program manager 2. Task force member

You will notice that in many cases the acquisition program responsibilities listed in this form mention participation as a member of a committee, team, or task force. Later in this chapter there is a discussion of these groups which you should set up to work on your acquisition program and the specific responsibilities which should be assigned to each.

HOW TO COMPLETE AND USE YOUR ACQUISITION WORK PLAN

To complete and use your acquisition work plan, you use the following procedure:

1. Review each work assignment on your list and analyze the minimum level of experience and talent required for each work assignment.

2. Review your list of personnel resources (company executives and outside specialists) and analyze the experience and talent offered by each of these individuals.

3. For each work assignment, give one of your executives or outside experts responsibility for managing or coordinating that work assignment. Select one of your senior executives to manage or coordinate a particular work assignment only when none of your lower-level executives or outside specialists can handle this responsibility. Other guidelines for selecting the individuals who you should use to manage or coordinate particular work assignments are discussed in the following sections of this chapter.

4. After you select the individual who will be responsible for managing or coordinating a particular work assignment, insert his or her name in the second column of your work assignment list next to the work assignment for which he or she will be responsible. Unless you make these notations, you are likely to forget to assign someone the responsibility for managing or coordinating some of your work assignments.

5. On your second list form (which indicates the executives and outside experts who you could use to work on your acquisition program), insert in the second column next to their names and/or titles the work assignment manager and coordinator responsibilities which you assigned to that individual. This will enable you to keep track of how much management and coordination responsibility you have assigned to each of these individuals. This then helps you to avoid burdening an individual executive or outside specialists with too many work assignment management and coordination responsibilities and also helps you to identify executives and outside specialists who are being underutilized.

6. The individual assigned responsibility for managing or coordinating a work assignment analyzes the support staff required to carry out this work assignment and proposes which individuals should provide this staff support.

7. On your second list which indicates the individuals who are available to work on your acquisition program, you note these proposed staff support assignments. This helps you to identify individuals who would be overburdened or underutilized. Then you can reallocate staff support assignments to even out this work load. When your proposed staff support assignments require more help than your present executives and outside experts have the time to provide, you should begin looking for ways to supplement these personnel resources. For example, you may be able to utilize nonexecutive personnel, retired executives, or additional outside experts.

TECHNIQUES WHICH REDUCE THE ACQUISITION PROGRAM WORK LOAD OF YOUR SENIOR EXECUTIVES

1. Develop your acquisition candidate screening criteria before you start looking for acquisition candidates. This yields the following benefits:

    a. It reduces the number of executive laborhours required to carry out your acquisition search program. This was discussed in Chapters 3 and 4.

    b. It involves your senior executives in your acquisition program right at the start. This begins the process of giving your senior executives a "stake" in making any business which you acquire successful after you own it. Yet it does not require a major commitment of their time.

2. Utilize staff executives and outside acquisition specialists to handle time-consuming acquisition work assignments which do not require senior management expertise. Examples of these work assignments include:

    a. Acquisition search

    b. Initial meetings with acquisition candidates

    c. Information gathering and analysis

    d. Investigating acquisition candidates

3. Assign acquisition program management responsibilities before you begin searching for acquisition candidates. This avoids confusion and duplicate efforts once your acquisition program is underway.

4. Select and begin working with outside acquisition specialists before you begin analyzing acquisition opportunities. These outside acquisition specialists should include an acquisition consultant, an acquisition accountant, and an acquisition attorney. Once those specialists understand your company, and its corporate development goals, objectives, and preferences, they can assume staff responsibilities which otherwise would have to be handled by your own executives. For example, your acquisition consultant and your accountant can then do most of the analysis required to estimate the fair market value of an acquisition candidate. Otherwise, this work would probably have to be done by your company's chief financial officer.

HOW TO INCREASE THE AMOUNT OF TIME WHICH YOUR SENIOR EXECUTIVES CAN DEVOTE TO YOUR ACQUISITION PROGRAM

1. Prior to launching your acquisition program, fill any vacant executive positions, either through internal promotions or recruiting. Due to the additional executive work load created by your acquisition program, such vacant positions would become weak links in your management structure once your acquisition program is underway.

2. Identify those of your executives who will be the most actively involved in carrying out your acquisition program. Generally, these executives will include your president, your chief financial officer, and the junior or midlevel executive who will be your acquisition program manager. Then reduce the administrative work load of these individuals by:

   a. Reassigning some of their responsibilities to other executives
   b. Providing these individuals with additional staff support personnel

The following is an example of this approach.

Alpha Distribution Company's sales manager has been selected to be their acquisition program manager. His present responsibilities are to supervise five salesmen, each of whom covers a different territory. He shares a secretary with his boss, the vice president for marketing. Since the acquisition manager position is a temporary one which will end when its acquisition program is completed in six to nine months, Alpha would not want to hire a new sales manager. In order to permit its present sales manager to devote 50% of his time to the company's acquisition program, Alpha makes the following changes:

1. One of its top salesman is promoted to assistant sales manager.

2. A junior salesman is hired to assist the assistant sales manager in covering his current territory. After one year this junior salesman will be ready to replace one of Alpha's other salesman who is nearing retirement age.

3. The executive secretary who works for both the vice president for marketing and Alpha's sales manager handles many administrative support responsibilities for these executives. The sales manager will need additional administrative support to handle his acquisition program responsibilites. Alpha therefore promotes this executive secretary to an administrative assistant position so that she can provide this assistance. Simultaneously, Alpha hires a junior secretary who will handle some of the secretarial duties formerly handled by its newly promoted administrative assistant.

In this example you will notice that neither of the two new individuals hired was assigned to work on Alpha's acquisition program. As a general rule only your company's present employees should be assigned to work on your acquisition program. The reasons are:

1. Acquisition program responsibilities are handled more effectively by executives and administrative support personnel who are already familiar with your company's operations and its personnel.
2. Involvement in your company's acquisition program will be considered a reward by your present employees. This is because this work seems interesting and exciting since it offers new challenges and variety. There will be considerable resentment and morale problems created if newly hired junior executives or support personnel are permitted to work primarily on your company's acquisition program.

ELEMENTS OF YOUR ACQUISITION PROGRAM ORGANIZATION

Your acquisition program management and staff support should consist of the following:

1. An acquisition committee
2. Your chief executive
3. Your acquisition (program) manager
4. An acquisition search team
5. An acquisition task force
6. A negotiating team
7. An acquisition consultant
8. Lawyers, accountants, and other outside experts

WHO SHOULD BE ON YOUR COMPANY'S ACQUISITION COMMITTEE

1. Your chief executive.
2. Those of your senior executives who would be involved in managing or providing critical support services to a business which your company ac-

quired. They will generally include your company's senior executives who are responsible for:

  a. Financial management (e.g., your chief financial officer)
  b. Marketing and sales
  c. Production and distribution of goods or services
  d. Personnel and administration
  e. Legal work (e.g., your general counsel)

3. When your chief executive frequently relies on a nonemployee (an accountant, lawyer, management consultant, board member, etc.) for business strategy advice, he or she should also be included as a member of your acquisition committee.

WHO SHOULD PROVIDE STAFF SUPPORT FOR YOUR ACQUISITION COMMITTEE

1. The company executive who acts as your acquisition manager
2. Your acquisition consultant

THE ROLE OF YOUR ACQUISITION COMMITTEE

Your acquisition committee is responsible for making decisions regarding which businesses, and types of businesses, your company should try to acquire. This decision-making role occurs at three different stages of your acquisition program. These are:

1. *Acquisition (search) planning.* Your committee chooses your company's initial screening criteria. After your company has had an opportunity to consider 8 to 12 acquisition candidates which met, or partly met, these screening criteria, your committee should again review these screening criteria and revise them if they are either

  a. Eliminating acquisition candidates which your company found attractive
  b. Failing to screen out less attractive acquisition candidates which your company does not have the time and personnel to pursue actively

2. *Commencement of acquisition price negotiations.* Your committee selects your company's acquisition selection criteria. Then it uses these criteria to compare the relative attractiveness of acquisition candidates and authorizes your negotiating team to begin price negotiations with individual acquisition candidates which appear to be the most attractive.

3. *Purchase recommendation.* After your company has completed its negotiations with an acquisition candidate, your acquisition committee decides whether or not to recommend the purchase of this business to your board of directors.

WHY YOU SHOULD LIMIT THE INVOLVEMENT OF YOUR ACQUISITION COMMITTEE

It is important to limit your acquisition committee's role in your acquisition program to the responsibilities just outlined. The reason is that your acquisition committee membership consists primarily of your senior executives who are responsible for managing your company's existing business. Therefore you cannot afford to have your committee become involved in those phases of your acquisition program which are very time consuming. Fortunately these phases of your acquisition program can be handled in a satisfactory manner by your company's staff, lower-level executives, and outside acquisition specialists. These phases of your acquisition program include:

1. Implementing your acquisition search program
2. Gathering information on and investigating acquisition candidates

THE ROLE OF YOUR COMPANY'S CHIEF EXECUTIVE

Your chief executive must assume primary responsibility for the success of your company's acquisition program. Companies which assign this responsibility to other individuals (e.g., another senior executive, or a board member, or a consultant) rarely make acquisitions.

The following are the acquisition program functions of your company's chief executive:

1. Select the members of your acquisitions committee.
2. Act as chairman of your acquisitions committee.
3. Select and supervise your acquisition (program) manager. The acquisition manager is one of your company's executives. He or she should be able to spend at least half of the time working on acquisition program assignments.

4. Select the outside acquisition experts to be employed by your company. These will generally include an acquisition consultant, an attorney, and an accountant.

5. Select and supervise your task force coordinator.

6. Select and control your negotiating team.

7. Meet with the principals of acquisition candidates and attempt to make them receptive to being acquired by your company.

WHY THE ROLE OF YOUR CHIEF EXECUTIVE OFTEN CREATES PROBLEMS

Implementing and coordinating an acquisition program is far more time consuming than most chief executives realize. There will be a tendency for your chief executive to try to be directly involved in all the phases of your acquisition program. When your chief executive fails to limit his involvement to the responsibilities described in the preceding section, he will quickly become overloaded. Then your company's acquisition program will be unable to proceed in a timely, efficient manner.

RESPONSIBILITIES OF YOUR ACQUISITION MANAGER

Your acquisition manager is one of your company's executives. He should be available to spend at least half of his time working on your acquisition program for a period of up to nine months.

The specific responsibilities assigned to your acquisition manager should include:

1. Attending the meetings of your acquisition committee.

2. Providing staff support to your chief executive and your acquisition committee.

3. Coordinating your acquisition search program.

4. Representing your company at exploratory meetings with the owners and senior executives of selling businesses.

5. Serving as a member of your acquisition task force. (The acquisition manager may also be the executive who your company selects to act as its task force coordinator. The responsibilities of the task force coordinator are described later in this chapter.)

6. Participate in your acquisition negotiations either as a member of your negotiating team or in the role of the "honest broker." The "honest broker" acts as an intermediary between your negotiating team and the owners of the selling business. He provides an alternative channel of communication between the seller and your company so that each side can explore issues and concerns which are difficult or embarrassing to handle in face-to-face negotiations. The "honest broker" will suggest compromises when negotiations become stalemated and works to defuse personality conflicts between the buyers and the sellers. (When the acquisition manager is a member of your negotiating team your corporate development consultant, or a finder/broker usually assumes this "honest broker" role.)

QUALIFICATIONS FOR YOUR COMPANY'S ACQUISITION MANAGER

Your acquisition manager must have the complete confidence and trust of your company's chief executive. He or she should be familiar with your company's business and have good personal relationships with your company's senior executives. Prior experience in planning or acquisition is helpful but not essential. It is necessary, however, that your acquisitions manager be detail oriented, be able to communicate well in writing, and understand business accounting.

The individual selected to be your acquisitions program manager may be either a junior- or a senior-level executive. This is an excellent position for a younger executive being prepared to join senior management over the next 12 to 18 months. It is also an ideal position for a senior executive who is nearing the completion of his or her career. In the event that you select such a senior executive to act as acquisitions manager, you should also designate the executive who will be his or her replacement. In this way they can begin assuming their new duties and free up the time of the senior executive to work on acquisitions. After the senior executive retires, he or she can continue to work as your acquisitions manager on an "as-needed" basis.

One common arrangement is to give the company's former (e.g., retired) chief executive responsibility for acquisitions program management. (This is especially common when the company is a family-owned business and a younger relative is now the chief executive.) Unfortunately, this arrangement frequently creates management problems because the former chief executive begins to interfere in the company's management. Companies which assign acquisition manager responsibilities to the former chief executive (who may now be the company's chairman) are often forced to cancel their acquisition program due to management and personality conflicts which develop within the company.

Your decision whether to use a lower-level executive or a senior executive to act as your acquisition manager will generally determine the role which this individual will play in your acquisition negotiations and your acquisition task force. When you select a senior executive as your acquisition manager, this individual will usually have the stature and power within your company which will enable him to serve as a member of your negotiating team and, if you choose, to also act as the coordinator of your acquisition task force. When you choose a lower-level executive as your acquisition manager he will usually play the role of "honest broker" in your acquisition negotiations and will serve as the principal assistant to your task force coordinator.

THE ROLE OF YOUR ACQUISITION SEARCH TEAM

Your acquisition search team plans and implements your acquisition search program. These responsibilities include:

1. Finding acquisition opportunities by directly contacting companies which appear likely to meet your company's screening criteria.

2. Finding acquisition opportunities by contacting intermediaries (e.g., finder/brokers and investment bankers) who have listings of selling businesses.

3. Finding acquisition opportunities by encouraging referrals from your own employees and outside sources which are likely to be aware of companies which seek to be acquired in your target industry (e.g., lawyers, accountants, bankers, consultants).

4. Gathering information on acquisition candidates in your target industry and market area.

5. Determining whether an acquisition candidate appears to meet your company's screening criteria.

6. Preparing written profiles describing individual acquisition candidates which appear to meet your company's screening criteria. These are then presented to your acquisition committee.

WHY YOU NEED AN ACQUISITION SEARCH TEAM

The reasons why you need an acquisition search team include:

1. The work load associated with planning and implementing your acquisition search program is too great to be handled by a single individual.

2. Planning and implementing your acquisition search program effectively requires an understanding of your company and its key personnel, along with prior acquisition search experience. Most companies do not employ a single executive who meets both these requirements.

3. Your company needs to follow up quickly when you find an acquisition candidate which may meet your acquisition screening criteria. This is because the first prospective acquirer which has two exploratory meetings with an acquisition candidate and then makes a reasonable initial price offer usually obtains an exclusive opportunity to negotiate to purchase that selling business. In order to follow up quickly after you find an acquisition candidate which may meet your screening criteria, you need at least two individuals, since one of them may be unavailable at a given point in time.

WHO SHOULD BE ON YOUR ACQUISITION SEARCH TEAM

1. Your acquisition manager.
2. Your acquisition consultant.
3. An acquisition search team alternate. This is a second executive or an outside specialist (e.g., your outside accountant) who has been trained to fill in if your regular team members are unavailable.

THE ROLE OF YOUR ACQUISITION TASK FORCE

Your acquisition task force conducts a thorough investigation of an acquisition candidate which your company is negotiating to purchase. This is called a "due-diligence" investigation. The task force cannot conduct this investigation until after the seller has given your company access to its financial records and its key executives. Therefore, the task force generally begins its work after your company and the seller have executed a "letter of intent." This is a nonbinding memorandum of understanding which outlines the principal terms and conditions of the acquisition transaction.

WHO SHOULD BE ON YOUR ACQUISITION TASK FORCE

Your acquisition task force should consist of one junior or midlevel executive who works for, and represents, each of the senior executives on your acquisition committee. For example, your chief financial officer (who serves on your acquisition committee) might select the company's comptroller to serve on the task force. (Your acquisition manager serves as your chief executive's representative on the task force.) This arrangement has the following benefits:

1. It permits each of your senior executives of your acquisition committee to guide the area of the acquisition candidate investigation about which they are most concerned without requiring a major commitment of their own time.

2. It keeps each senior executive on your acquisition committee informed regarding the ongoing acquisition candidate investigations.

3. It provides valuable training and experience for the junior and midlevel executives who serve on the acquisition task force.

4. Executives and key employees at the selling company will often be more open and candid when dealing with your lower-level executives. One of the reasons is that they feel less threatened and defensive when they are not dealing with a senior executive who is likely to be their new boss after their company is acquired.

In addition to the junior and midlevel executives who represent the senior executives who serve on your company's acquisition committee, your task force should include an accountant and an attorney who are experienced at investigating acquisition candidates.

THE ROLE OF YOUR TASK FORCE COORDINATOR

Your task force coordinator is responsible for:

1. Monitoring and coordinating the work of the task force members

2. Assigning acquisition candidate investigation and analysis responsibilities to the individual task force members

3. Convincing your company's senior executives to select their more talented subordinates to serve on the task force, and to permit these individuals to devote the time necessary to handle their acquisition task force duties

WHO SHOULD BE YOUR TASK FORCE
COORDINATOR

Your task force coordinator should be one of your senior executives who is powerful enough to:

1. Obtain the cooperation of the executives and outside acquisition specialists who the task force members normally report to.
2. Command the respect of the task force members.

Your task force coordinator should, therefore:

1. Be selected by, and have the full confidence and support of, your company's chief executive.
2. Hold an important position in your company's management hierarchy.

In most companies the executive who meets these requirements will hold one of the following positions:

- Executive vice president
- Chief financial officer
- Principal assistant to your chief executive
- Director of corporate development

This executive who is selected to be your company's task force coordinator may also be a senior executive who is also your acquisition manager. The advantages of having the same individual fill both these positions is that it makes it easier to coordinate the acquisition search and the acquisition candidate investigation phases of your acquisition program. The disadvantage of having one of your senior executives fill both roles in your acquisition program management is that it would leave that individual with little time to devote to his or her other ongoing management responsibilities.

THE ROLE OF YOUR COMPANY'S
NEGOTIATING TEAM

Your negotiating team is responsible for the face-to-face negotiations with the owners and senior executives of the selling business. These negotiations begin after your company has made its initial price offer for the seller's business and they have responded with the counteroffer. However, your negotiating team needs to become familiar with the seller's business and needs to begin to develop a relationship and rapport with the owners and senior executives of the acquisition candidate prior to the start of these negotiations. Therefore, at least one member of your negotiating team should participate in your second meeting with the owners and executives of the selling business. As will be discussed in the next chapter, this second meeting with the sellers precedes your making an initial price offer for the seller's business.

THE COMPOSITION OF YOUR NEGOTIATING TEAM

The preferred approach is to start out with a two-person mininegotiating team which includes neither your chief executive nor your outside attorney. The role of this mininegotiating team is to reach agreement with the sellers on the basic outline of an acquisition transaction. The two members of your company's mininegotiating team should include one of your company's senior executives. The second team member may be your acquisition program manager, an acquisition consultant, or a second senior executive. Once your mininegotiating team is close to negotiating the final terms of a preliminary written agreement (called a letter of intent), your negotiating team is temporarily expanded to include your chief executive. After you obtain a letter of intent, your chief executive should withdraw from your negotiating team, which is now expanded to included your outside acquisition attorney. Your chief executive should again rejoin your negotiating team when you are getting close to negotiating the final terms of a purchase agreement.

THE SPECIALISTS YOU WILL NEED TO HELP IMPLEMENT YOUR ACQUISITION PROGRAM

In order to implement your acquisition program, your company will need to employ individuals who are experienced in each of the following areas:

1. Acquisition search
2. Field (accounting) audits of acquisition candidates
3. Structuring of acquisition transactions
4. Legal audits of acquisition candidates
5. Preparing letters of intent, employment agreements, and business purchase contracts

Large companies which are continuously actively seeking acquisition opportunities may employ full-time professionals who are experienced in some or all of these areas of expertise. However, most companies will need to rely on outside experts. The next sections of this chapter will discuss three types of outside experts which you should utilize if your company's own employees are not experienced in these five areas. They are:

1. An acquisition consultant
2. An acquisition accountant
3. An acquisition attorney

QUALIFICATIONS OF YOUR ACQUISITION CONSULTANT

Your acquisition consultant should be an individual or a firm experienced in the following areas:

1. Acquisition planning.
2. Finding selling businesses (acquisition search).
3. Investigating acquisition candidates.
4. Valuing selling businesses.
5. Structuring acquisition transactions.
6. Negotating acquisitions.

THE ROLE OF YOUR ACQUISITION CONSULTANT

The responsibilities of your acquisition consultant should include:

1. Advising your chief executive
2. Advising and providing staff support to your acquisition committee
3. Serving on your acquisition search team
4. Assisting in the valuation of acquisition candidates
5. Advising your task force coordinator
6. Advising and providing staff support to your negotiating team.

WHY YOUR COMPANY NEEDS AN
ACQUISITION CONSULTANT

1. Your consultant helps your chief executive to be more objective in his acquisition decision making. Chief executives tend to be more willing to accept acquisition advice and guidance from an outside acquisition expert than from their company's own executives.

2. It is somewhat difficult and very time consuming for your company to develop its own network of qualified acquisition intermediaries who have listings of suitable selling businesses. An acquisition consultant will usually already have a network of such intermediaries.

3. Your acquisition consultant handles most of the initial acquisition candidate information gathering and the preliminary screening of acquisition candidates. Those functions are very time consuming. Therefore you want to avoid having your company executives perform this work. Otherwise your executives will not have enough time to handle their more important acquisition program and ongoing management responsibilities.

4. Your acquisition consultant can help you select and control the other outside acquistion specialists. These include intermediaries, lawyers, accountants, and appraisers.

5. Your acquisition consultant is a valuable source of advice and assistance of your acquisition manager, task force coordinator, and negotiating team.

TWO TYPES OF INDIVIDUALS AND FIRMS
WHICH YOU CAN USE AS YOUR
ACQUISITION CONSULTANT

1. Acquisition finder/brokers
2. Management consultants who specialize in acquisition work

CHOOSING BETWEEN THESE TWO TYPES OF
ACQUISITION CONSULTANTS

The better acquisition finder/brokers and most acquisition-oriented management consultants are capable of handling the responsibilities of your acquisition consultant. Each tends to be somewhat stronger in handling some of these responsibilities. These are indicated in the following chart:

FINDER/BROKERS	MANAGEMENT CONSULTANTS
acquisition search	acquisition planning
structuring transactions	acquisition candidate investigation
acquisition negotiations	acquisition candidate valuation

Your choice between using a finder/broker or a management consultant to act as your acquisition consultant should therefore be influenced by your analysis of which of these acquisition consultant capabilities are the most important for your company.

HOW TO SELECT YOUR ACQUISITION CONSULTANT

The acquisition consultant who you select should meet each of the following three criteria:

1. Your chief executive likes, respects, and will accept advice from that acquisition consultant.
2. The acquisition consultant has performed satisfactory work for at least six companies which completed an acquisition. (You should confirm this by contacting some of the companies for which the consultant has worked.)
3. The consultant is somewhat familiar with the industry in which you seek to make acquisitions. Whenever possible, you should try to find an acquisition consultant who specializes in this target industry.

HOW TO FIND QUALIFIED ACQUISITION CONSULTANTS

Three of the techniques which you can use are:

1. Contact companies which have made acquisitions in your target industry.
2. Contact the executive secretary of the trade association in your target industry.
3. Solicit recommendations from other acquisition specialists such as attorneys, accountants, and appraisers.

WHY YOU SHOULD CONSIDER USING OUTSIDE ACCOUNTANTS WHO SPECIALIZE IN ACQUISITION WORK

1. Your ability to value an acquisition candidate depends upon your obtaining an accurate understanding of the financial condition and the financial strengths and weaknesses of the selling company. This is a difficult task which requires special expertise. This is especially true when the seller is privately owned. Most privately owned companies do not have audited financial statements. Even when they have audited financial statements, they are likely to be misleading. For example:

   a. Privately owned companies which are very profitable often understate their reported earnings in order to save taxes.

   b. You can expect the financial statements of companies which are having financial difficulties to camouflage these problems skillfully.

2. There are dozens of different ways to structure an acquisition. Each alternative deal structure will produce different short-term and long-term tax consequences for the buyer and for the seller. In many instances it is possible to develop a deal structure which meets the needs of both the buyer and the seller. Special expertise is required to deal with this area. Unless your negotiating team can call upon this expert accounting assistance, their chances of success will be significantly reduced.

3. Investigating and analyzing the financial condition of an acquisition candidate can be done by your company's present outside accounting firm. They will become quite good at performing this role after they have done it a few times. However, over the near term, their lack of experience will slow down your acquisition process and cost you more money than using accountants who specialize in acquisitions work. Even though acquisition accountants may cost more on a per hour basis, they usually will carry out an assignment more rapidly and at lower cost because they require fewer hours to complete a project. This is because they already have in place the necessary data base and systems to conduct acquisition candidate field audits.

WHY MANY PROSPECTIVE ACQUIRERS DO NOT USE ACCOUNTING FIRMS WHICH SPECIALIZE IN ACQUISITIONS WORK

Most companies instead choose to use their present accounting firm to support their acquisition program. The following are some of the reasons:

1. Many companies do not realize that large accounting firms which have merger/ acquisition departments will agree to discount their hourly rates for smaller companies.

2. The company's owner/manager is fearful of alienating his present accounting firm. Frequently this firm is a valuable resource because it provides a great deal of helpful business advice and guidance which they are not directly compensated for.

3. The company is not located in a major metropolitan area. It cannot, therefore, find accounts who specialize in acquisitions in its area. It is more difficult for the company to work with firms which are not conveniently located nearby.

HOW TO CHOOSE ACQUISITION SPECIALIZED ACCOUNTANTS WHO ARE BEST FOR YOUR COMPANY

Your objectives should be to find accountants who meet **five criteria:**

1. They are acquisition specialists.
2. They are experienced working with companies your size.
3. They are familiar with your industry.
4. They are located where you are located.
5. Their acquisition partners are personally compatible with the executives at your company with whom they will be working.

All five criteria are important. However, you may be forced to choose an out-of-town firm in order to get the expertise you will need.

TWO TECHNIQUES FOR LOCATING THESE ACCOUNTING FIRMS

The following sources can help you to find accountants who can support your acquisition program.

1. Your own local accountants are likely to be affiliated with a larger accounting firm which has an acquisitions department.
2. Your industry trade association can identify accounting firms which specialize in your industry and may have acquisitions experience.

WHAT TO DO ONCE YOU HAVE IDENTIFIED SEVERAL ACCOUNTING FIRMS WHICH YOU MIGHT EMPLOY FOR YOUR ACQUISITION PROGRAM

Go and meet with all of them. Discuss your company and its acquisition plans. Ask them what experience they have had that would be relevant to your needs. Act a little naive and helpless. You will come away from these meetings with thousands of dollars worth of valuable advice, and you will also, it is hoped, find the firm which will do the best job for your company.

ANOTHER ACQUISITION PROFESSIONAL YOU WILL NEED TO EMPLOY

• An experienced acquisition attorney.

THE ROLE OF YOUR ACQUISITION ATTORNEY

1. Prepare the standard finder's fee agreement which you will use to employ intermediaries to search for acquisition opportunities.
2. Prepare or review contracts and agreements with consultants, accountants, and other professionals whom you employ to work on your acquisition program.
3. Prepare "letter of intent" agreements. These are preliminary agreements of sale between the prospective acquirer and the acquisition candidate.
4. Prepare or review acquisition agreements between the acquisition candidate and your company. These agreements will typically include the purchase contract, noncompete agreements, and consulting contracts with the former owners.
5. Identify and analyze the potential legal problems and risks of your owning the selling company. The following are examples:

   a. Contracts with suppliers and customers
   b. Loan agreements
   c. Franchise agreements
   d. Employment contracts
   e. Lawsuits (ongoing and prospective)

6. Advise and assist your negotiating team.

WHY YOU SHOULD EMPLOY AN ATTORNEY
WHO IS AN ACQUISITIONS EXPERT

1. The attorney will be able to prepare the legal agreements you need more rapidly. This is important. Many companies lose excellent acquisition opportunities because the principals of the selling company begin looking elsewhere for a purchaser when the prospective acquirer's attorneys take too long to prepare agreements or take too long to respond to those prepared by the seller's counsel.

2. It is less expensive. Though an acquisition attorney may charge a higher hourly rate, bills will be lower because it takes him or her far less time to do the work than it takes a good business attorney who has limited acquisition experience.

3. An experienced acquisition attorney can provide you with valuable free acquisition advice based on his or her involvement with other companies which faced the same problems that you will encounter in implementing your acquisition program.

DO NOT USE YOUR ACQUISITION ATTORNEY
AS YOUR NEGOTIATOR

This is a danger area for many companies. Since the principals of your company usually have limited experience acquiring other companies, there is a tendency to rely on attorneys to negotiate with the seller. This virtually guarantees that the negotiations will be unsuccessful.

The role of your acquisition attorney in the negotiation process is to identify the hundreds of different legal risks and problems that may occur if you purchase the selling company. His job is not to balance potential benefits, costs, and risks; only you can make these decisions. If your attorney handles your negotiations, he will insist on eliminating all your risks by making the seller remain responsible for anything that goes wrong after you own the seller's company. If the seller wanted to continue to be responsible for its business it wouldn't be selling it. As a result the negotiations will fail.

WHEN YOU CAN USE YOUR COMPANY'S
REGULAR ATTORNEY TO SERVE ON
YOUR NEGOTIATING TEAM

When your attorney is one of your key business advisors, who coincidentally has a law degree, he or she can frequently be effective as one member of your two-person negotiating team. However, when your attorney is primarily a legal expert, rather than business advisor, he or she should not be placed in a negotiating role.

HOW TO AVOID CONFLICTS BETWEEN YOUR COMPANY'S REGULAR ATTORNEY AND YOUR ACQUISITIONS ATTORNEY

Have your regular outside attorney help you find and select an acquisitions attorney. Most local law firms have good contacts at larger firms which have acquisition specialists.

C·H·A·P·T·E·R T·E·N

HOW TO NEGOTIATE THE ACQUISITION

WHAT THIS CHAPTER COVERS

This chapter describes the techniques and procedures which will help your company proceed from the time you find selling businesses which you might want to own to your completion of acquisition negotiations.

HOW THIS CHAPTER IS ORGANIZED

This chapter consists of two parts. The first sections describe the goals, objectives, and characteristics of acquisition negotiations. In combination with the previous chapter, Staffing and Managing Your Acquisition Program, this will help you to understand and use the techniques and procedures recommended in the later sections of this chapter. These later sections discuss your acquisition program in roughly chronological order, starting with when you find an acquisition candidate which appears to be somewhat attractive and concluding with some guidelines to help you negotiate a final agreement to purchase a business.

THE PURPOSE OF ACQUISITION NEGOTIATIONS

Acquisition negotiations seek to define and narrow the issues so that the acquirer and the selling company can reach agreement on a basis that both parties find acceptable. Since the prospective acquirer does not need to acquire a particular selling business, and the owners of a profitable selling business can usually choose not to sell at this time, neither party will reach final agreement unless they each feel that the purchase and sale of the business will achieve most of their financial, personal, and business objectives.

HOW ACQUISITION NEGOTIATIONS ARE CONDUCTED

Contrary to popular belief, acquisition negotiations rarely consist of two groups of negotiators seated on opposite sides of a table, hammering out the terms and conditions of the acquisition. Acquisition negotiations involve the interchange of information, ideas, and positions. This usually occurs during many meetings, telephone calls, brief conversations, and exchanges of written proposals, spread over a period of several weeks or months.

YOUR FOUR ACQUISITION NEGOTIATION OBJECTIVES

1. To convince the owners and senior executives of the selling business that your company is a legitimate (serious) potential purchaser for their business. Until the sellers view your company in this way, they will withhold the confidential business and financial information you need to evaluate their business. There are three factors which cause the owners and senior executives of a selling business to consider your company as a legitimate potential purchaser. These are:

   a. Your company appears to have the financial resources necessary to acquire their business for a fair price.

   b. Your company has a logical business reason for wanting to own and operate their business. (When there is no logical business reason for a prospective acquirer to purchase their business, the sellers will suspect that this prospective acquirer will be unwilling to offer a fair price for their business since it is likely to be of less value to that purchaser.)

   c. Your company demonstrates its preliminary interest in purchasing the seller's business by sending your representative to meet with the owners and senior executives of the selling business.

2. To obtain from the owners and senior executives of the selling business the information you need to analyze their assets, liabilities, current revenues and

current earnings, and to make a preliminary estimate of the future revenue and earnings producing potential of the seller's business. (This is the information which you need to estimate the fair market value of the seller's business so that you can prepare a preliminary price offer.) It includes the seller's financial statements for the past two or three years and supplemental information which will help you to understand and interpret the information contained in their financial statements. Examples of this supplemental information include:

a. Direct and indirect compensation paid to the seller's owner/executives.
b. Accounting policies and inventory practices.
c. The identification and estimated values for hidden assets. These are assets which are not listed or which are undervalued on the seller's balance sheet.
d. The identification of potential liabilities which are not shown on the seller's balance sheet. These types of liabilities include contingent liabilities, unfavorable long-term sales contracts, pending litigation, unfunded pension liabilities, and the expiration of favorable long-term leases and supply contracts.

3. To convince the owners and senior executives of the selling business that your company is the one with which they should commence serious price negotiations. Once the seller commences price negotiations with your company, it will usually postpone starting negotiations with other prospective purchasers while your negotiations with them are still continuing. The factors which cause the owner of the selling business to commence serious price negotiations with your company include those outlined in the first negotiation objective and one other important factor. This is:

> *Your company makes a preliminary price offer which the seller considers too low, but somewhat reasonable.* The seller will consider any initial price offer which you make to be too low. Usually it will consider a preliminary price offer that is 70% to 80% of the estimated fair market value of its business to be reasonable enough to warrant its making a counterproposal. This constitutes the commencement of serious price negotiations.

4. To encourage the owner of the selling business to moderate (lower) its selling price expectations. Most owners start out with inflated or overly optimistic selling price expectations. It generally takes several weeks or months of discussions before the owner of a business becomes realistic in its selling price expectations.

Stretching out the price negotiating process and other techniques which will encourage the seller to lower the price expectations are discussed later in this chapter.

THREE UNIQUE CHARACTERISTICS OF ACQUISITION NEGOTIATIONS

1. The owners of the selling business will decide whether or not they want your company to be the new owner of their business. Unless the owners of the selling business decide that your company would be a suitable owner of their business, they will sabotage your negotiations. For example, the sellers will:

   a. Withhold access to key information
   b. Require difficult payment terms (e.g., all cash at closing)
   c. Constantly reopen negotiations of issues which had apparently been resolved

2. The price for which a business is finally sold is rarely an important issue. Businesses are almost always sold for prices which are close to (plus or minus 20%) their fair market value. Acquirers who claim to have negotiated a bargain purchase price for a business usually overlooked hidden problems and, therefore, overestimated the fair market value of the seller's business.

3. Acquisition price negotiations usually require considerably more buyer patience and persistence than do other types of price negotiations.

WHY THE BUYER'S PATIENCE AND PERSISTENCE ARE CRITICAL TO NEGOTIATING SUCCESS

The owners of a selling business usually develop their initial asking price in either of two ways. These are:

1. The amount of money which they would like to receive so that they can achieve all of their personal financial objectives (e.g., becoming millionaires)

2. A price which they would be happy to accept because it exceeds by a considerable margin their own estimate of how much their business is worth

In either case the seller's initial asking price is generally at least 50% higher than the price which any prospective buyer would be willing to pay.

The owners of a business who have a serious desire to sell that business will eventually, reluctantly, reduce their price expectations to a level which approximates fair market value. This process generally takes several weeks or months. Once the sellers' price expectations approach (decline to) the fair market value of their business, whichever buyer with which they are negotiating at the time usually has the first opportunity to purchase the business for this more reasonable price. When your company is the first prospective acquirer to commence serious negotiations with a selling business, your goal is to still be negotiating with the sellers when their selling price expectations finally decline to a reasonable price level. When some other company has already been involved in unsuccessful price negotiations with the sellers (due to their unreasonably high price expectations), your strategy is to move in quickly, since the sellers are likely to be more reasonable the second time around.

WHY SELLERS CARE ABOUT WHO WILL BE THE NEW OWNER OF THEIR BUSINESS

The owner/executives of a business often have a great deal of affection and loyalty for and pride in that business. This emotional attachment makes sense when you consider that most of the owner/executives' waking hours have probably been devoted to that business for many years. Due to this emotional attachment to their business, the sellers would usually prefer to sell their business to a company which they find attractive.

FACTORS WHICH MAKE A PROSPECTIVE ACQUIRER MORE ATTRACTIVE TO THE OWNER/EXECUTIVES OF A SELLING BUSINESS

1. The prospective acquirer appears to have the financial resources to purchase the selling business for a fair price.
2. The prospective acquirer shows a complimentary attitude toward both the seller's business and its owner/executives.
3. The prospective acquirer does not indicate a desire to make changes in the seller's business which would irritate or embarrass its selling owners. For example, the prospective acquirer does not indicate that it plans to relocate the seller's business, dismiss trusted employees, replace long-time suppliers, or change the name of the seller's company.
4. The prospective acquirer has a respectful attitude toward the owner/executives and their ideas and suggestions.
5. The prospective acquirer offers to provide those former owner/executives who do not desire to separate fully from their business with executive positions or consulting assignments.

A prospective purchaser which has made itself attractive to the owner/executives of the selling business is called a "preferred buyer." Some of the factors which help a prospective acquirer to become a preferred buyer were outlined in this section. Additional techniques are presented in later sections of this chapter.

THE ADVANTAGE OF BECOMING THE "PREFERRED BUYER" OF A SELLING BUSINESS

There are three advantages to becoming the preferred buyer of a selling business. Prior to discussing these advantages it is important to recognize that becoming the preferred buyer of a selling business will not cause the owners to sell that business to you for a significant discount below its fair market value. The reason is that the owners of a selling business are first and foremost practical business executives. They would prefer to sell their business to a company which they feel would be a good owner for their business, but only if it would not cost them much money. For example, give the choice between selling their business to a "preferred buyer" for $10 million, or selling to a prospective purchaser who would pay $15 million, but embarrass the former owners by dismissing long-time employees and moving the business to Haiti, most sellers will choose the $15 million offer.

There are three potential advantages to becoming the "preferred acquirer" of a seller's business. These are:

1. You can generally purchase the seller's business for 5% to 10% less than it would require some other prospective purchaser to pay for the business.
2. The seller is more likely to accept payment terms which will make it easier for your company to finance its acquisition of the business. For example, the seller may agree to accept a lower cash down payment than it would accept from some other prospective purchaser.
3. The seller will make it easier for you to analyze its business by providing you with more accurate and complete information.

THE SIX STAGES OF THE ACQUISITION CANDIDATE INVESTIGATION-ANALYSIS-NEGOTIATION PROCESS

1. Exploratory meetings with the owners and senior executives of the selling business (information gathering)
2. Preliminary price negotiations
3. "Letter of intent" negotiations

4. Due diligence investigation (information gathering)

5. "Purchase contract" negotiations

6. Renegotiation and closing

WHY YOU NEED TO SET UP AN ACQUISITION PROGRAM ORGANIZATION

When your acquisition program is underway, your company will be simultaneously involved in several of these six negotiating stages while also continuing to search for acquisition candidates. For example, your company may be reviewing nine acquisition candidates which responded to a recent direct-mail solicitation, having exploratory meetings with four acquisition candidates, conducting preliminary price negotiations with three acquisition candidates, conducting letter of intent negotiations with two acquisition candidates, and carrying out a due diligence investigation of one acquisition candidate. Even though you may only be seeking to acquire one or two businesses, all this activity is necessary since experience has shown that a company must find and pursue ten suitable acquisition candidates in order to be assured of completing at least one acquisition.

Simultaneously searching for acquisition candidates, while being involved in several different stages of the acquisition negotiating process, creates a tremendous management and staff work load and will require expertise in many different areas. At the same time your company must continue to manage and operate its present business. The solution to this severe staffing and management problem is to create an acquisition program organization which:

1. Uses outside acquisition specialists to supplement your company's staff resources

2. Uses outside acquisition specialists to provide expertise and guidance in areas in which your own executives may lack suitable experience or training (e.g., conducting accounting and legal field audits of selling businesses)

3. Spreads out the remaining acquisition program work load among your company's executives

4. Assigns clear responsibility for each of the key areas of your acquisition program

The strategies and techniques used to create an acquisition program organization which accomplishes these objectives were described in the previous chapter, Staffing and Managing Your Acquisition Program.

AVOID PREMATURE ACQUISITION
CANDIDATE SELECTION

As soon as your company's acquisition search program begins to uncover selling businesses in your target industry segment, the natural response of your senior executives will be to try to use an attractiveness rating system to rate these companies. Typically, they will choose to use a three-tier rating system such as:

- Excellent–good–fair
- Very attractive–attractive–unattractive

Their reason for desiring to employ a rating system at this early stage in your acquisition program is to pick out the most attractive candidates for your company to meet with. This is neither a reasonable nor an effective approach. Some of the reasons why you should not use this approach are:

1. Your company will rarely have the information and insights required to analyze the relative attractiveness of a selling business until after your representative has had a face-to-face meeting with the owners and senior executives of a selling business.

2. It is fun and interesting for your senior executives to sit around discussing how to rate acquisition candidates for which you have only sketchy information. Each of your senior executives gets a chance to present his or her own views on how your company should grow and prosper, while pretending to be discussing the merits and weaknesses of the individual acquisition candidates. These meetings frequently lead to poor choices regarding which acquisition candidates you should visit. This is because when you have only limited information describing individual acquisition candidates, your attractiveness ratings will tend to reflect the power and influence of the executives who liked or disliked a particular acquisition candidate.

3. Your senior executives will become excited about the prospects of owning a particular acquisition candidate. Then they will often be disappointed when they meet with the owners and senior executives of that selling business and find that it is less attractive than their imaginations led them to expect. After riding this emotional roller coaster a few times, your senior executives are likely to become frustrated and lose interest in your acquisition program.

HOW TO PROCEED AFTER YOU FIND A SELLING BUSINESS WHICH MAY MEET YOUR SCREENING CRITERIA

The correct approach is to have one of your representatives meet with the owners and senior executives of the selling business. Then following this meeting your company should have enough additional information about the selling business to analyze whether it is attractive enough to merit a follow-up visit by one or more of your senior executives.

EXPLORATORY MEETINGS WITH THE OWNERS AND SENIOR EXECUTIVES OF THE SELLING BUSINESS

The initial stage of the acquisition negotiating process consists of the first two meetings between representatives from your company and the owners and senior executives of the selling business. It is important that you limit discussions to an exchange of information and delay making an initial price offer. The reasons are:

1. Until you have an opportunity to review, analyze, and ask questions about the seller's financial statements, you are likely to either overestimate or underestimate its value. When you overestimate its value, you may make a preliminary price offer which is too high. The sellers will resent it if your subsequent price offers are lower and will feel that you "tricked" them. On the other hand, when you underestimate the value of the seller's business, you may make a price offer which is significantly below its fair market value. The normal response of the seller to such a price offer will be to refuse to provide your company with additional information about the business and to start negotiating with someone else.

2. The seller is more likely to accept your initial price offer as the basis for beginning serious negotiations if the structure of this offer is tailored to the seller's personal financial and psychological objectives. For example, if the owner/executive of the selling business is 67 years old and in poor health, he would find an earnout arrangement which requires him to continue managing the business for five years rather unattractive. On the other hand, if the owner/executives of the selling business would prefer to stay and use your financial resources to grow their business, an earnout arrangement which offered the

prospect of a higher price over three years might be more attractive than a significantly lower price offer which would be paid in cash at closing. Until you have had two meetings with the seller (the second of which was attended by your chief executive), you will usually not have enough understanding of the seller's financial and nonfinancial objectives to structure a price offer to make it attractive to the sellers.

3. Price negotiations will proceed more smoothly and successfully when you have developed a rapport with the owners and senior executives of the selling business. This relationship building process stops when price negotiations begin. Therefore, you do not want to begin price negotiations too quickly.

THREE PRIMARY GOALS OF YOUR EXPLORATORY MEETINGS WITH THE SELLERS

1. Your first goal is to confirm that the seller's business does in fact meet your company's acquisition screening criteria. This may seem unnecessary since you would not be meeting with the seller unless you thought that its business met your screening criteria. Often, however, you will find that the information which you received describing a selling business is inaccurate. For example:

   a. Revenues are often overstated.
   b. A business reported as being "profitable" may not yet be profitable.
   c. Significant revenues and earnings may come from unexpected sources. For example, a business which you thought was primarily a manufacturer might be deriving a substantial portion of its sales and revenues from marketing finished goods produced by other manufacturers.
   d. Indications that the management wants to stay, or plans to leave the business after it is sold, are often incorrect. In face-to-face discussions with the owners and senior executives of a selling business you might learn that:
      (1) Even though the owner/executives plan to retire in a year, the real senior management consists of nonowner/executives who will stay on.
      (2) Though the seller indicated that management would stay following the sale, key senior executives have outside business interests which make this unlikely.

2. Your second goal is to gather information about the seller's business which will help your acquisition committee determine how well that business meets your company's selection criteria. Examples of this type of information include:

   a. Management quality
   b. Management depth
   c. Product and service reputation
   d. Growth potential
   e. Profitability
   f. Marketing skill
   g. Manufacturing efficiency
   h. Manufacturing capacity
   i. Competitive strengths and weaknesses
   j. Product development capabilities
   k. Supplier relationships

3. Your third goal is to gather additional information about the seller's business which you need to estimate its fair market value. This information would include:
   a. Current and historical financial statements (balance sheet, income statements, and cash flow statements)
   b. Explanations of accounting policies and financial practices (e.g., leasing fixed assets) which affected the seller's reported net worth, earnings, and cash flow.
   c. Projected revenues, income, and cash flow for the next two years.

TWO IMPORTANT SECONDARY GOALS

While pursuing the three primary goals already described, you should also use your first two meetings with the owners and senior executives of the selling business to pursue two important secondary goals. These are:

1. Establishing your credibility as a legitimate purchaser of the seller's business
2. Developing a rapport (positive personal relationships) with the owners and senior executives of the selling business

TECHNIQUES WHICH HELP YOUR COMPANY ESTABLISH CREDIBILITY AND DEVELOP A RAPPORT WITH THE SELLERS

Some of the techniques which will help you use your exploratory meetings with the sellers to establish your credibility and to build a rapport with the owners and senior executives of the selling business include:

1. Praise the seller's business. Express open admiration for the job which they have done building and preserving this business.

2. Do not suggest changes or improvements which your company plans to make after it owns the seller's business.

3. Mention a weakness or problem which your company has, which purchasing the seller's business would help correct.

4. Describe the proposed transaction as a combination of two businesses which would benefit both businesses.

5. Provide the seller with a written description of your company's business. Suggestions for items to include in this description are discussed later in this chapter.

6. Whenever the seller inquires about price, respond that your company is prepared to pay a fair price and has the financial resources to do so.

7. Do not indicate that you might require financing (e.g., a deferred payout arrangement) from the seller. Indicate that your company intends to make its own financing arrangements through its banks. (Later if you propose that the seller finances a portion of the purchase price, this will be presented as a means of providing the seller with a higher price, which you feel is justified but which your bank doesn't understand.)

HOW MANY REPRESENTATIVES TO SEND TO YOUR INITIAL MEETING WITH THE SELLERS

You should send either one or two representatives to meet with the owners and senior executives of a selling business. The advantages of sending two representatives are threefold:

1. It will make a better impression than if you only send one representative.

2. One of your representatives can concentrate on making notes and preparing follow-up questions while the other is speaking.

3. A single representative may feel intimidated meeting simultaneously with the owners and several executives from the selling business.

The disadvantages of having two of your representatives, rather than a single representative meet with the seller, are:

1. It increases your personnel requirements.
2. It doubles your travel expenses.
3. It may be difficult to coordinate the schedules and availability of two representatives.

FACTORS TO CONSIDER WHEN DECIDING WHO TO SEND TO VISIT A SELLING BUSINESS

Your first meeting with the owners and senior executives of a selling business should be a reconnaissance mission. Therefore, you want to send a representative or representatives who:

1. Understand the information you need
2. Have good information gathering skills

Your secondary goals for the first meeting are to establish your credibility as a legitimate purchaser of the seller's business and to begin to develop a rapport with the owners and senior executives of the selling business. Therefore, your representative or representatives should be an individual or individuals who:

1. Will make a good impression
2. Are familiar with your company
3. Have good marketing skills

As discussed earlier in this chapter, it is important that your initial meeting with the seller not turn into a negotiating session. Therefore, you do not want to send a representative or representatives whom the seller:

1. Would consider senior enough to begin price negotiations on your behalf
2. Would expect to be a member of your negotiating team

WHY YOUR CHIEF EXECUTIVE SHOULD NOT REPRESENT YOU AT YOUR FIRST MEETING WITH THE SELLER

The owners of a selling business will always prefer to meet with your company's chief executive. You may be tempted to have your chief executive make this initial visit since he is likely to be your most effective sales representative. It is important that you delay having your chief executive meet with the seller until your initial meeting with the seller has confirmed that its business meets your company's acquisition screening criteria. This avoids three potential problems. They are:

1. *Overburdening your chief executive.* Visiting acquisition candidates is very time consuming. You do not want to waste the limited time which your company's chief executive by having him meet with the selling businesses which may turn out to be unsuitable (e.g., it does not meet your company's screening criteria).

2. *Indicating a desire to acquire a selling business which may be unsuitable.* The sellers will assume that a visit by your chief executive indicates that you have decided that you wish to purchase their business. Then if the sellers' business does not meet your screening criteria and you therefore terminate further discussions, the sellers will feel that you acted in bad faith. This will hurt your company's reputation as a legitimate purchaser of businesses in the seller's industry segment.

3. *Making a premature price offer.* The seller will expect your chief executive to give some indication of how much your company is prepared to pay for the business. Your chief executive will often be forced to give a purchase price indication even though you have not had an opportunity to gather and analyze the information needed to make a reasonably accurate estimate of the selling company's fair market value.

4. *Less information gathering.* The seller will always view your senior executive as your company's top negotiator. His presence at your first meeting with the seller shifts the focus from information gathering to preliminary negotiation. Following an initial meeting with the seller which was attended by your company's chief executive you will often find that you spent much of your time answering the seller's questions rather than learning about the seller's business and the financial and personal goals of the seller's owners and senior executives.

WHY YOU SHOULD NOT HAVE ONE OF YOUR OTHER SENIOR EXECUTIVES REPRESENT YOU.

Another approach would be to send one of your company's other senior executives to have the initial meeting with the owners and senior executives of the selling business. This approach should however also be avoided. The reasons are:

1. The seller will feel slighted that a senior executive other than your chief executive came to meet with it.

2. When your senior executive displays candor in discussing your business, this may be interpreted as disloyalty. However, if your senior executive is reticent, this will make the seller less likely to disclose its company's weaknesses and problems.

3. Your senior executive cannot "sell" the seller on how wonderful your company is without appearing to be bragging.

4. Though your senior executive may be a fine manager, he may not have the personality of an effective salesman.

WHO YOU SHOULD SEND TO YOUR FIRST MEETING WITH THE OWNERS OF THE SELLING BUSINESS

Your best choice is to send one or two of the following types of individuals to make the initial visit to meet with the owners and senior executives of a selling business:

1. Staff executives who handle special projects for your company's chief executive (This may include your acquisition program manager.)

2. Your acquisition consultant(s)

3. Your attorney(s)

4. Your accountant(s)

5. Your outside director(s)

HOW THIS CHOICE OF REPRESENTATIVES HELPS YOUR COMPANY

There are several advantages to sending these types of individuals rather than your chief executive or one of your other senior executives, to meet with the sellers. They include:

1. This establishes the initial meeting as an opportunity to exchange information rather than as an initial negotiating session.

2. Your representative(s) can mention one or two of your company's weaknesses or problems without appearing to be disloyal. Mentioning one or two of your company's weaknesses or problems encourages the seller to be more candid in responding to your representative's questions.

3. Your representatives can give a complimentary description of your company without appearing to be "bragging."

4. Your company will not be held responsible for your representative's comments and statements since they are not part of your company's senior management.

HOW TO PREPARE FOR YOUR INITIAL MEETING, WITH THE OWNERS AND EXECUTIVES OF SELLING BUSINESSES

1. Select your representatives who will be available to visit selling businesses.

2. Develop an acquisition candidate profile form.

3. Prepare an information package describing your own company.

THE NUMBER OF REPRESENTATIVES YOU WILL NEED

The number of representatives whom you will need to have available to make initial visits to meet with the owners and senior executives of selling businesses depends upon whether you will usually send one or two representatives to meet with each seller. When your company will usually be sending a single representative you will need two representatives. When you will usually be sending two representatives to each initial meeting, you will need three representatives. Each of your representatives should be able to devote four days per month to making these visits.

The reason you need to have an extra representative available to make initial visits to meet with selling businesses is that acquisition search programs tend to work in spurts. You can expect to find no suitable acquisition candidates for several weeks and then find five or six suitable candidates over a two-week period. Once you find a suitable acquisition candidate, it is important that you follow up and meet with the seller within two weeks. This rapid follow-up automatically gains credibility for your company as a legitimate purchaser of the seller's business. By having more representatives who are available to represent you at initial meetings with the seller, you will be able to handle this work load in a timely manner. This multiple representative arrangement also provides you with backup for times when one of your regular representatives is not available to visit selling businesses due to vacations, illness, or nonacquisition program work responsibilities.

HOW TO PREPARE AN ACQUISITION
CANDIDATE PROFILE

An acquisition candidate profile is a one- or two-page questionnaire-type form which is used to organize and record mostly nonfinancial information about a selling business. The information categories and questions on your form should represent the key types of information which you would like to have in order to determine:

1. Whether the acquisition candidate meets your screening criteria
2. To what extent the acquisition candidate fits your company's selection (comparative attractiveness) criteria

It works best if you can fit this profile form on a single 8 ½" x 14" page. The reason is that there is a tendency for your busy executives who will be reviewing these write-ups not to flip over and read the second page. When the information which you need to include on your acquisition candidate profile will not fit on a single page, you should put the most important categories and questions on the first page of your two-page form.

The following are examples of the information categories and questions a company might consider including on its acquisition candidate profile form if it is was interested in purchasing a manufacturing business:

- Company name, address, and telephone number
- Contact person at company (name and title)
- Type of business (industry segment and principal products)
- How large are they? (number of employees and estimated annual revenues)
- Profitable? (check "yes" or "no" and indicate annual income)
- Where do they market? (list geographic markets and percentage or proportion of sales made in each of these market areas)
- To whom do they sell? (list types of customers and percentage, or proportion of sales made to each type of customer and identify largest customers)
- How do they market? (describe marketing network and resources, sales practices, distribution methods, etc.)
- How large is their market share?
- Who are their principal competitors?
- How large are these competitors?

- How do they produce or obtain each of the principal products or services which they produce?
- What do they buy and who do they buy from? (key suppliers)
- Describe their manufacturing facilities and capabilities.
- Do they have unused manufacturing capacity? how much?
- What are their expansion plans?
- How much would it cost to implement these plans?
- Who manages the business? (list principal executives, titles, or functions and provide brief profiles)
- How well do they manage it? (e.g., excellent, good, or fair)
- Who owns the business?
- Why do they want to sell?
- What follow up is required? (include actions taken and dates)

THREE REASONS TO PREPARE ACQUISITION CANDIDATE PROFILE FORMS

Your acquisition candidate form serves three purposes. These are:

1. It provides a checklist to guide your information gathering efforts.
2. It summarizes the important information on an acquisition candidate.
3. It becomes the cover sheet(s) for your file on that acquisition candidate. Financial statements and supplementary information such as product catalogs are placed in a file folder with the profile attached to the outside of the folder.

HOW TO USE ACQUISITION PROFILE FORMS

1. Begin to fill in an acquisition candidate profile form as soon as your acquisition search program uncovers a selling business.
2. Order a Dun & Bradstreet credit report for the acquisition candidate. Use the information contained in the D&B report to fill in missing information on your acquisition candidate profile form.
3. When an acquisition candidate clearly does not meet your screening criteria,

indicate the reason (e.g., too small) on your profile form and place the profile in a "dead deal" file.

4. When an acquisition candidate appears to meet your screening criteria, make a list of the missing information on their profile form and use this list to guide your questioning at your initial meeting with the owners and senior executives of the selling business.

5. Following his or her first meeting with the seller, your representative fills in as much of the remaining missing information on the profile form as possible.

6. Whenever you obtain the financial statements for the seller's business, these are attached to their acquisition candidate profile form.

7. The acquisition candidate profiles (with attached financial statements if available) are presented to your chief executive. When a profile indicates that a selling business appears to meet your company's acquisition screening criteria, a second exploratory meeting with the seller's owners and senior executives is arranged.

8. Your representatives who will attend your second meeting with the seller (e.g., your chief executive) review that company's acquisition candidate profile to prepare themselves for this meeting. A list of the missing information on the profile form is prepared and is used by your representatives to guide their questioning at this second meeting with the owners and senior executives of the selling business.

9. Following their second meeting with the seller, your representatives add to the acquisition candidate profile form any missing information which they obtained.

10. The acquisition candidate profiles of those selling businesses which you have met with two times are submitted to your acquisition committee.

11. Your acquisition committee compares those selling businesses and ranks them in order of relative attractiveness. The committee authorizes your company to make a preliminary price offer for the higher ranking of these selling businesses.

WHY YOU SHOULD DEVELOP AN INFORMATION PACKAGE DESCRIBING YOUR OWN COMPANY

1. Providing the owners and senior executives of a selling company with segments of this information package describing your business encourages them to reciprocate by providing your representatives with the information you desire

describing the selling business. It also helps your company establish its credibility as a legitimate purchaser of the sellers' business.

2. Providing the information package to acquisition search intermediaries (e.g., finders and brokers) helps them to understand better your company and its acquisition criteria. It encourages these intermediaries to refer suitable acquisition opportunities to your company, but discourages them from referring acquisition candidates which would not fit your acquisition objectives.

HOW TO PREPARE AN INFORMATION PACKAGE DESCRIBING YOUR OWN COMPANY

A convenient and effective way to prepare this information package is to fill in your acquisition candidate profile form for your own company. Then add to this (unless it is already included on your profile form) the following information:

1. A one- or two-paragraph company history

2. A description of your management philosophy and growth plans

3. An organization chart and brief biographies of your senior executives

4. Product catalogs and brochures

5. Business, professional, and credit references

6. A brief ownership description

7. Your acquisition criteria (stated in general terms)

HOW TO USE YOUR INFORMATION PACKAGE

There are two ways in which you should use your information package to support your acquisition program. These are:

1. To develop a buyer's profile of your company. This is a two-page summary which describes your company and its acquisition objectives.

2. To provide a pool of written information from which you will select segments to send to a selling company which you are negotiating to purchase. During your negotiations to acquire a selling business, you will get more cooperation and information if you exchange information, rather than requesting the seller to provide you with written information describing their business, without ever reciprocating.

TYPES OF INFORMATION TO INCLUDE IN YOUR BUYER'S PROFILE

Some of the types of information which you should include in your two-page buyer's profile include:

1. A brief description and history of your business
2. A description of your principal products and services
3. A description of where you operate and the types of customers you sell to
4. A list indicating the locations and providing a brief description of your principal manufacturing, distribution, and sales facilities
5. A list of your senior management personnel with their titles and responsibilities (e.g., Harold Golderg, vice president, Eastern sales manager)
6. An indication of how large your company is. For example, you could indicate your annual sales or number of employees
7. A description of your company's growth plans and acquisition objectives

HOW TO USE YOUR BUYER'S PROFILE

There are two ways in which you can use your two-page buyer's profile. These are:

1. To provide your representatives and intermediaries (e.g., finders and brokers) with a document which they can send to selling companies which respond to your acquisition search solicitations (e.g., advertising and direct mail). Sending this document encourages a seller to reciprocate by providing you with information describing their business. It also makes the seller more receptive to meeting with your representative.
2. When your representative visits a selling business which has not already been provided with your profile, he or she provides the sellers with your summary profile at this initial meeting. This encourages the seller to view your company as a legitimate (serious) prospective purchaser of their business.

WHAT YOUR REPRESENTATIVE SHOULD DO FOLLOWING HIS FIRST MEETING WITH THE SELLER

1. As soon as he leaves the seller's offices, he should write down any new facts which he learned about the seller's business and the names and short profiles

of the individuals who he met with. The important thing is for your representative to write down everything which he remembers before he forgets. Later, he can sort through these notes and pick out the more important information.

2. Upon returning to his home or office, your representative should add the key information which he learned about the seller's business to the one- or two-page acquisition candidate profile form for that company. This is the form which was used to record information about the selling business when it first responded to your acquisition search efforts.

3. In addition to the information added to the acquisition candidate profile form, your representative should prepare and attach a brief narrative description of his visit. This should include the names and brief profiles of the people he met with at the selling business.

4. Within two days following the meeting with the seller, your representative should send a one-page letter to the chief executive of the selling business. This letter should thank him for taking the time to meet, indicate that he was impressed with the seller's company, and indicate that he will be contacting him again in a few days. Receiving this courtesy letter tends to make a good impression for your company with the seller.

5. Following your company's decision to either proceed or delay further discussions with this selling business, your representative should phone the seller's chief executive. When you wish to continue discussions he should arrange a second visit. When you do not wish to continue discussions, your representative should indicate a logical reason why your company has chosen not to proceed further *at this time*. For example:

> "They (your Company) want to try to find a larger business for their first acquisition."
>
> "They want to try to find a business which could use their existing marketing network."
>
> "They want to delay until after they complete their refinancing."
>
> "They have decided that they should first try to find a business located closer to their present operations."

It is better that someone other than one of your senior executives be the one to advise a seller that your company is not interested in pursuing the seller's business at this time. The reason is that the seller will feel that your representative was the one who didn't understand exactly what you wanted, rather than that your company doesn't know exactly what it wants to buy and therefore wasted the seller's time. Thus, your representative rather than your company becomes the focus of the seller's disappointment hostility. This will make it easier for your company to revive conversations with the seller in the event that you later change your mind. This is an additional reason why it is better to have a representative who is not one of your company's senior executives have the first meeting with the owners and senior executives of a selling business.

THE OBJECTIVES OF YOUR SECOND MEETING WITH THE SELLER

Usually your first meeting with the seller will have provided you with information which confirmed that the selling business meets your company's acquisition screening criteria. Therefore, the primary objective of your second meeting with the seller is to obtain the information which you need to make a preliminary price offer. This information includes:

1. Current financial statements (balance sheet and income statements)
2. An explanation of the accounting policies which were used to prepare these statements
3. Information which would help you to interpret and analyze these statements, for example, excess compensation paid to owner/executives, transactions with affiliates, tax avoidance practices
4. Projected revenues and expenses for the next 12- to 24-month period
5. Anticipated capital expenditure requirements (e.g., plant modernization) over the next two years
6. Factors affecting the seller's growth prospects (e.g., import competition, technological change, competitive environment, industry trends)

In addition to this primary objective your second meeting with the sellers should continue the process of pursuing three other objectives. These are:

1. Learning more about the seller's business
2. Increasing your company's credibility as a legitimate purchaser of the seller's business
3. Developing a rapport between your representatives and the owners and executives of the selling business

WHO SHOULD REPRESENT YOUR COMPANY AT THE SECOND MEETING WITH THE SELLER

Your delegation should consist of the following representatives:

1. Your representative who had the initial meeting with the owners and senior executives of the selling business
2. Your company's chief executive
3. One other senior executive from your company

THE ROLES WHICH THESE INDIVIDUALS SHOULD PLAY AT YOUR SECOND MEETING WITH THE SELLER

1. Your representative who had the initial meeting with the sellers should play the role of the "honest broker," even though he may be an employee or consultant paid by your company. The "honest broker's" role is:

  a. To arrange the meeting.
  b. To ask questions of the seller which will provide it with opportunities to mention positive features of its business. For example, if the selling business has a large diversified customer base, he would ask the seller to describe its customer base.
  c. To take notes.

2. Your chief executive acts as the quiet somewhat remote boss of your company. He rarely asks questions of the seller but does indicate that:

  a. The seller has developed a fine business.
  b. Your company would use its financial resources to expand the seller's business if you owned it.
  c. Combining your business and the seller's business could help both businesses to be more successful in the future.

3. Your other senior executive's role is to be the "bad guy" who asks the seller tough questions. For example:
  "Why are your earnings only 2% of sales?"
  "Why did your selling costs decline from $3,000,000 two years ago to $2,500,000 last year?"

"How are your labor relations? Why did you have a strike in 1986? When does your present union contract expire?"

"Why did you change accounting firms in 1988?"

"Are you involved in any litigation?"

"How often do you take a physical inventory? What were your write-offs for damaged and obsolescent inventory?"

"Why haven't your revenues increased for the past two years?"

"When does your lease expire?"

HOW THIS ROLE PLAYING HELPS YOUR SUBSEQUENT NEGOTIATIONS

1. Your representative who plays the "honest broker" role provides an informal communication channel for the sellers to raise issues and concerns which are difficult to discuss in face-to-face negotiations. For example:

   "Would the purchasers be willing to continue employing my son-in-law who helps out in the office?"

   "Will the purchasers let me (e.g., the chief executive of the selling business) serve on their board of directors for a few years?"

   "Can our business keep its present name after it becomes part of their company?"

   Disclosing a side agreement with one of their distributors who helped them out when they had financial problems in 1985.

   "Would the business be permitted to continue paying for our country club memberships?"

   "Even though I will be retiring next year, could I continue to keep my office and my secretary?"

2. Your representative who plays the "honest broker" role also provides an informal communication channel for your company to raise questions which may be difficult or embarrassing to ask in face-to-face negotiations. For example:

   "Are there special arrangements with the purchasing agents at the XYZ Corporation, which is your largest customer?"

   "Why is a 2% sales commission on export sales paid to ABC Associates? Can this arrangement be terminated?"

   "Why are the real estate tax assessments so low? Will this continue?"

   "Why did you back out of your deal to sell to C&G, Inc.?"

"Why do you have a sales office in Palm Springs? Who works there?"

"Why did three of your senior executives resign in 1987?"

3. The seller will not expect your chief executive to participate in the interim negotiating sessions since he apparently limits his management role to policy making and delegates day-to-day decision making to your company's other senior executives.

4. Your senior executive who plays the "bad guy" role will become the focus of the seller's hostility. This is intentional because it diverts this hostility away from your company's chief executive so that he can develop a rapport with the owners and senior executives of the selling business. (After your second meeting with the seller, this senior executive will drop out of the direct discussion with the seller so that there will be time for the seller's hostility toward him to fade away before the two businesses are combined. The "bad guy" role during the subsequent meetings with the seller should be assigned to either your outside attorney or your outside accountant.)

WHY IT IS IMPORTANT TO HAVE TWO EXPLORATORY MEETINGS BEFORE COMMENCING PRICE NEGOTIATIONS

When your acquisition search program uncovers a selling business which appears attractive to your company, you will be tempted to speed up the negotiating process by skipping one or both of these exploratory meetings. This is particularly true if an intermediary representing the seller (e.g., a finder/broker) has already provided you with a reasonably comprehensive written description of the selling business. It is important that you resist this temptation to commence price negotiations prematurely with the owners of a selling business. The reasons are:

1. The information you obtained describing a selling business prior to your first meeting with the seller will always be incomplete and will often be misunderstood.

2. Your two meetings with the owners and senior executives of the selling business almost always help your company to improve its credibility as a legitimate purchaser of the seller's business. The reason is that the seller is usually impressed that you took the time and effort to meet with its owners twice at their offices.

3. Your two meetings almost always help your company to develop some rapport with the owners and senior executives of the selling business. The reason is

that the sellers begin to view your company as consisting of real people who have reasonable personal and business goals rather than as faceless strangers who want to take away their business which they took many years creating and protecting.

4. Your exploratory meetings with the owners and senior executives of a selling business will often provide you with a great deal of useful information regarding competitive market conditions and industry trends. This will help you to improve your company's acquisition screening and selection criteria. It will also help you to understand and evaluate better other selling businesses which you are considering purchasing, which are in the same industry segments as the selling business which you have met with.

HOW TO PROCEED FOLLOWING YOUR SECOND EXPLORATORY MEETING WITH A SELLING BUSINESS

Your first objective after your second meeting with a selling business is to maintain good relations with the seller while your company decides whether you should seek to acquire that business. (When you do decide to try to acquire a business, your company's next step would be to make a preliminary price offer.) To help accomplish this objective:

1. Your chief executive should send a letter to the chief executive of the selling business. This letter should:

   a. Thank him for taking the time to meet.
   b. Mention that you were impressed with his (the seller's) business.
   c. Explain that your senior management will be meeting to discuss how your company and the seller's company might fit together.

2. Your representative who attended your two exploratory meetings with the seller should send it some additional written information describing your company. For example, if you have not already done so, this is a good time to supply them with copies of your product catalogs and brochures or your management organization chart.

Your second objective is to "complete" your acquisition candidate profile for the selling business. The procedures for completing this acquisition profile are as follows:

1. Upon returning from your second meeting with the seller, gather the new information which you obtained at that meeting and enter it on your acquisition candidate profile form.

2. Next make a list of the information which you are still missing on your acquisition profile form for that selling business. Pick out one or two of these missing information items which you would most like to have. Your representative now phones his contact at the selling business. He thanks them for taking the time to meet with you and asks one of two questions designed to uncover this missing information. The answers are then inserted on the acquisition profile form.

3. Analyze the financial statements of the selling business. Then add to your acquisition candidate profile a financial summary section. This section should contain the following information:

   a. Current and projected annual revenues.
   b. The pretax income which you expect the sellers' business to produce the first year you owned it.
   c. Adjusted net worth. This is the net worth shown on the seller's balance sheet plus an adjustment for assets which were undervalued on this balance sheet. For example, you should substitute the fair market value of fixed assets for their depreciated book value.
   d. An estimate of the likely selling price of this business. (You use a fair market value appraisal to make this price estimate.)

4. Make a list of the potential benefits of your owning the seller's business. Add this to your acquisition candidate profile (at the end).

WHY YOU SHOULD NOT PROVIDE YOUR ACQUISITION COMMITTEE WITH THE SELLER'S FINANCIAL STATEMENTS

There are two reasons why you should not include the seller's financial statements in the information package on the selling business which you provide to the members of your acquisition committee. These are:

1. The financial statements of privately owned companies frequently give an inaccurate view of the seller's business. Most of your committee members will lack the experience, skill, and supplemental information required to analyze and interpret these financial statements.

2. You want your committee members to focus on applying your company's acquisition screening and selection criteria rather than playing the role of

amateur financial experts. Whenever the acquisition committee members of a prospective acquirer are provided with the seller's financial statements, they tend to spend most of their time showing off their ability (or inability) to analyze and interpret financial statements instead of concentrating on examining how combining your present business and the seller's business would improve (or fail to improve) your profitability, competitive position, and growth prospects.

WHEN YOU SHOULD BEGIN TO SUBMIT ACQUISITION CANDIDATE PROFILES TO YOUR ACQUISITION COMMITTEE

You should delay submitting your first "completed" acquisition candidate profiles to your acquisition committee until you have at least three "completed" profiles which meet the criteria outlined in the previous section. Then, whenever you subsequently have additional "completed" profiles on selling businesses for your acquisition committee to consider, your committee members should also again be presented with the candidate profiles which they considered at their earlier committee meetings. The reasons for following these procedures are:

1. It is much easier for your committee members to analyze the attractiveness of a selling business when they can compare it with other selling businesses which met your company's screening criteria.

2. Your acquisition committee members usually start out with somewhat unrealistic expectations. Therefore, they are likely to assign low attractiveness rating to the first few selling businesses which are presented for their consideration. Their expectations tend to become more realistic after they have considered seven to ten acquisition candidates. Therefore, by reviewing the older completed acquisition candidate profiles, your committee members have an opportunity to reconsider, and reevaluate, these earlier presentations.

HOW OFTEN SHOULD YOUR ACQUISITION COMMITTEE MEET

Your acquisition committee should first meet to analyze and evaluate completed acquisition candidate profiles when there are at least three of these profiles for them to compare and consider.

Thereafter your acquisition committee should meet approximately every three weeks. At these meetings your committee members should also be briefed on the status of your negotiations with selling businesses. The reason why your committee should not meet more frequently is that your committee members need to spend most of their time managing your company's present business. The reasons why your acquisition committee should not meet less frequently is that it is important to maintain the members' interest and involvement in your acquisition program.

WHAT YOU WANT YOUR ACQUISITION COMMITTEE MEETING TO ACCOMPLISH

The objectives of your acquisition committee meeting are for your committee members to reach a consensus regarding which selling businesses are sufficiently attractive to warrant your company commencing price negotiations with these selling businesses. You want to achieve this consensus as quickly as possible because:

1. Your acquisition committee members have a limited amount of time which they can devote to your acquisition program.
2. The owners and senior executives of a selling business will become less receptive to dealing with your company the longer it takes for you to make a preliminary price offer to acquire their business.

WHY YOUR ACQUISITION COMMITTEE MEETINGS MAY FAIL TO ACHIEVE THIS OBJECTIVE IN A TIMELY MANNER

There are two problems which your company is likely to encounter when attempting to achieve your acquisition committee meeting objective. These are:

1. Acquisition committees are often reluctant to decide which selling businesses your company should commence price negotiations with.
2. Acquisition committee meetings have a tendency to drag out and become unproductive philosophical discussions. Some of the reasons why these problems occur are:

    a. Members may view committee meetings primarily as offering opportunity to impress their company's chief executive. They, therefore, focus on making a good impression rather than trying to reach a group decision.
    b. Committee members often assume, incorrectly, that your company will go out and acquire a business if they recommend that you begin price

negotiations with that particular selling business. Therefore, they become fearful and hesitate to make these recommendations. This assumption is incorrect because the final decision whether to acquire a particular business is months away. During the interim your company's task force will be conducting a thorough investigation of the seller's business which provides your acquisition committee with a great deal of additional information and insights. Only after your negotiating team completes its price negotiations and your task force completes its investigation will your company's acquisition committee need to decide whether to proceed with the acquisition of a particular business.

c. Unless your company generally uses senior executive committees to make other strategic policy decisions, your acquisition committee members will be inexperienced at making these types of decisions as a group.

d. Each selling business which meets your acquisition screening criteria offers a different combination of potential benefits and problems. Analyzing and comparing different acquisition candidates is therefore a potentially complex, confusing, and time-consuming job.

HOW TO PREPARE YOUR ACQUISITION COMMITTEE TO WORK EFFECTIVELY

The following policies and techniques will help prepare your company's acquisition committee to reach objective decisions regarding which selling businesses your company should commence price negotiations with. They will also reduce the time and effort required to make these decisions.

1. Completed acquisition profiles for selling businesses are only presented to your acquisition committee when your chief executive has already decided that the selling businesses are somewhat attractive. This policy is made clear to each of your acquisition committee members.

2. Your acquisition committee is not asked to select directly the selling businesses with whom you should commence price negotiations. Instead, they are given the responsibility of placing each selling businesses into one of the following three categories:

a. Most attractive

b. Attractive

c. Least attractive

3. When you present additional completed acquisition candidate profiles to your acquisition committee, your committee will be given the opportunity to reconsider the categories which they assigned to the selling businesses which they analyzed and reviewed at earlier meetings. This policy is made clear to each of your acquisition committee members.

4. Prior to your first acquisition committee meeting to consider completed acquisition candidate profiles, your company develops an attractiveness rating sheet and an attractiveness rating report form. The attractiveness rating sheets will be used by your committee members when they review individual completed acquisition candidate profiles. The attractiveness rating report form will be presented to your committee at the beginning of its meetings.

HOW TO DEVELOP YOUR ATTRACTIVENESS RATING SHEET

This is the form which each of your committee members prepares for each acquisition candidate. To develop your attractiveness rating form, you use the following format.

Acquisition candidate:	XYZ Corporation
Committee member:	William Smith
Date prepared:	June 24, 1989

	DOES THE CANDIDATE MEET THIS CRITERION?		
	YES	**PARTLY**	**NO**
A. Selection criteria			
1. Profitable operation			X
2. Good growth potential	X		
3. Marketing synergy		X	
4. Management will stay		X	
5. Excellent product reputation	X		
6.			
7.			
8.			
9.			
10.			

B. Other reasons why we should buy this business

C. Other reasons why I don't like this acquisition candidate

D. Overall rating (check one)
   Attractive _____   Somewhat attractive _____
   Unattractive _____

HOW TO USE YOUR ATTRACTIVENESS RATING SHEETS

1. An attractiveness rating sheet is attached to each completed acquisition candidate profile. The profiles and the attached rating sheets are distributed to your committee members approximately five business days before your scheduled committee meeting.

2. Each committee member is responsible for filling in his or her rating sheets within two days after receipt. This timing is designed to give your committee members enough time to review the completed acquisition candidate profiles and fill in their attractiveness rating sheets but is intended to make it difficult for them to consult with one another prior to filling in their attractiveness rating sheets. The reason that this is desirable is that you want to obtain your committee members individual impressions.

3. During the two days prior to your acquisition committee meeting, your acquisition consultant and your acquisition coordinator meet individually with each committee member. The purpose of these discussions is:

a. To assure that the committee members' filled-in rating sheets accurately reflect his or her views and preferences

b. To make your acquisition consultant and your acquisition coordinator aware of the issues which will need to be discussed at the committee meeting

The reasons why your committee member may have difficulty using the attractiveness rating sheets are:

a. Even though the committee member was involved in choosing your company's selection criteria, this was several months ago. By now he has probably forgotten exactly what was meant by each of these selection criteria (which are the basis for the categories on the attractiveness rating form).

b. Senior executives (most of your committee members are your company's senior executives) tend to have a hard time filling in written forms which ask them to give their opinions and make judgments. The principal reason is that they automatically view any question as a "test question" for which there must be some "right" answer.

As your committee members, and your acquisition coordinator, and your acquisition consultant become more experienced, it will continue to be helpful, but will not be as necessary, to have these preliminary discussions prior to your committee meetings.

4. Your acquisition coordinator and your acquisition consultant use the filled in attractiveness rating sheets to compile and fill in an attractiveness rating report form for each acquisition candidate. These forms are then presented individually at your acquisition committee meeting.

HOW TO DEVELOP AN ATTRACTIVENESS RATING REPORT FORM

This report form is designed to summarize the information contained in the attractiveness rating sheets prepared by each acquisition committee member. To develop your attractiveness rating summary report form, you use the following format:

Acquisition candidate: XYZ Corporation
Committee members (initials):   JL, WS, PG, WW, HR, and
                                    ST
Date prepared: June 27, 1989

	NO. OF "YES" ANSWERS	NO OF "PARTLY" ANSWERS	NO. OF "NO" ANSWERS
A. Selection criteria			
1. Profitable operation	4	2	0
2. Good growth potential	3	1	2
3. Marketing synergy	2	3	1
4. Management will stay	4	0	2
5. Excellent product reputation	1	1	4
6.			
7.			
8.			
9.			
10.			
Totals	_____	_____	_____

B. Other reasons why we should buy this business

C. Other reasons why we should NOT buy this business

HOW TO FILL IN THIS ATTRACTIVENESS RATING SUMMARY REPORT FORM

Your company's selection criteria are listed in the first column, just as they were on your attractiveness rating sheets. Then you count up and insert the number of "yes," "partly," and "no" answers indicated on your committee members on the filled-in attractiveness rating sheets. Finally, you list the other reasons why your committee members felt that your company should buy or not buy this selling business. Your acquisition coordinator and your acquisition consultant are responsible for selecting the items to be included in these two final parts of the summary report form.

HOW TO USE THIS ATTRACTIVENESS RATING REPORT FORM

Each summary report form is presented to your acquisition committee one at a time by your acquisition coordinator or your acquisition consultant. Your committee should then discuss each summary report one at a time. The objective of these discussions is to reach a consensus regarding whether the selling business meets, partly meets, or does not meet each of your company's selection criteria. After your acquisition committee has completed these discussions, your acquisition coordinator or acquisition consultant then produces a "revised" summary report for each selling business. Instead of indicating the number of "yes," "partly," and "no" answers, this revised form has a checkmark in the appropriate column. Generally, this indicates the consensus rating of your acquisition committee. However, when your committee members are unable to reach a consensus view regarding how well a selling business meets one of your company's selection criteria, you put a checkmark in the appropriate column which represents the majority rating of your acquisition committee members.

Next your committee reviews and discusses the other reasons listed on your summary form for buying or not buying that selling business. The objective of this discussion is to determine whether any of these items are important enough to add to your selection criteria for evaluating the attractiveness of that acquisition candidate. When your committee feels that one of these items is particularly important, it is added to your selection criteria list, and the appropriate column is checked indicating whether the selling business meets, partly meets, or does not meet that selection criteria. The following is an example of what this filled in "revised" summary form looks like. In this example the acquisition committee felt that the "new product development expertise" of the selling business was a very important potential benefit of owning that business. Though "new product development expertise" had not been one of their company's selection criteria, the committee decided it should be added to their selection criteria.

"REVISED" ATTRACTIVENESS RATING
REPORT FORM

Acquisition candidate: XYZ Corporation
Date:

Selection criteria	DOES THE CANDIDATE MEET THIS CRITERION?		
	YES	PARTLY	NO
1. Profitable operation		X	
2. Good growth potential	X		
3. Marketing synergy		X	
4. Management will stay	X		
5. Excellent product reputation			X
6. New product development expertise	X		

When you add a new selection criterion to your list for one selling business, you need to also add it to the selection criteria listed on your "revised" report forms for each of the other selling businesses which your committee is considering. This includes the filled-in "revised" report forms which were prepared for selling businesses which your committee considered at its previous meetings. Your committee discusses whether each of the other selling businesses which they are considering at their present meeting meets, partly meets, or does not meet this new selection criteria item. A checkmark is then placed in the appropriate column on the "revised" report form.

Since your "revised" attractiveness rating report form duplicates the first section of your attractiveness rating sheet form, it is not necessary to prepare a new form. Instead you can simply mark "Revised Report Form" on your attractiveness rating sheet form and use the first section of this form to indicate the consensus or majority views of your committee members regarding how well a selling business meets each of your company's selection criteria.

WHAT TO DO NEXT

Once your acquisition committee has completed the process of filling in your revised attractiveness report form, it is time to call a recess. The reasons are:

1. Your committee members will likely be fatigued and irritable from several hours of discussion and debate.

2. Your acquisition coordinator and your acquisition consultant need two to three hours to develop a preliminary list which places each selling business in three different categories. These three categories are:

a. Most attractive

b. Attractive

c. Least attractive

The selling businesses placed on this preliminary "attractiveness category listing" include both the new selling businesses presented at this acquisition committee meeting and those considered at your previous acquisition committee meetings.

HOW TO PREPARE YOUR PRELIMINARY ATTRACTIVENESS CATEGORY LISTING

This listing which divides all the selling businesses into three categories (most attractive, attractive, and least attractive) is prepared by your acquisition coordinator and your acquisition consultant. The procedure which is used is as follows:

1. Any new selection criteria added at this committee meeting are added to the revised attractiveness report forms for selling businesses considered at previous acquisition committee meetings.

2. Your consultant and your coordinator decide whether these selling businesses which were considered at previous committee meetings meet, partly meet, or do not meet these new selection criteria. Then a checkmark is inserted under the appropriate column heading on these forms.

3. Your consultant and your coordinator compute a numerical attractiveness rating for each of the selling businesses. The procedure for computing these numerical ratings is described in the next section.

4. Then your consultant and coordinator list these selling businesses in descending order. The selling business which has the highest numerical score is at the top of your list and the selling business which has the lowest numerical score is at the bottom. For example:

	NUMERICAL SCORE
A&G Associates	10 points
WCG Corp.	10 points
Alpha Plumbing	9 points
Beta & Sigma, Inc.	7 points
West Side Supply	6 points
Wilson & Smith	5 points
Southern Corp.	4 points
Old Stone Supply	3 points
New Guys Wholesale	3 points
Johnson Brothers	3 points

5. After you complete this numerical ranking list, you take the top (highest numerically rated) 25% to 35% of these selling businesses and place them in the "most attractive" category. Then you take the next 35%-45% of these selling businesses and place them in the "attractive category." The remaining selling businesses are placed in the "least attractive" category. For example, using the sample numerical rating, the preliminary attractiveness category listing would be as follows:

MOST ATTRACTIVE	ATTRACTIVE	LEAST ATTRACTIVE
Wilson & Smith	A&G Associates	Old Stone Supply
Southern Corp.	WCG Corp.	New Guys Wholesale
Good Quality Corp.	Alpha Plumbing	Johnson Brothers
	Beta & Sigma Inc.	
	West Side Supply	

HOW TO COMPUTE YOUR NUMERICAL ATTRACTIVENESS RATINGS

To compute your numerical attractiveness ratings, your acquisition coordinator and your acquisition consultant use the following procedure:

For each of the selling businesses which your acquisition committee considered at its previous meetings and its present meeting, add up the number of "yes," "partly," and "no" answers indicated on the "revised" attractiveness report form. For each "yes" answer, the selling business is awarded three rating points. For each "partly" answer, the selling business is awarded one rating point. For each "no" answer, one rating point is subtracted. Then total up these rating points to get your numerical rating for each selling business.

The reasons for using this particular numerical rating system are:

1. To give greater priority to those businesses which fully meet particular selection criteria rather than to businesses which partly meet particular selection criteria.

2. To give a lower priority to those selling businesses which do not even partly meet a selection criteria.

Experience has shown that this works best because:

1. Rather than acquiring a single business which partly met several selection criteria, a purchaser will generally obtain better results if it acquires two businesses each of which *completely* met a smaller number of its selection criteria.

2. It is riskier to purchase a business which does not even partly meet a significant number of your selection criteria. This is because it reduces the chances that a newly acquired business will perform better than you expected due to its fully meeting a particular selection criteria after you own it, which it apparently would only partly meet based upon its operation under its former ownership.

The following is an example of how to compute the numerical attractiveness rating for a selling business.

$$
\begin{array}{ll}
\text{No. of ``yes'' answers} \times 3 \text{ rating points} & = \text{ ?} \\
\text{No. of ``partly'' answers} \times 1 \text{ rating point} & = \text{ ?} \\
\text{No. of ``no'' answers} \times -1 \text{ rating point} & = \text{ ?} \\
\quad \text{Total}
\end{array}
$$

HOW TO PROCEED AFTER YOU PREPARE YOUR PRELIMINARY ATTRACTIVENESS CATEGORY LISTING

Your preliminary attractiveness category listing will be presented to your acquisition committee when it reconvenes. Then the committee will review the categories which each selling business was placed in and make any changes which they feel are appropriate. There are three final adjustments which you should make to your preliminary category listing prior to presenting it to your acquisition committee. These are:

1. Your acquisition coordinator and your acquisition consultant may select a business which they especially liked and shift it to the "most attractive" category even though its numerical ranking would have placed it in the "attractive" category.

2. Those selling businesses which are being considered for the first time at this meeting are indicated by typing them in capital letters.

3. Any selling businesses which were previously considered but are now listed in the "most attractive" category for the first time are underlined. There are several reasons why a selling business which was previously placed in the "attractive" category may now be placed in the "most attractive" category. They include:

a. As the number of selling businesses which your committee has considered increases, the number which are in the top 25% to 35% also increases.

b. The numerical rating of selling business may have changed due to your obtaining new information or deciding to expand your list of selection criteria.
4. Your acquisition committee reconvenes and has an opportunity to discuss and change the attractiveness categories assigned to individual acquisition candidates.

WHEN SHOULD YOUR ACQUISITION COMMITTEE MEETING RECONVENE

It is important that your acquisition committee reconvene either the same day or the following day. The reason is that their discussions regarding the new selling businesses being considered need to be fresh in their minds. Otherwise, the committee members will be likely to repeat their earlier discussions, which slows down the decision-making process.

A useful technique is to reconvene your acquisition committee meeting at 4 P.M. This prevents the final phase of your acquisition committee meeting from dragging out. Late-afternoon committee meetings have a tendency to accomplish their decision making quite rapidly because the committee members want to go home at their normal quitting hour.

HOW TO PROCEED FOLLOWING YOUR ACQUISITION COMMITTEE MEETING

Your acquisition coordinator contacts each of the selling businesses which have been placed in your "most attractive" category for the first time. He confirms that these selling businesses are still available and would consider selling to your company. Then your company prepares and submits a preliminary price offer to these selling businesses.

Your acquisition consultant contacts those selling businesses which were considered for the first time at this committee meeting, but were not placed in the "most attractive category." When one of these selling businesses was placed in the "attractive" category, your consultant advises the seller that your company is still interested in its business but has decided to first conclude its discussions with some other acquisition candidates. When one of these selling businesses was placed in the "least attractive" category, your consultant advises the seller that your company has changed its priorities and will probably purchase a different type of business.

HOW TO DEVELOP YOUR PRELIMINARY PRICE OFFER

Your preliminary price offer for a selling business should be not less than 70% of its estimated fair market value. Therefore, using the valuation techniques from

Chapter 8 you first compute the fair market value of the seller's business. Then you should offer 70% to 80% of this estimated fair market value depending upon how valuable the seller's business would be to your company if you owned it.

HOW TO PRESENT YOUR PRELIMINARY PRICE OFFER

Your representative (e.g., your acquisition coordinator or consultant) who had the initial meeting with the owners and senior executives of the selling business should make your preliminary price offer. This offer should be made in person, at the sellers offices. Regardless of how much you offer, the seller will usually be disappointed since unrealistic selling price expectations are the "norm" rather than the exception. Your representative should explain how your company estimated the value of the sellers business. Then he should indicate that if it (the seller) feel that it can justify being paid a higher price based upon its earnings or assets, your company would welcome a counterproposal.

HOW TO RESPOND TO THE SELLER'S COUNTERPROPOSAL

The seller will either respond with an asking price which is ridiculously high (e.g., 150% of fair market value) or an asking price which is somewhat (e.g., 25%) more than you think the business is worth. When the seller's price demands are still unreasonable, your approach should be to prolong your negotiations while the seller becomes more realistic. When the seller's asking price is within 25% of the amount you think the business is worth, you should move quickly and aggressively to try to obtain a letter of intent. Both these price negotiating strategies will be described in the following sections.

HOW TO MAINTAIN AND PROLONG YOUR PRICE NEGOTIATIONS

When the seller responds to your preliminary price offer with an asking price which is too high to warrant serious consideration, your response should consist of three parts. These are:

1. Your asking price seems high, but we could afford to pay it.
2. We are prepared to pay your asking price if your company's future earnings, asset values, and expected growth rate will justify that price.

3. We want to learn more about your business so that we can reevaluate our price offer.

This approach begins to shift to the seller the responsibility of justifying its asking price and gives it an incentive to continue talking to your company rather than entering into negotiations with another prospective acquirer. From this point on you use the following techniques to maintain and prolong your negotiations with the seller:

1. Each week or two you request some additional information about the seller's business. For example:

   a. Its income tax returns for the past two years
   b. Details of its leases
   c. A description of its machinery and equipment
   d. Copies of its franchise and marketing agreements

   The information gathering checklists which are used to guide your task force investigation of a selling business will provide you with hundreds of ideas of different types of information which you can request. (The procedure for developing your task force investigation checklist is described later in this chapter.)

2. As you get more information from the sellers, you demonstrate your continued interest by:

   a. Sending them some more information describing your company and its business. You take this information from the information package which you prepared prior to the commencement of the negotiating stage of your acquisition program. This information package was described earlier in this chapter.
   b. Every three to four weeks sending one of your line executives (e.g., your sales manager, production manager, chief engineer), or outside experts (e.g., your marketing consultant, accountant, advertising agency account officer) or a member of your board of directors to visit the selling company.
   c. Having the seller visit your company, tour its facilities, and meet with your executives.

These are three procedures which you would also employ if you had reached a preliminary price agreement with the seller. The difference is that you are spreading it out over a longer period. For example, if you had reached a preliminary price agreement with the seller, you would:

1. Request most of the additional information you would like to have right away rather than in dribs and drabs over many weeks.
2. Send several of your executives and outside experts to visit the seller's business over a four- to six-week period rather than sending them one at a time over a period of three to four months.

The fourth procedure which your company should use is to make a new price offer every three weeks. Though each of these seems to be a new price offer, they are actually simply different versions of your initial price offer. For example, you would offer:

1. A higher price but with the seller being paid long-term notes at a below-market interest rate.
2. A higher price offer which takes the form of a long-term consulting contract. The difference in the price offer represents your tax savings. (Consulting fees are expensed for tax purposes while the price you pay for goodwill cannot be used to offset taxable earnings.)
3. A higher price which is subject to the seller's business producing a future level of earnings or revenues which would justify that price.
4. Increase your price offer to include assets such as real estate which are used by the seller's business but which are owned by the principals.

The final procedures which your company should use is to utilize quasi-legitimate excuses to slow down the negotiating process. For example;
"We want to resume discussions after

- our accountants complete their annual audit."
- our chairman returns from Europe."
- our board of directors meet."
- we complete our labor contract negotiations."

HOW TO HANDLE CONTINUED UNREASONABLE SELLER PRICE DEMANDS

When you have used the techniques outlined in the previous section for three months but the seller still insists on an unreasonably high asking price, your approach should be:

1. Explain to the seller that you are still very much interested in acquiring its business. However, since you and it are still far apart regarding price, you want to go back and rethink your company's growth plan.

2. Then, after waiting two or three months your representative should contact the seller and make a price offer which is 10% higher than your initial price offer.

In almost 40% of the instances where this approach is used, you will find that the seller has reduced its price expectations to a more reasonable level. When this is not the case, you can usually assume that the owners of the acquisition candidate are not really serious about selling at this time.

HOW TO PROCEED WHEN THE OWNERS WILL ACCEPT A SOMEWHAT REASONABLE PRICE FOR THEIR BUSINESS

When the owners of a selling business are willing to accept a purchase price which is no more than 25% higher than the price you would be willing to pay, you should move quickly to negotiate a "letter of intent." A letter of intent is a nonbinding purchase agreement. It outlines the principal terms of the acquisition but contains conditions which enable the buyer or the seller to back out prior to closing without incurring any additional financial liability. Examples of these conditions include:

- Satisfactory employment contracts
- Appraisals
- Transfer of franchises and license agreements
- Satisfactory accounting audit
- Legal review
- Board approval
- Financing

WHY YOU WANT TO EXECUTE A LETTER OF INTENT

Once the seller and your company agree to a letter of intent, you can expect that the seller will:

1. Not consider acquisition inquiries or proposals from other prospective acquirers.
2. Permit your task force to conduct an in-depth, on-site investigation of its business.
3. Provide you with confidential information which was withheld for competitive reasons and/or because it could expose the seller to tax liabilities and penalties. Examples of this type of information include:

    a. Customer lists
    b. Detailed manufacturing costs analysis
    c. New products or services being developed
    d. Excess compensation paid to owners and their relatives
    e. Owners' personal expenses paid by the business
    f. Usable inventories written off for tax purposes
    g. Capital improvements expensed as "repairs and maintenance"
    h. Hidden ownership
    i. Secret agreements (e.g., payments to customer's purchasing agents)

HOW DETAILED TO MAKE YOUR LETTER OF INTENT

The best letter of intent should be no longer than two pages. It is a waste of time to go into too much detail since the terms of the purchase will be renegotiated several times prior to the closing. Also, you run the risk of raising areas of disagreement which may prevent the seller from executing (signing) the letter of intent.

THE ROLE OF THE GOOD FAITH DEPOSIT

When the prospective purchaser and the owners of the selling business execute (sign) a letter of intent, it is often expected that the prospective purchaser will make a good faith deposit to demonstrate the seriousness of the intent to purchase the seller's business. Though the good faith deposit is theoretically designed to protect the seller, making a large enough good faith deposit usually assures that the seller will feel honor bound to reject inquiries from other prospective acquirers and negotiate exclusively with your company. The amount of your good faith deposit should be not less than $25,000 or more than $100,000. Generally, you should offer a good faith deposit of $25,000 when the proposed purchase price is less than $3 million, $50,000 when the proposed purchase price is between $3 and $5 million, $75,000 when the proposed purchase price is between $5 million and $7 million, and $100,000 when the proposed purchase price is over $7 million.

The good faith deposit should be held in escrow by the seller's attorney. A separate agreement should be added to your letter of intent which outlines the conditions under which all or a portion of the good faith deposit would be returned to your company. A reasonable arrangement would be to use a sliding scale to determine the proportion of the good faith deposit which is to be returned to your company. For example:

- Ninety percent of the good faith deposit is returned to your company if acquisition negotiations are terminated within 30 days.
- Eighty percent of the good faith deposit is returned to your company if acquisition negotiations are terminated within 60 days.

When acquisition negotiations are terminated after 60 days, 50% of the actual legal fees paid by the seller are deducted from the good faith deposit, and the balance of the good faith deposit is returned to your company. When there is a disagreement regarding the reasonableness of these legal fees, they would be determined by an impartial arbitrator.

Some prospective acquirers seek to have an arrangement whereby 100% of the good faith deposit is returned to them if acquisition negotiations are terminated within 60 days. Though this approach would save your company a nominal amount of money, it is unwise to seek this arrangement. The reason is that it gives the seller the impression that you are not a serious acquirer.

HOW TO PREPARE FOR LETTER OF INTENT NEGOTIATIONS

Your company's acquisition attorney should develop a standard two-page letter of intent form, and a good faith deposit escrow agreement, which you can use for all your letter of intent negotiations. These documents will have blank spaces where the information which will vary from deal to deal would be inserted. Examples of this information are the legal description of the selling business, the amount, terms and conditions of the purchase price, and the amount of the good faith deposit.

Your objective in using these standard documents is to enable your company to obtain the seller's signature on a letter of intent agreement the same day you reach agreement regarding the purchase price and related terms of the proposed acquisition transaction. Any delay increases the likelihood that the seller will get "cold feet" and start making unreasonable demands. Therefore, it is important that when the seller read these documents it feels that they already include adequate safeguards to protect its interests. For example:

1. The acquisition is contingent upon the approval of the final purchase agreement by the board of directors of both your company and the seller's company.
2. A confidentiality agreement protecting any sensitive information which is provided to you by the seller.

It is a good idea to have your standard letter of intent form and escrow agreement set in type and then printed. The reason is that this discourages the seller and its attorney from making minor changes in these documents, because there isn't any room to insert them. Such minor changes are a potential problem because they give the seller an opportunity to delay signing the documents.

WHO SHOULD REPRESENT YOUR COMPANY AT THE LETTER OF INTENT NEGOTIATIONS

Your company should be represented by the following individuals:

1. Your chief executive.
2. The person from your company who has developed the greatest rapport and has had the most prior contact with the seller. Usually this will be your acquisition coordinator or your acquisition consultant.
3. One member of your two-person negotiating team. Your negotiation team will have the responsibility of attempting to work out the details of your final purchase contract to acquire the seller's business. Generally, this will be your company's chief financial officer.
4. When your chief financial officer is not a member of your negotiating team, he or she should be added to your representatives attending the letter of intent negotiating session.

The two individuals who you should *not* have represent your company are your attorney and your accountant. The reason is that they rarely control their desire to begin negotiating the final purchase agreement. The last thing you want to do is to have your representatives raise any issues at this negotiating session which cannot be immediately resolved between you and the sellers. Your chances of acquiring a selling business are significantly reduced if you cannot obtain a signed letter of intent at a single negotiating session with the sellers. Remember that even though the letter of intent looks like a short form purchase agreement, neither you nor the seller are really going to be bound by its terms. The entire proposed transaction will be renegotiated many times between the time you have an executed letter of intent and when you and the seller reach agreement on a final purchase contract.

HOW TO PROCEED AFTER YOU OBTAIN A SIGNED LETTER OF INTENT

After you obtain a letter of intent, your task force conducts its investigation of the seller's business. The objectives of this investigation are:

1. To obtain a thorough understanding of the seller's present business and its future earnings and growth prospects.
2. To identify problems and issues which should be negotiated with the seller.
3. To provide the information needed to make the various value estimates described in Chapter 8.
4. To identify the executives and other key personnel who are important to the successful operation of the seller's business.

HOW TO PREPARE AND GUIDE YOUR TASK FORCE INVESTIGATION

The key to preparing and guiding your task force's investigation is to develop and use checklists which outline all the types of information which may be needed to achieve the objectives mentioned in the previous section. Most books on mergers and acquisitions include example of such checklists. A good source of items which you might use for your company's task force information checklists is the following publication:

A Checklist Guide to Successful Acquisitions
Victor Harold
Pilot Books, 103 Cooper Street, Babylon, NY 11702

To use your checklists, first identify those items which will be handled by your acquisition accountant and your acquisition attorney. Then, assign responsibility for gathering the remaining types of information to the other members of your company's task force.

MANAGING YOUR COMPANY'S ACQUISITION TASK FORCE

In order to manage the work of your company's task force members, you will need to:

1. Assign to individual task force members the responsibility for gathering the different types of information listed on your acquisition candidate investigation checklists.
2. Monitor the performance of these information gathering assignments by your individual task force members. This is the responsibility of your company's task force coordinator.

HOW TO ASSIGN INFORMATION GATHERING RESPONSIBILITIES

Your task force coordinator should be responsible for recommending which of your task force members should be assigned responsibility for gathering each information item listed on your company's acquisition investigation checklists. To prepare these recommendations, your task force coordinator first provides copies of your checklists to each of your task force members. Then each task force member indicates on his or her checklists the information items for which he or she would be willing to accept responsibility. Your acquisition coordinator then reviews these suggestions and prepares his or her recommendations.

Though you task force coordinator recommends which of your task force members should be assigned each information gathering responsibility, the actual choices should be made by your company's chief executive. This assures that the individual task force members will assign a high priority to these assignments.

Once your company has assigned responsibility for gathering each information item listed on your checklists to one of its task force members, copies of your checklists indicating these assignments should be distributed to all of your task force members and also to your acquisition committee members.

RESPONSIBILITIES OF YOUR COMPANY'S NEGOTIATING TEAM

Your company's negotiating team is responsible for negotiating the terms and conditions of your agreement to acquire the sellers' business. Some of the items which are included in this agreement include:

1. The purchase price
2. Payment terms
3. Seller warranties
4. Management contracts and consulting agreements with the sellers' owners and key executives
5. Arrangements for postacquisition purchase price adjustments

INFORMATION NEEDED BY YOUR COMPANY'S NEGOTIATING TEAM

In order to perform their responsibilities effectively, your negotiating team will need:

1. To have an in-depth understanding of the sellers' business.
2. To become aware of financial and nonfinancial issues and problems which should be discussed with the owners and senior executives of the selling business.

   This information will be gathered by your company's task force. Your task force will also gather the information which is used by your company's chief financial executive, accountants, and your acquisition consultant to develop the third type of information needed by your negotiating team. This is:
3. Valuation estimates for the seller's business.

YOUR PRICE NEGOTIATION GOALS

In order to make good acquisitions, your company should pursue two goals in your price negotiations. These are:

1. Avoid paying too much for a selling business. Your company has usually paid too high a price for an acquisition candidate when:

   a. You pay more than 120% of its fair market value. This is the price which the selling business would be likely to sell for based on market conditions. The reason why you should avoid paying a higher price for a selling business than its fair market value is that you can often acquire a similar business without paying a premium over its fair market value. However, when a selling business has unique characteristics which would make it especially profitable for your company to own it, a premium of up to 20% over its fair market value may be justified.

b. You pay more than its acquisition investment value. This is how much the selling business is likely to be worth to your company after you owned it.

2. Avoid missing out on purchasing a selling business which you would like to own because you did not offer a high enough price. Prospective acquirers often fail to purchase selling businesses which would have been attractive investments for the following reasons:

a. They had not estimated how much the selling business would have been worth to their company if they owned it. This is the acquisition investment value of the selling business.

b. When they found that the selling business had unexpected serious problems and weaknesses, they didn't know how much they could still pay without taking too much risk. This fail-safe price for a selling business is its "forced liquidation value."

c. They become frustrated and angry when the seller kept reopening price negotiations. This is normal seller behavior. The key for the prospective purchaser is to remember that as long as the final purchase price for a business which they would like to own is less than its acquisition investment value, and is not more than 120% of its fair market value, it is still a worthwhile purchase.

THE THREE TYPES OF ACQUISITION CANDIDATE VALUE ESTIMATES YOU SHOULD USE TO GUIDE YOUR PRICE NEGOTIATIONS

There are three types of acquisition value estimates which your company should use to guide its price negotiations. The procedures and techniques for developing and using these selling business value estimates were described in Chapter 8. The three value estimates are:

1. *Fair market value.* This is the estimated selling price of the business based upon market conditions.

2. *Acquisition investment value.* This is an estimate of how much the selling business would be worth to your company if you owned it.

3. *Forced liquidation value.* This is an estimate of how much money you would recover if you acquired the sellers' business and then subsequently closed and

liquidated it because it performed poorly (e.g., produced low profits) after you owned it.

THE ROLE OF YOUR NEGOTIATING TEAM

At this point in your acquisition negotiating process, your company has obtained a signed letter of intent and has determined the maximum price that you would be willing to pay. Your negotiating team now begins working with its counterparts at the selling business to reach preliminary agreement on most of the terms and conditions of the proposed acquisition. When your negotiating team has accomplished this objective, your "expanded negotiating team" will meet with the sellers and attempt to reach agreement on the remaining terms and conditions of the proposed acquisition. Your "expanded negotiating team" consists of your negotiating team members and your chief executive. It may also include your attorney, your accountant, and other executives from your company.

CONCENTRATE ON THE PRINCIPAL TERMS AND CONDITIONS OF THE ACQUISITION TRANSACTION

There are dozens of terms and conditions which will be included in your final agreement to purchase a business. This written sales contract is usually a lengthy legal document. However, your negotiating team should concentrate on five key aspects of your purchase agreement. The reason is that once the buyer and the seller have reached agreement on these "principal terms and conditions" of your purchasing agreement, you will usually be able to reach agreement on the remaining purchase agreement terms and conditions when your chief executive rejoins the negotiations.

The five aspects of your purchase agreement on which your negotiating team should focus their efforts are:

1. *The purchase price to be paid for the assets (tangible and intangible) of the selling business.* This purchase price includes the assumption of any liabilities (e.g., accounts payable, bank loans, etc.) by your company and all the compensation which would be paid to the present owners of the selling business. For example, this compensation might include generous consulting agreements and employment contracts and future payments under noncompete agreements.

2. *The manner in which the purchase price will be paid. Some of the alternative purchase price payment arrangements which might be used include:*

a. Cash to be paid at closing

b. The assumption of debts owed by the owners of the selling business

c. Promissory notes from the purchaser, to be held by the present owners of the selling business

d. Additional future payments which are contingent upon the future performance of the selling business

e. The portion of consulting fees and salaries to be paid to the former owners which exceeds the value of the post acquisition services which they are to provide

f. Future payments for noncompete agreements

3. *The seller's postacquisition contingent liabilities.* For example, the sellers might be responsible for reimbursing the new owners for bad-debt losses on accounts receivable which exceed the loss reserve shown on its balance sheet.

4. *The form of the business ownership transfer.* A business may be acquired by either purchasing all its assets (tangible and intangible) or all its outstanding stock.

5. *The role of the selling business's senior executives following the change in ownership.* When the senior executives desire to retain their present positions, or the acquirer seeks to retain the seller's present management, it will be important to negotiate the postacquisition duties, responsibilities, and management authority of senior executives of the selling business who are expected to remain following the change in ownership.

SOME LEGAL TERMS AND CONCEPTS USED IN ACQUISITION NEGOTIATIONS AND AGREEMENTS

Your executives involved in acquisition negotiations should become familiar with the legal terms and concepts used in acquisition negotiations and agreements. This will also help them to communicate more effectively with the sellers and with your own attorney. Some of these key legal terms and concepts include:

- An *acquisition* is any transaction in which a buyer acquires all or part of the assets or business of a seller. Acquisitions may be structured as an asset purchase, or a merger, or a consolidation.

- An *asset purchase* involves the purchase by your company of assets now owned by the selling corporation, partnership, or sole proprietorship. These assets may be subject to liabilities which you assume (e.g., bank loans, lease obligations) or the selling entity may continue to be responsible for paying (discharging) some or all of these liabilities. When a company is selling most of its assets, the transaction is subject to the *bulk sales act* of the state in which it is incorporated or was set up to operate. The *bulk sales act* is a set of laws and regulations designed to protect the creditors of the selling company. Though the *bulk sales act* applies to the seller rather than the purchaser of assets, you want to be sure that the sellers have complied with it. The reason is that otherwise the seller's creditors can sue to have your asset purchase contract ruled invalid. This is called "recission."

- Most acquirers would prefer to make *asset purchases* rather than *stock purchases*. The reasons are that in a stock purchase the acquirer assumes all the liabilities of the seller while in an asset purchase the acquirer assumes specific liabilities as provided for in the purchase agreement. Any other liabilities remain with the seller's corporation.

- *Mergers and consolidations* are combinations of two corporations pursuant to the requirements and procedures set forth in the corporation laws of their states of incorporation. Mergers and consolidations involve the purchase of the selling company's stock whether for cash, notes, stock in the acquiring company, or other considerations. When one corporation is absorbed into the other, this is called a merger. A consolidation occurs when two corporations are combined to form a third corporation. Mergers and consolidations are also called "stock purchase" acquisitions.

- A *takeover* is an unfriendly acquisition.

- A *tender offer* is an offer to purchase the stock of a public corporation for cash. No SEC registration is required, but an information purposes filing with the SEC is required.

- In an *exchange offer* the acquiring company offers stock or other securities (e.g., preferred stock, bonds, subordinated debentures) for the stock of the selling company SEC registration is required unless the transaction qualifies as a private placement. Generally, if the selling company has fewer than 35 shareholders, the transaction will qualify as a private placement. Registration may be required if the selling company has more than 35 shareholders, even though both the seller and the buyer are privately owned corporations.

- A *letter of intent* is a written document which outlines the preliminary acquisition agreement between the seller and the prospective acquirer. It contains numerous provisions which are designed to enable either the buyer or the seller to pull out of the deal without incurring any liability. For example, the acquisition is usually subject to the approval of both boards of directors.

- The *purchase agreement* is a document which contains all the conditions and terms of the acquisition. When signed by the buyer and the seller, it is legally enforceable, but the time and expense of doing so usually exceeds the financial compensation recovered from successful litigation.

  There are differing views as to whether your attorneys or the sellers' attorneys should prepare the first draft of the purchase agreement. The party whose lawyers prepare the first draft will incur the higher legal cost but will have a slight advantage in affecting the form and content of the final purchase agreement. The reasons that the preparer of the first draft has only a slight advantage is that the purchase agreements are usually renegotiated and revised several times prior to closing.

- *Representations and warranties* are contained in the purchase agreement. They are a list of commitments and promises which the seller makes to the purchaser. For example, the seller may agree (warranty) that it will be responsible for dealing with any lawsuits which arise from their company's activities prior to the transfer of ownership.

- A *purchase option* is a purchase agreement which is contingent upon the completion of some important aspect of the transaction by the purchaser, such as obtaining a bank loan. The purchaser is usually required to pay a portion of the purchase price into an escrow account. (The seller will want 10% but will usually agree to 5%.) This good faith deposit is nonrefundable if the purchaser does not perform but is refundable if the terms covered by the seller's representations and warranties change adversely and cannot be remedied.

- A *management contract* outlines the terms and conditions of the continued employment of the selling company's owner/executives. Management contracts are enforceable only on the employer, not on the employee. Therefore, from the acquiring company's point of view they are gentlemen's agreements.

- A *noncompete agreement* is an agreement by the seller not to engage in a similar business activity for a fixed period of time. Noncompete agreements are very enforceable so long as they are not unreasonable. Noncompete agreements are an effective way of increasing the likelihood that the selling company's owner/executives will honor their employment contracts.

- *Contingent liabilities* are financial obligations which may arise in the future based upon the actions and agreements of the selling business prior to your purchasing that business. Examples of agreements which may create future obligations for the new owner of a business include:

  Guarantees
  Leases
  Franchise agreements
  Sales agent contracts

Product warranties

Collective bargaining agreements (e.g., union contracts)

Examples of actions of the selling business which may create future obligations for the new owners include:

Employment discrimination

Environmental pollution

Zoning and building code violations

Antitrust violations

Inadequate funding of pension plans

• *Collective bargaining* refers to the labor union agreements and the responsibilities of an employer under the U.S. labor laws to bargain in good faith with unions representing employees. Often you can structure the purchase of a business in a way which either:

Permits you to avoid assuming the seller's existing union contracts, or

Permits you to keep the seller's contracts with its union employees in effect.

WHY ACQUIRERS OFTEN PREFER TO ASSUME THE SELLING COMPANY'S COLLECTIVE BARGAINING AGREEMENTS

This avoids the need to enter into new collective bargaining negotiations, and to take the risk of a strike, when management's time is concentrated on solving other types of problems at the acquired company (e.g., replacing key executives, revising marketing programs, restructuring finances).

WHY ACQUIRERS SOMETIMES PREFER NOT TO ASSUME THE SELLING COMPANY'S COLLECTIVE BARGAINING AGREEMENT

When the acquiring company will seek salary, fringe benefit, or work rule concessions from the union, a new owner's threats to make substantial employment cutbacks if these concessions are not made tend to be taken more seriously by the union, than would similar threats made by a management team whose own jobs would be lost if the business were liquidated.

COLLECTIVE BARGAINING RESPONSIBILITIES OF THE SELLING BUSINESS

Unless specifically required in its union contract, the selling business does not need to obtain approval from its unions for a change in ownership. The selling company is, however, required to "bargain in good faith" regarding the effect of this action on the employees who the union represents. For example, if the transfer of any ownership would result in a cutback in employment, the bargaining will generally cover topics such as pay for accrued vacations, early retirement, severance pay, and continuation or conversation of health insurance coverage.

COLLECTIVE BARGAINING OBLIGATIONS OF THE NEW OWNERS

Though you can generally structure your purchase of a business so that the old union contracts are no longer in force, this does not eliminate your obligation to bargain in good faith with the unions representing these employees. When the employees of the acquired business will remain substantially the same after you own that business, you automatically assume the collective bargaining obligations of the selling company.

PREPARING THE WRITTEN PURCHASE AGREEMENT

After you and the sellers have reached oral agreement on those terms and conditions of the acquisition transaction which come up in your negotiations, the next step is usually for your attorney to prepare a written purchase agreement (contract). Your attorney will include in this agreement additional terms and conditions which he or she, and your accountant, feel would "protect" your company.

WHY YOUR OWN LAWYERS AND ACCOUNTANTS OFTEN ARE A MAJOR OBSTACLE TO CONCLUDING AN ACQUISITION AGREEMENT

Your lawyer and your accountant want the seller to be responsible for anything that goes wrong for the next 20 years.

The seller does not want to be responsible for the business after it has sold it. If it wanted to remain responsible, it wouldn't be selling.

Many mutually advantageous acquisition transactions are never consummated because the seller is "turned off" by the representations and warranties section of the purchase agreement which was prepared by your lawyer and your accountant.

HOW YOU SHOULD HANDLE THIS POTENTIAL PROBLEM

1. Don't do business with a seller unless your investigation of his or her company confirms the reliability of his oral representations. No purchase agreement can adequately protect you if the sellers are not honorable businesspersons.

2. Carefully review the representations and warranties section of the purchase agreement which your lawyer prepared *before* it is sent to the seller. Once you alienate the seller, you will not be able to regain its trust and confidence. Therefore, eliminate from your proposed warranties and representations any items which either (a) are not of significant dollar value or (b) can be confirmed independently by your attorney or accountant.

3. Have a portion of the purchase price (usually 10%) escrowed for six months to take care of any postacquisition adjustments covered by the seller's warranties and representations. Agree to limit the adjustments to the escrow amount.

THE ROLE USUALLY PLAYED BY THE SELLER'S ATTORNEY

The seller's attorney expects to lose a client if you purchase the seller's business. This tends to make the seller's attorney rather zealous in his or her efforts to protect his client from making a "bad deal" by selling to your company. For this reason the seller's attorney can often be a "deal killer."

HOW TO HANDLE THE SELLER'S ATTORNEY

Your objective is to make the seller's attorney feel that he or she is not going to lose a client if you purchase the seller's business. To do this you, or your attorney, indicate that you intend to utilize his or her services and expertise after you acquire the client's business. It would be unethical to employ the seller's attorney to do work for your company while you are negotiating with his or her client. However, there are opportunities during the final negotiations to indicate your future needs which would require the services of a local attorney. For example, you can ask them questions regarding:

1. Zoning regulations
2. Building codes
3. Tax assessments
4. Personalities and attitudes of the union executives who represent the seller's union employees
5. The administration of pension plans for the seller's employees
6. Local firms such as residential real estate brokers who they would recommend

HOW THE SELLER WILL RESPOND TO THE WRITTEN PURCHASE AGREEMENT PREPARED BY YOUR ATTORNEY

After your attorney drafts the written purchase agreement, or revises and expands the written purchase agreement prepared by the seller's attorney, this document is submitted to the seller for review. In some rare instances the seller will make only minor changes in your written contract, and you can proceed to closing. However, the usual seller response will be to come back with numerous requested changes, including important items which you thought had already been agreed to (e.g., the purchase price).

RENEGOTIATING THE PURCHASE AGREEMENT

When the seller responds to your proposed written purchase agreement by requesting numerous changes, you should respond in kind by requesting new concessions from the seller. For example, you should request a reduction in your cash down payment.

The key to dealing with this final stage of the negotiating process is not to become angry, frustrated, or anxious. It is normal for the seller to get "cold feet" when it is about to sell its business and to worry that it may have made a "bad deal." You handle this situation by having your negotiating team and the seller's representatives resume their discussions. Once they have again reached a tentative agreement on the terms and conditions of the acquisition transaction, you have the seller's attorney draft a new revised purchase agreement. Now if you respond with only minor changes, the seller will usually agree to it.

Even after your company and the seller have reached agreement on the final purchase agreement, you can expect one final round of purchase contract renegotiations before it is signed. The day before the scheduled closing, the seller will almost always insist that they must receive a higher purchase price or more favorable payment terms from your company. Your response should be to insist that the closing take place as scheduled but agree to make a minor improvement in the purchase price or payment terms. Then the deal will usually close. A 5% increase in the purchase price or cash down payment is usually adequate, but you run the risk of encouraging the seller to reopen negotiations on other terms and conditions. A better technique which accomplishes the same objective is to increase your purchase price and down payment slightly by agreeing to pay a portion of the seller's legal or accounting costs or a portion of the fee which the seller is obligated to pay a finder/broker. The advantage of this arrangement is that it is less likely to encourage the seller to reopen negotiations on other acquisition terms and conditions on which agreement has already been reached.

INDEX

389

B